A Comfortable Boy

Sam Pickering

A Comfortable Boy

A Memoir

Mercer University Press
Macon, Georgia

MUP/H773

© 2010 Mercer University Press
1400 Coleman Avenue
Macon, Georgia 31207

First Edition.

Books published by Mercer University Press are printed on acid free paper that meets the requirements of American National Standard for Information Sciences—Permanence of Paper for Printed Library Materials.

Mercer University Press is a member of Green Press initiative (greenpressinitiative.org), a nonprofit organization working to help publishers and printers increase their use of recycled paper and decrease their use of fiber derived from endangered forests. This book is printed on recycled paper.

Cataloging-in-Publication Data is available from the Library of Congress

ISBN: 978-0-88146-182-4

"For auld lang syne, my dear.

For auld lang syne,

We'll take a cup of kindness yet,

For auld lang syne."

For thirty years I have written essays describing my life and wanderings. As a result some of the stories in this book first appeared in slightly different form in collections of my writings published by several presses, including the University Press of New England, the University of Georgia Press, the University of Iowa Press, the University of Missouri Press, the University Press of Florida, Ohio University Press, the University of Tennessee Press, and the University of Michigan Press. I am proud of those volumes, a list of which appears in the front of this book.

Contents

PICKERINGS

William Blackstone Pickering—Civil War soldier. My great grandfather.

Sam Pickering—Born in Carthage. My grandfather.

Samuel Francis Pickering—My father.

Samuel Francis Pickering, Jr.—Me.

↓↓

Nannie Brown—My great grandmother. She married Bud Griffin from Georgia.

Frances Sue Griffin—My grandmother. She married Sam Pickering.

Samuel Francis Pickering—My father.

RATCLIFFES

Hampden Francis Ratcliffe—My great grandfather. He married Alice Garthright, my great grandmother.

John Leigh Ratcliffe of Cabin Hill—My grandfather. He married Ida Catlin, my grandmother.

Katherine Winston Ratcliffe—My mother. She married Samuel Francis Pickering.

Samuel Francis Pickering, Jr.—Me.

Christmas circa 1946. Sammy Pickering with his mother and father.

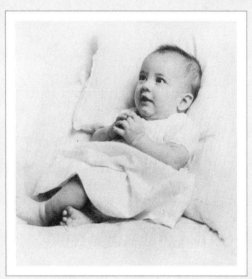

Sammy Pickering at about three months.

Sammy Pickering and his first cousin,
Sherry Ratcliffe.

Katherine Ratcliffe at twenty before she married Sammy's father.

Sammy's grandmother Frances Griffin before she married Sam Pickering.

Frances Griffin Pickering with her two boys, Coleman Pickering leaning on her lap and Sam Pickering, Sammy's father, standing beside her.

William Blackstone Pickering, the Union
Veteran, in old age.

The Pickering house in Carthage, Tennessee. Standing in front of it are Coleman
Pickering, the smaller child, and Sam Pickering, Sammy's father.

Sammy's father just over three years old.

Sammy Pickering almost three years old.

John L. Ratcliffe with his mother-in-law,
Hattie Catlin.

Sam Pickering, Sammy Pickering's grandfather
at about 20.

Katherine Ratcliffe in Arizona when she was about twenty.

Introduction

In "My Heart Leaps Up," William Wordsworth declared "The Child is the Father of the Man." In a memoir, this lineage is reversed: the man is the father of the child. Instead of the past determining the present, the present determines how a person sees the past. The child who frolics on the page is conceived in an attic, not a bedroom, his life shaped by what lurks tattered and mildewing in boxes and trunks. Moreover time changes the past. Personality is recollection. Events that the twenty-year-old thinks significant may not matter to the sixty-year-old.

In "Intimations of Immortality," Wordsworth got closer to the truth when he wrote, "Our birth is but a sleep and a forgetting." Although I have forgotten much, I know a bit about my birth. I was born at 11:30 at night on September 30, 1941. Some years ago a local newspaper interviewed me. In the article, the reporter mentioned my birthday. The next day while I stood in line in a café a stranger approached me. "We have the same birthday," he said, "September 30." "Have you ever thought," he continued, "that you were conceived on New Year's Eve and your parents were probably drunk as hell?" The thought had never before crossed my mind. For a time, it bothered me, and I couldn't push the picture of Mother and Father out of my imagination, eyes glazed, tossing streamers to the ceiling, little red party hats falling down over their ears. Now, I like thinking that a happy frolicking knitted together rather than routine, a dull doubling sandwiched between lights out and the wonderless bread of an onerous day. "There is no duty we so much underrate as the duty of being happy," Robert Louis Stevenson wrote. "By being happy, we sow anonymous benefits upon the world." Although I have occasionally sunk into selfish petulance, that lively conception has determined my days, and I'm never depressed for long and have skipped through years smiling, thinking, as a new year's baby should, that life is always new.

Along with the birds and the honeyed bees of my birth, I know the facts. I cost $65.25, Vanderbilt University Hospital charging my parents $48 for room and board, $15 for use of the delivery room, $1.25 for drugs, and $1 for a guest tray. As a comfortable boy, I wasn't eager to leap into the light, and I appeared only after Mother spent twenty-three hours in labor. A flock of telegrams accompanied my birth. "Congratulations to Momma and Poppa Pickle and Welcome to the Little Dill Pickle," Adelaide wrote from Richmond. "Vanderbilt has a Great New Fullback," the Gang wrote from Washington. Both telegrams proved inaccurate. I despise all pickles except pickled peaches, and as a boy I was a terrible athlete, not a condition corrected by manhood. Uncle Wilbur, really my great uncle and my grandfather's brother, sent me $10. "Enclosed you will find a check. At present it will be of little value to you but as time goes on it will come in handy for nothing but ice cream cones. Don't let anyone kid you about saving it. You only save it until you get to the ice cream stage and then you have a good time. I would not advise using it all at once; it would probably be better to take at least one or two weeks for the ordeal."

Many years ago I published an essay in the *Kenyon Review*. The essay contained some untoward paragraphs, and for a while I thought about withdrawing it from publication. Eventually, however, I decided no one in my family was likely to read the *Kenyon Review*. I was mistaken. Words will out, particularly if they involve, as mine did, youthful indiscretions. A week after the essay appeared, Mother telephoned. A friend had sent her the *Review*. The essay did not go down well in Tennessee. "We are," Mother said, "people of some reputation in this town, and this kind of thing…." Before mother could sink her teeth into the piece and spit out all the rotten kernels, I interrupted. "Mama," I said, straining to shift the grounds of the conversation, "Mama, don't think of the essay as truth; think of it as literature." "Literature," Mother exclaimed after a slight pause. "It's not literature. It's bullshit." In this book I haven't tried hard to winnow the manuré, as the French put such matters. I tell many stories, most told to me and of doubtful provenance. The stories, however, were and are part of my life as I see it, even amid the dense glaucoma of years. And, of course, anything dredged from the murk of memory always smacks of fiction and fertilizing literary turns of thought and phrase. Perhaps my greatest distortion for the page is calling my parents Mother and Father. When they were living, I addressed them as Mommy and Daddy. Now that they are dead, I talk to them more than I did when they were alive, and I call them Mommy and Daddy, this despite my aging into becoming them, or if not them, at least into someone as old as they were when they died, a contemporary, almost a member of their generation.

I stop this book at the end of the eighth grade. No philosophic reason motivated me to do so. High school and college did not change the tenor of my days. "I know why you stopped after the eighth grade," my friend Josh said. "You didn't want to write about sex." Josh was wrong. In kindergarten I kissed Mary Corrine, and although I blush to say it, I didn't get beyond kissing until after college. I had girl friends, but they were real friends, not bedmates. In researching this book, I was delighted to discover that Alice Orr and I were King and Queen of the seventh grade at Parmer School. I was crazy about Alice, so much so I named my baseball glove after her in the sixth grade writing, "The Alice" across the heel. For me Alices have always inhabited Wonderland, and holding the glove was the closest I've ever come to laying a hand on any Alice. Still, the book contains a couple of paragraphs about girls, for I adored them, always, however, from afar except in Red Rover. Indeed I write little about sexual matters. In the seventh grade at a sleeping party at Rock Island, Hayes explained masturbation, startling me but providing a skill that for most men comes in handier after marriage than before.

Researching this book was fun. At times I felt like Jim Hawkins wandering Treasure Island in the company of Ben Gunn. I dug up wire-rimmed glasses, bundles of keys, the plate for my first calling card—Samuel Francis Pickering, Jr.—and scores of pictures, among others. The pictures were often of people whom I could not identify—balding, bearded men framed in gold, children in white dresses and smocks, Union and Confederate soldiers, and steep-roofed brick houses with long porches, families stretched across them, colored servants containing them like bookends. I discovered more childhood pictures of Father than of Mother, wearing knickers and a velvet coat in third grade in Carthage and pushing a lawn mower in 1919, his hair a meringue atop his head, the lawn mower now in my basement behind a stack of cardboard boxes beside the washing machine. I found more pictures of Father because Grandfather Ratcliffe's house in Richmond burned down when Mother was a young woman. Almost nothing was saved from the blaze. Mother blamed the fire on her pet alligator, saying it had escaped its tank and disappeared into the walls to gnaw through wires, creating a short circuit. Not many girls have pet alligators, and I suspect Mother filched the idea of such a pet from the Jefferson Hotel in Richmond. In the lobby of the hotel was a shallow white tiled pool, home to a small alligator. After the fire and maybe before, Grandfather and Grandmother Ratcliffe, henceforth called Big Ga and Ga, spent winters in a suite in the Jefferson, bartering rent for a year's supply of flowers, Big Ga being a florist.

The book contains much about schools, not simply matter pertaining to Ransom and Parmer, schools I went to, but to schools my parents attended. In the first grade Father received a 100 for this composition: "It makes me happy when Christmas comes. It makes me sorry when Daddy is sick. It is right to mind mother. It is wrong to fight." Father appears to have been a better student than I, at least if early assignments are an indication. On May 4,

A Comfortable Boy

1949, when I was eight, I wrote mother a letter from Ransom. "Dear Mother," I wrote, "I am going to send you a surprise for Mother's day. It will be a big surprise. I am glad that Mother's day is coming. You will find out what the big surprise is on Sunday. You will like it. The surprise is not candy. The big surprise will have a card tied on. Father will like the surprise that I am going to send you. You have some like the surprise. I think that the surprise will be green. Some people will not like surprises." What startles and assures me that I haven't yet succumbed to old-timer's disease is that I remember the surprise, a pot of African violets.

In the last issue of Parmer's school paper, *The WOP*, published on June 3, 1955, just before my class graduated from Walter O. Parmer School, students wrote reminiscences. Hayes described lunch one day in Mrs. Bonney's fourth grade class: "We were in the lunchroom and three or four boys and I were eating at one end of the table. For a few days we had been making our famous Goulash Deluxe to annoy the cooks. Now in case you don't know what a Goulash Deluxe is, it's a strange mixture of food. Well, today we had a very weird combination mixed up. It was composed of meat loaf, milk, salad, cherry pie, sugar, salt, ice cream, beans, spinach slaw, and peanut butter sandwiches. Just as soon as I got ready to take the tray back to the kitchen, Mrs. Bonney came up and said, 'Boys, since you made it, you eat it.' We ate it but very reluctantly." I remember that day. I sat across from Hayes at the same table. Although this book is a goulash, I did not help him hash lunch. Only after decades of scribbling am I able to blend the appetizing and unappetizing on the same page. At Parmer, alas, I wrote editorials for the school paper celebrating order, typically beginning, "We should try to be quieter in the halls and coming in from recess because it disturbs the other classes." In any case Mrs. Bonney's chefs threw up, something that delighted the class, not because we disliked Hayes and his compatriots but because for fourth graders, especially boys, vomiting was a hilarious disturbance.

I have written much about family. Shortly before Father died, I dedicated a book to him inscribing it, "For that other and better Sam Pickering, my father, with respect and love." Platitudes govern writing and thinking. Two decades ago I started an essay describing my unhappy childhood. I did not get beyond the first sentence, a lie, "My childhood was unhappy." In truth my childhood was wondrously happy. No incest, alcoholism, quarrels, divorce, eating disorders, or questions of identity made my days relentlessly unforgettable. My parents and indeed my grandparents were sane, decent, and unfailingly loving. Feigning unhappiness was impossible, so I tossed my unhappy childhood into the waste can and wrote a book called *Deprived of Unhappiness.*

By exploring the past of my family, I wander the present, discovering that matters that relatives thought important marked the pages of my mind. Grandmother Pickering studied small matters in hopes of discovering beauty. "Life," she said in a report to the grand chapter of the Eastern Star, "is made up of little things; little books so dearly read, little songs so dearly sung, and when nature made anything especially rare and beautiful, she made it little—little diamonds, little pearls, and little dew." I, too, have long celebrated the small and the ordinary. In my most recent book I wrote, "As sappy as it sounds, I hope my writing slows readers so that they will pause, examine their lives, and find days wonderful." Although time erases people, the doings behind words remain pressed onto genes. I despise the word *nurture*, associating it with silly people, goony teachers who say they learn as much from their students, "even more," than their students learn from them. Yet, Big Ga was a gardener, a grower of fine flowers, the heading on his stationary declared. He and his brothers and sisters, several of whom were unmarried, endlessly nurtured me and enlivened my days. "Dear Sammy," Big Ga wrote me before my fourth birthday:

> it has been a very long time since I have seen you, and I miss you very much. I hope you will have a fine Birthday, and I am sure you will have, and I am going to try to ship you two

wild cats—very large ones, and if the man on the train will take them, they will be in a cage, and they should get to Nashville about the time of your Birthday, but I am afraid they are going to kill everybody in Nashville because they are very wild and very vicious.

I killed seven wolves the other night. They most chewed a little boy up, but we got him to the hospital, and he is all right now, and if these wild cats do not kill everybody in Nashville, I will send you two large wolves that will, so you had better tell your Mother about this at once to see whether she wants them sent down because I do not want to build a cage for these wolves and wild cats unless you have some place to put them…. I am sorry we cannot come down to the Circus with you. I have to stay here to keep the wild animals out of our yard. Pumas are coming up from the river, and you know they are pretty bad unless somebody is there that they are scared of, and they are scared to death of me.

The circus was Ringling Bros. and Barnum & Bailey and featured twenty "Performances," among others the program stated, the Leopard Women; the Wallendas on the trapeze; Captain Roland Tiebor's Sea Lions; Tagadore Hilding's Boxing Stallions; Amazonia, "A Con*glamor*ation of Girls in the Ancient Olympic Tradition"; and Alice in Circus Wonderland with an entourage that included the Mad Hatter, White Rabbit, March Hare, and the Mock Turtle. My favorite performers were clowns, and when a small car darted into the arena and clowns began clambering out of its doors and windows, I laughed with joy. Just when I was certain the car was empty, another clown stuck his head up. Mother, Father, and I roamed the animal tents, straw thick on the ground, a grove of poles supporting the canvas, lions and tigers in brightly colored cages, elephants and camels chained together in lines, separated from patrons by a rail of long ropes. Once while I was feeding peanuts to an elephant, he sneezed on me. After wiping me off, Father bought me a red cane with a gold ball on top.

I have drifted. But like many children born in my privileged place and time, I had leisure enough to drift or perhaps wander, ambling from collecting lead soldiers to baseball cards, from catching frogs and turtles to reading libraries of books. Moreover I have grown into a meandering adult, Big Ga's grandson, plucking not greenhouse flowers, but simpler, less commercial flowers, tamed wildflowers, buttercups and daisies, yarrow, blue flag, dame's rocket, and purple clovers with heads as big as hands. "Sam," a friend once said, "there are more flowers in your books than there are mouse turds in a meal barrel."

At Cabin Hill in Virginia, Big Ga bred Jerseys and Guernseys, and he concluded his letter, writing, "The brown cow bull asks every day if you are still drinking your milk, and I told him that you were a very good boy and I felt sure you were drinking your milk and behaving yourself like a man because you know we men have to stick together." In *The Prelude* Wordsworth said that his soul had a "fair seed-time" and that he grew up "fostered alike by beauty and by fear." The letters I received did not make me fearful, but they awakened the imagination. When my own children were small, occasionally I battled a troll in the basement of our house. I made a hullabaloo then staggered up the stairs and grabbing the children, pulled them down below, showing them the remains of the dead troll: warty rubber hands I'd slid under boxes, fingers sticking out long nailed and red. After a moment or two I spun around and clambered back up the stairs shrieking, "I hear another troll. It's alive and coming after us. Run for your lives. Warn your mother." The children followed fast on my heels, terrified and not sure whether they should be crying or laughing.

No boy of my generation, of my background, Southern American of British descent, at least no such boy in Nashville, escaped the Civil War. Trenches still cut across yards. Conversations about the war and family decorated vacant hours. In the attic I found letters and memorabilia from the war. Southern soldiers and families wrote most of the letters. Great Grandfather Pickering, however, was a Union soldier from Ohio. At the outbreak of the war he was a junior at Ohio University. Almost immediately he stopped his studies and joined the Ohio Volunteer Infantry. Levi, a brother, was killed at Perryville; another brother "Uncle Joe" was captured by Stonewall Jackson's troops at Harper's Ferry "when Jackson was storming through the Shenandoah Valley." My great great grandfather in Ohio sent Joe a new coat just before he was captured. "That's a mighty nice coat you have there, Yank," a Confederate soldier said to him. "I hope you enjoy it Reb," Joe answered.

On June 9, 1863, my great grandfather left the Ohio Infantry and joined the First Regiment of "Cavr Middle Tennessee Volunteers" stationed in Carthage, Tennessee, as lieutenant and adjutant. He enlisted for "three years or during the war," and he did not bring a horse or "horse equiptments [sic]" with him. Pickerings generally behave sensibly, and toward the end of the war, Great Grandfather, Father told me, reached an agreement with Confederates in the hills above Carthage that they would avoid shooting at each other.

Great Grandfather died in 1919. The Good Samaritan Colored Society sent flowers to his funeral. "These flowers," the accompanying card read, "are sent in grateful remembrance by the descendents of Slaves you helped to free. They will remember that through all the intervening years you have been their faithful guide and friend. May thy slumbers be peaceful and thy awakening pleasant in the arms of a liberty loving God." I write much about colored people. In the 1940s and 50s, African Americans were colored. I like the sound of the word *colored*; it is a soft, gentle word and frees me to get at the heart of my Southern life, the real heart, better than another phrase. Since I was a child, times, of course, have changed, in many ways for the better. Only after college did I realize that the society I loved passionately was raised on unconscionable injustice. That awareness has made me a doubter, maybe even a curmudgeon. Every semester I ask students, "What do you suppose are the aspects of our society that we accept without thought that later generations will think so horrific that they will wonder what was wrong with us?" My children have grown up in a different world. They have not known impoverished or colored people, and their lives are narrower for that. In this book I try to describe the society in which I grew up and truths by which I lived. What was true for me in race relations will not be true for others because they have lived in different times in different places. I have not written an apologia for my childhood. I simply want readers to realize that amid the injustice there was much humor and decency, complexity, and love. I would probably be a lawyer today if it were not for Wilna who for decades worked for Mother and Father, and me. My senior year in college I won a scholarship to law school at the University of Virginia. The scholarship covered fees and tuition, books, room and board, even a salary. When I told Wilna about it, she said, "Mr. Sammy, please don't be no lawyer. Lawyers don't do right." I loved Wilna, and her words sank to the taproot of my being.

Sometimes I think that it was Wilna who caused the deep conservatism in my character to crumble. Cancer killed Wilna. When she worked for us, Wilna was gloriously round and must have weighed 280 pounds. At her death she was a wraith. In 1965 I returned to Nashville after spending two years in Britain studying at Cambridge University. Wilna lay dying in the hospital. Mother told me she had not moved for days and was unable to recognize people. The morning after I returned to Nashville, I hurried to the hospital. Wilna was in an oxygen tent. When I walked into her room, she sat upright and stared at me. She didn't speak. She looked at me for a moment then fell back onto the mattress. That evening Wilna died. At eight the next morning I went back to the hospital to see her. Her door was shut, and a nurse said, her tone harsh and strident, at least to my ears, "Mrs. Hall expired last night." "Oh, God," I thought. As I stood in the corridor, I balled my hands into tight fists and something hard within me broke.

Other sections of the book don't touch on matters as interesting as race is to contemporary readers. Childhood, however, is not a political time. Children simply live in the world in which they were born. I have written pages on toys and pets, sports, and Nashville, Carthage, and Hanover, Virginia, where I spent summers on Big Ga's farm. I write little about religion. My people have been active in churches, but they don't seem to have been religious, that is, believers or acceptors of doctrine. For them the spirit of Christianity has always mattered more than the law. The messages of the Sermon on the Mount have remained constant, but the tincture of denomination has changed with place. My Pickering ancestor arrived on the Winthrop Fleet and settled in Salem, Massachusetts, in 1630s. Fifty years later, my line drifted to Pennsylvania and Virginia where we were Quakers. In Ohio we were Methodists; in Tennessee Methodists, members of the Christian Church, then finally Episcopalians.

The big question is clearly why I wrote this book. Perhaps the best way to approach an answer is roundabout through the negative. I did not write to discover a self. I have long been at home in the world, and, yes, also with one of the world's two companions, the flesh, and in truth, maybe the devil in his playful clown-like moods. Years ago a friend said, "The difference between us, Sam, is that you are always comfortable. You can walk into any room and not feel uneasy. Because I'm black, I always study new places and wonder if I will fit in." Almost never have I felt uncomfortable in a group of people, no matter if I am in Europe, the Mid-East, or, the love of my later life, Australia. Additionally, I didn't write to solve the mysterious. Mysteries abound in families, usually resulting from discretion and mannered restraint. I do not know, for example, why Uncle Earl was buried at the corner of the family plot in Carthage far from every other Pickering. In pictures he looks like other family members except that he is taller and his ears stick out from his head like sails. What neurological disease did Mother's brother suffer from that led him to commit suicide? Mother and Ga talked endlessly about Uncle Buster, but never in my hearing did they mention his illness.

I haven't written a self-help book. My readers are likely to be old and content, their muscles corpses of themselves, their thinking realistic, beyond believing in reformation by sentence. Still, for readers intent on nosing up lessons, the book is filled with little, forgettable accounts of decency and love, stories that nudge the funny bone and provoke soft smiles. Perhaps a few readers will close this book and scrolling back through their years discover the stuff of their happiness, material that will make them appreciate the present more. "Greatness of soul," Montaigne wrote, "is not so much pressing upward and forward as knowing how to set oneself in order and circumscribe oneself. It regards as great whatever is adequate and shows its elevation by liking moderate things better than eminent ones." As a retired Christian, one who retired at age ten but did not tell his mother, and one, paradoxically, who wishes he could hear "Whispering Hope" on the breeze, I don't have much truck with the soul. Moreover, I think the greatest soul is that which is satisfied with small things. Greatness seems the spawn of ambition and is dangerous and ruinous. When asked what I am most proud of, I usually say "resisting ambition." When big opportunity knocked on my front door, I ran out the back and wandered hill and field catching snakes and traipsing after butterflies until opportunity, and temptation, vanished. As a result I have not had to shape my words or life to corporate needs or expectations. Of course I have tied myself into knots to suit the needs of family and friends. Not to have done so would have been to live selfishly, so without compassion and sensibility that I would have been no better than a savage, hunkered over a fire, sucking the marrow out of his neighbor's days or, in this moneyed world, his bank account.

Many years ago an old friend in Carthage cleared out a bureau. Lining the bottom of a drawer was a copy of a weekly newspaper published in 1953. On the front page appeared the obituary of my grandfather. "Rites set Friday for Sam Pickering," the headline declared. The friend clipped out the obituary and sent it to me. The next morning I tacked the obituary to the bulletin board outside the office of the English Department at the University of Connecticut where I teach. As I admired my work, a student started reading clippings on the board. "Oh, no," she said, seeing the obituary. "I planned to take Pickering's course in the fall. Now I will have to redo my schedule." "Is he really dead?" she asked turning toward me. "Plucked and fried," I said. "He's roosting in the holy sanctum now. Never again will he teach writing." "Damn," the girl exclaimed. "What an inconvenience! My friend told me getting an *A* from him was easy. Now I'll have to find some other gut course." I am an easy teacher, tolerant of ne'er do wells, people who wander beyond margins, often into disaster but sometimes into happiness. I always give students half a grade higher than they could ever imagine receiving in hopes that they will have time enough to explore books and music, things I mention in class but which have little to do with a course syllabus. This book resembles one of my classes, starting to go one way then suddenly stopping and spinning in several other directions simultaneously, a bit like life itself.

I have written twenty-one books, and *A Comfortable Boy* is probably my literary obituary, or metaphorically perhaps, my swan song. My hearing isn't as acute as it once was. Songs that quicken others often swirl silently around me. Consequently, I might not hear the verses of the final gospel hymn sung for me, say "Will the Circle Be Unbroken," and I just might compose one or two other things. Rarely does impossibility, particularly the thought of being called up yonder, inhibit an optimistic boy, the sort of boy who always made do and has had fun no matter place or time, or, as a poem put it in the *Seventh Grade Spotlight* "published" on March 26, 1954 at Parmer School, "I was sitting in my chair / I knew the bottom wasn't there. / No legs, no back, but I just sat / Ignoring little things like that." Now that I look at the poem, I wonder if its source came from somewhere other than the author's mind. Oh, well, that's a little thing, the sort of matter that would bother an adult but shouldn't concern a seventh grader. Little things brighten life, especially, in contradiction to the song, when they don't mean a lot, just like the big things, whatever these last may be.

Family in Tennessee and the War

On January 12, 1899, my great-great grandfather's obituary appeared on the front page of the *Athens Messenger* (Ohio). "During the last week," the article recounted, "he grew gradually more infirm, and early Sunday morning, after he had journeyed long and journeyed far, there came for him the twilight and the dusk, the mist gathered over the mirror of memory, the pulse throbbed faint and low, and finally ceased to beat forever." Family bibles are mausoleums, entombing beginnings and endings of lives but not middles hearty with stories. If a person travels too far back in time, his memory will resemble Alice's looking glass and reflecting hagiography will transform mud huts into castles and weeds into family trees. I grew up surrounded by relatives, most disembodied but still wandering quick through small talk. Rarely, however, were family members from my great-great grandparents' generation the stuff of paragraphs, and so I start this chapter with my great grandparents, people whom I never met but who occasionally strolled into my life.

I knew my great grandfather William B. Pickering only as an adult. I first met him as a picture when he was nineteen years old and a Union Cavalry Captain. He was handsome, his hair slicked back from his forehead, and had brown eyes, and round, almost sensuous cheeks. Forty years later he had a mustache. His cheekbones rose prominent and dignified, and he appeared extraordinarily kind, the sort of person who would listen and advise selflessly. The toys he left me were military: his Colt .44 pistol, a pen used to sign his commission in the Company C, 3rd Regiment, Ohio Volunteer Infantry; spurs decorated by eagles with eyes fashioned from rubies; a diary in which he occasionally noted that he was "fired on"; and then three leather-bound photograph albums, the largest six and a half inches tall, five and a half wide and three thick. The pictures themselves were small, two and a half by three and a half inches and slotted between pages into frames resembling windows. Some of the pictures were of family members, most of whom have vanished into the twilight. Others depicted friends in the army. Still other pictures were of generals, soldiers collecting them, it seems, like boys of my generation collected Topps baseball cards: Sheridan, O. M. Mitchell, Joe Hooker, McPherson, Rosecrans, Ben Butler, Rousseau, and George Thomas, the Rock of Chickamauga, the majority of these last pictures taken from negatives in Brady's National Portrait Gallery and published by E. & H. T. Anthony, 501 Broadway, New York.

Five years ago I reviewed a book in which a critic discussed the education of women in the nineteenth century. Consisting in part of lessons in penmanship, music, language, and painting, such education, the author argued, turned women into ornaments and by not teaching them useful skills ensured they would be dependant on men for their livelihoods. The author had not read widely enough. I am alive because of penmanship. Good handwriting served both men and women well. William Pickering wrote a beautiful hand and because of it he became company clerk and clerk to the general commanding his division, surviving Cheat Mountain, Murfreesboro, and Perryville, among many small battles and skirmishes. Family story says that to become clerk Great Grandfather submitted a sample of his penmanship, writing a stanza from Longfellow's "Psalm of Life." "Lives of great men all remind us / We can make our lives sublime, / And, departing, leave behind us / Footprints on the sands of time."

In 1881, Great Grandfather was chief clerk of the Tennessee House of Representatives. At the end of the session he applied "To the Honorable Secretary of War" for a place as "Investigating Agent of the Quartermasters Department." Accompanying the application was a petition signed by all members of the house "present at the session, those not signing being absent on account of sickness." Great Grandfather wrote the petition, and the script flowered like a garden over the page. Heavy stems of letters swept upward in airy blossoms. Words stretched in lines like boxwood hedges trim and thick. Capitals rose in the middle of pages, resembling bronze statues in lily ponds: Athena, a helmet pushed high on her forehead, or Hercules, a knobby club hanging from his right hand and draped over his shoulders, the skin of the Nemean Lion. When I read the petition, its ink had faded, turning red and Georgian. From a distance words appeared bricks, the margins of the pages stone dressing atop walls. Like pavilions at the end of gravel walks, Great Grandfather's signature loomed at the bottom of pages, the letters of his initials *W, B,* and *P* ornamental urns, the other letters lattice work.

Mr. Billy Pickering, as a correspondent called him in a letter, seems to have been the sort person who believed that trying to leave footprints was important, something that I no longer think possible but which I probably accepted without thought in the eighth grade. I, or Sammy Pickering, as I was then, was president of my eighth grade class and gave the farewell speech at graduation. The speech was prosaic. But, of course, it couldn't have been otherwise. Eighth graders in 1955 did not rise above platitudes. The speech was 221 words long. I began saying it was a privilege to speak for the graduating class. "While our graduation is what we have been studying and working for, yet now that the time has come, I know we all have mixed feelings. We have a feeling of satisfaction at having reached our goal, yet we also have many regrets at leaving. So to be saying goodbye is in many ways a sad duty." I thanked the teachers for helping us learn and for understanding our problems and said that we knew our education at Parmer would mean a lot to us in the future. "And so," I concluded, "we leave with appreciation and regret—appreciation for what has been done for us and regret to be leaving our school, our teachers, and our classmates." The prose was clean, and looking at the speech now makes me wonder if I wrote it, or wrote it without Father's guiding eraser. An adult was more likely to mention problems than a child. Aware of the fragility of life and happiness, Mother and Father would have worried about me, as I did and still do about my own children. They would have imagined futures beset by the problematic if not actual problems. For my part I was a carefree thirteen-year-old.

"Few men in Smith County, or in the Fourth Congressional District, were better or more favorably known than Mr. Pickering," the *Carthage Courier* wrote on Great Grandfather's death in 1919. Mr. Billy was active in local affairs. In addition to being clerk of the legislature, he was postmaster and county court clerk. For thirty years he was superintendent of the Methodist Sunday school. He filled all his positions, the paper said, "with unusual accuracy, care and neatness, wrote a splendid hand, and was ever obliging to the public." He was a "Republican in politics and has been prominent in his party's councils, having been nominated for congress, a delegate to national conventions and chairman of district and county committees."

Buried in the obituary are the seeds of story. My grandmother, not a Pickering but a Griffin, belonged to and insisted that her children attend the Christian Church. Every Sunday my father and his brother Coleman walked past their grandfather who stood outside the Methodist Church on their way to attend the Christian Church down the street. "That was unforgivable," Father told me once shaking his head. "Why Daddy let that happen, I don't know." Great Grandfather himself ran against Cordell Hull for Congress. "Mr. Hull won because he had a rich wife," I was told. Later Mr. Hull was Roosevelt's secretary of state. He did not escape Carthage, however. In old age his father began to step out, and on occasion during the Second World War, Cordell Hull left Washington and returned to Carthage to shove his father back into line. Years later when I was in Carthage with Father, an old man stopped us on the street and talked about my grandfather, William's son, Sam, calling my grandfather the man who died in 1953, "The last of the good Republicans."

To compare the past favorably with the present is to slip into a commonplace; yet, remembrances shaped many years ago seem softer and more moving than today's accounts, which often seem tinny and pocked by acidic humor. My grandfather sold insurance, and his office was on the second floor of a building in Carthage. Eight years after his death, a note appeared in the *Carthage Courier*.

An unprepossessing, probably little noticed metal sign, its enamel chipped with age," the note said, "is fastened to a the stairway entrance of a business building here, proclaiming to his friends in life, the destiny of a man in eternity. The sign reads:
SAM PICKERING
UPSTAIRS.

I have long thought sentiment a high virtue, maybe the highest virtue. Of course when sentiment becomes divorced from deeds, it corrupts. As the old saying puts it, "Words are nice, but chickens lay eggs." Still words are a form of action and can so move a person that they better the spirit and the man himself. When my daughter Eliza was two, she often awoke at three or four in the morning to go to the potty. Almost always I heard her climb out of bed then pad rapidly through the hall to Vicki's and my room. "Daddy," she said, and I got out of bed, turned the bathroom light on for her, handed her a cup of apple juice then sat on the edge of the tub. When Eliza finished, I walked her back to her room holding her hand. I pulled the covers over her and once or twice she put her arms around my neck and said, "I love you, Daddy. You are the best daddy in the whole world." Nothing anyone has said since has meant more to me.

Great Grandfather's obituary ended, declaring, "He was a well-read, useful, substantial citizen, broad-minded, charitable, thoughtful and considerate of the feelings of others; he was a faithful and devoted companion, a tender, loving father; and hundreds of friends and admirers will be touched by the death of this grand and noble man of God." Reputation doesn't last long enough to be blighted. The last time I was in Carthage vandals had knocked over his tombstone. When I asked about the damage, a woman who ran a nearby business said, "I didn't know white people were buried in that graveyard."

On April 9, 1865, Lee surrendered to Grant at Appomattox Courthouse. On July 4, 1865, Great Grandfather married Eliza Jane McClarin in Carthage, the date signifying independence and freedom, this last from war. Both Eliza Jane and William lost brothers in the fighting, Eliza Jane's brother Robert fighting for the Confederacy. Eliza had been born in Pittsburgh in 1843, her family Scotch-Irish, having emigrated from Northern Ireland. Known as Pittsburgh Jim, her father was a blacksmith. For my part all I ever heard about Eliza was that she was beautiful and intelligent. Immediately after marriage Great Grandfather took Eliza away from Carthage back to his family in Athens where he finished his studies at Ohio University. Eliza was not happy in Athens, and eventually the couple returned to Carthage where in 1873 they bought five acres "more or less" for $2,800. In 1888 Eliza died after having given birth to six children, my grandfather Samuel the third child, born on Christmas Eve 1870.

I have always been a rummager. To me attics are caverns inviting exploration, and as a small boy whenever I visited a relative, I disappeared into the attic as soon as was politely possible. Nothing could discourage me. Wild women and knots of snakes infested the attic at Cabin Hill, Big Ga's farm in Virginia, mother said in the forlorn hope of keeping me from rummaging through boxes and trunks. Two minutes after her warning I was in the attic. Wild women were, incidentally, a staple of mother's cautionary conversation. They lurked in the woods on the farm in Virginia and behind the Sulgrave Apartments on West End Avenue in Nashville where I lived until the beginning of fourth grade. Once in Nashville I overheard wild women plotting to kidnap me, and I ran home. Alas, I was barefoot and jabbed a thorn into my heel. The thorn went so deep that a doctor had to dig it out. My experience of wild women in later life has been limited. When I was four years old, I played Ring Around the Rosie with the three little girls. At "tishoo, tishoo," we all fell down, I on the bottom and the girls on top snapping my collarbone. Despite untoward hankerings, never again did I play with a gaggle of girls. One girl, of course, is enough to batter a boy's heart, happily not something that can cause more than temporary angina, for in childhood one infatuation quickly replaces another.

In attics I discovered family lurking amid books and boxes of paper. At the beginning of the twentieth century, my grandfather Samuel Pickering married Frances Sue Griffin in her mother's house at 905 Fifth Avenue South in Nashville. Although the neighborhood deteriorated, the house remained in the family until my grandmother's sister Aunt Lula died in the 1950s. Two days after her death the house was burgled. Thieves had long given Aunt Lula a wide berth. They did not steal much, spooked, Father and I later decided, by what they found. For our part Father and I discovered thirty-nine loaded pistols in two rooms, a sitting room and a combination kitchen and pantry. We found pistols in a pot on the stove, in the oven and breadbox, under cushions, and in drawers. I wanted to keep a double-barreled derringer, but Father would not let me, and I had to settle for two .22 rifles and four shotguns, a .410, and 12-, 16-, and 20-gauge guns. I got rid of the guns after college, and the only gun I own now is a 20-gauge, made for mother by Abercrombie & Fitch in the 1930s, one barrel for birds, the other for skeet. I keep the gun in the basement, broken into three parts, each part wrapped in rags and locked in a truck far from the other two parts. I don't own shells, and I don't know in which of the many trunks in the basement I hid the parts. I am a cautious man, and I broke the gun down because I worried that anger might someday shred reason and I would behave foolishly, in a way other than verbally.

What appealed to me more than guns were letters I found. In a desk was a letter to Santa Claus mailed by Aunt Lula on December 12, 1885, from Bellevue, Tennessee. "Dear Santa

Claus," the letter began, "You are such a nice old man that I hate to ask you for many things but I hope you can bring me a Doll (china Doll) and an Orange, some Candy and Nuts, some Raisins and some fire Crackers. You may not remember me but I am the liveliest little girl in these woods. I am the Belle of three. You may bring me a Candy Dog, and a Ring Cup and Saucer and Plate. Please don't forget me for I would be greatly disappointed. Affectionately your little Girl. Lulie Griffin."

Life stripped hop from the step of the lively little girl. She married a doctor, who, so far as I could learn from eavesdropping on conversations, became addicted to his own prescriptions and during his last days may have been an abortionist. She had one son Jerdan who attended Hume-Fogg High School in Nashville then Vanderbilt. Jerdan was a good student, but at twenty he broke down and spent the rest of his life in and out of Central State, a mental institution. "Lula did not let him have any friends," Father told me in explanation. One December Jerdan disappeared on a farm Lula owned in Williamson County, the remnant of land owned by her mother's people, the Browns. The National Guard searched but could not find him. The following spring Mother smelled decay on the wind and discovered his body behind a fallen tree. Aunt Lula asked Mother to retrieve Jerdan's watch. "Not a pleasant chore," Mother said.

Mother was hardier than Father. Once in Virginia for the family of a farm worker she conducted a funeral for a stillborn child. At home Wilna dipped snuff. As a spittoon she kept a Maxwell House coffee can on the stove in the kitchen. Sometimes she missed the can, splattering the stove or in some cases the food, turnip greens and fried chicken. Once Father complained to Mother, "God damn it, Sam," Mother said. "Wilna is wonderful, and Sammy loves her. Don't be prissy. Think of the tobacco as seasoning. Besides it takes a peck of dirt to kill you."

Help was often the subject of story and of life itself. Years later in Virginia when Ga grew feeble Mother hired a colored woman to sit with Ga at night. Once when Mother and Father were visiting and were asleep upstairs, Mother was awakened by thumping downstairs. Assuming that the woman had dozed off and Ga had fallen out of the bed and was rolling on the floor, Mother hurried downstairs. Ga was asleep in bed. The hired woman, however, was awake and entertaining a gentlemen caller in the spare bedroom, the caller not her husband. "Did you fire her?" Father asked after Mother returned to bed. "Hell, no," Mother said. "Good help is impossible to find. Who would replace her?" Mother and Father were politically conservative; yet in ways beyond the political they were liberal and rarely reduced people to or lived according to narrow abstraction. Later in Nashville after we left the Sulgrave and moved to a house on Iroquois Avenue in Belle Meade, Mother hired Fred, a gardener and yard man who worked for her one or two days a week. In the newspaper one morning appeared a story in which Fred was accused of homosexual rape. Fred's other employers let him go. Mother did not. "He told me he wasn't guilty," Mother said to a friend. "Even so, Katharine," the friend began. "He said he was not guilty, and that's all that matters, aside from my liking him and his being a good yardman," Mother said. Time proved Fred innocent. Years later, shortly after Mother died, I received a package from Fred. Mother and Father spent the last years of their lives in an apartment, and I'd forgotten about Fred. He had not forgotten Mother. Fred returned to our old house, dug the bulbs of five lilies out of the backyard, and sent them to me. "Your mother," Fred wrote, "would want you to have these."

In Aunt Lula's attic I found a shoebox containing some 200 letters, written for the most part during the years 1858–1878. Most were written to and by girls and boys, then men and women, who lived on farms outside the small towns of Middle Tennessee: Columbia, Franklin, and White Bluff. Many of the correspondents were sisters or had been schoolmates and had attended small boarding schools together, places named Bethany or Minerva College, this last the school attended by my great grandmother Nannie Brown. Among the letters were school commencement exercises, calling cards, invitations to funerals, and accounts of quilting parties, dances, chicken fights, candy pullings, pet lambs, and war. In a trunk lay Nannie's diploma from Minerva, awarded on June 7, 1860, the college located, the diploma said, "Near Nashville." Nannie was born in 1844 and was fifteen and a half years old when she graduated. The degree was signed by S. E. Jones, "President and Professor of Biblical Science," as well as by the governess and teacher of English and French, the professor of Ancient Languages and Literature, the instructress in Mathematics, the instructress in Fancy Work, the mistress of the Preparatory School, and the professor of Instrumental and Social Music.

Also in the trunk were six small blue volumes, three and a half by four and three-quarters inches, published in New York by Geo. A Leavitt. The books were *The Lady of the Lake* by Sir Walter Scott, Felicia Hemans's *Poems* "With an Essay on Her Genius," Thomas Moore's *Lalla Rookh,* Lydia Sigourney's *Poems, Paradise Lost,* and *Poems from the Poetical Works of William Wordsworth.* In the front of each book, Nannie wrote her name, Nannie E. Brown, the calligraphy ornate. In one book curlicues floated like clouds around her name and in another while ivy spilled from the letters in a small waterfall, a bird perched on the *N* of her Christian name. In Hemans's poems Nannie's name ran upward across a ribbon binding a bouquet of roses. The names were so beautifully done, so classical in their order and delicacy that I hesitated to read the books. Sadly what lay ahead for Nannie was the disorder of war and life itself. To look at the names and not fall in love with Nannie was impossible.

Many of the letters I found were written by the Brown family in Williamson County during the Civil War, and I read these first, drawn, I suppose, by prurient curiosity, the sort of thing that in fourth grade drew me to pictorial accounts of the Second World War—books sensational with pictures of bodies dragging back and forth in the wash of waves, books which I'd refuse to look at now and would toss out of the house if I owned them, their horror stirring rage then grief for, as Wordsworth put it, "man's inhumanity to man." Little violence appeared in these letters, though. Instead with wonderful innocence they celebrated the ordinary. Early in summer 1861, Innis Brown wrote his sister Mary from Camp Cheatham. "If there is any fighting to be done," he declared, "I want to get at it as I think we can fatigue them very easy if we get afoul of them while the weather is warm." After mentioning the "fine times" he had recently enjoyed with "ladie visitors from Franklin," he turned to important matters in a postscript. "I forgot to tell you," he said, "to take care of my dogs. If you have not got them, I want you to get them." By December Innis was in Virginia. "On account of sickness," he had been away from his regiment for a month. On recovering, he wrote that he'd had "a fine time fox hunting." "There is a fellow that lives about a mile from here that has a pack of dogs and he comes up for us every time he goes a hunting."

In the letters daily life rivaled the war. "There was fighting at Bowling Green yesterday and the day before," one of Nannie's classmates at Minerva wrote. "My ardent wish is that the Southrons may be victorious, if the Linkhouners were to gain a battle there I would almost despair, for they would never stop till they were south of me or had driven us from our homes, but God will aid the side of justice, if any justice there be in war." The war was only part of what was on the girl's mind, and she did not write much about it. She was more interested in love. "Wars nor any thing else," she wrote brightly, "can stop this thing of marrying. We had three weddings in one day not long since." "I presume," she continued gaily, "you are not yet wed, as you believe in sending all *sweethearts* to battle. If it pleases you to answer this, write me a long, long letter, tell me something about your *favorites*."

Sweethearts wandered through the letters. "We have had great times, corresponding with Captains Gilbert and Ellis," Sallie wrote from Nashville in 1864. "The latter wanted me to open a correspondence with a friend of his, Lt. Victor Oliviér. Isn't that name pretty enough to keep a schoolgirl in a perfect fever of excitement for a whole week? I only lost one night's sleep by it, and eat as hearty a breakfast next day, as usual, I declined corresponding with him...though Capt. Ellis says that he is young, handsome, and accomplished and in short, a gentleman by birth and education. He was wealthy before the war, and belongs to one of the best Creole families in Louisiana. He is related to Genl. Beauregard both by blood and marriage. Still I declined a correspondence with him. Do you think me a simpleton or a prude?"

Not all doings, of course, were gay, and on the last page of the letter Sallie wrote, "I expect Aunt Mary will have to take some Yankee boarders in order to get coal. I will not be introduced. We will use the front stairs and they the others, and I will come to the second table. I don't know one, nor do I intend to." Sallie and the correspondents in the letters were all about eighteen years old in 1864 and despite the war were able to dream. "Sweet friend," a girl wrote from "Laurel Hill" in November 1864, "t'was a beautifull moonlight night; while seated alone by an open window with a halo of moonshine around me, and the breeze playing with my neglected tresses, and holding in my hand a letter I had just finished reading, that the thought very naturally arose, if Nannie were only here I could tell her of my joys and sorrows." Despite the moonshine and breezes, life at Laurel Hill was far from romantic. In the middle of the letter, a paragraph stood out in a noonday of realism. "The federals are very troublesome out here now," the girl wrote, "there has been a band of robbers going about through the country. Our house has been robbed twice. The last time they were here they presented a pistol at Pa's head and told him they would blow his brains out if he did not give them what gold and silver he had. They also threatened burning our house and made such wicked threats about me I thought very seriously about leaving the country." Still the girl ended her letter romantically. She had been to Columbia, she said, visiting a friend who was "full of music." When the friend "would warble in a rich sweet voice, *why do summer roses fade*, it reminded me of the blest days of yore when we were as two souls with but a single thought and two hearts that beat as one."

Rarely did I oppose my parents, and the one time I was unyielding in opposition, I now regret. I did not want to learn to play the piano, and when the time came for my first lesson, I hid in the small woods behind our house. As a result I am musically illiterate and cannot differentiate one note from another. In attics, though, I found three collections of tunes, each of the volumes bound in leather, two of them owned by Nannie and one by Bettie L. Ratcliffe, a great aunt in Virginia. Old favorites filled the books: among others, "Beautiful Dreamer," "Bella Donna Waltz," "Billy in the Low Grounds," "Maryland, My Maryland," "Softly Falls the Moonlight," "Minnehaha or the Laughing Water Polka," "Mary of the Wild Moor," "Juanita," "Kathleen Mavourneen," "Mocking Bird Quick Step" dedicated "To the Pupils of the Woodford Female Academy Versailles, Kentucky," and "Santa Anna's March" as "played on the field of Buena Vista the night previous to the battle." "NB," a note on the title page explained, "This beautiful air was brought home by some Kentucky Volunteers having heard it played by the Mexican Bands at Buena Vista while on sentry duty."

In the albums war was inescapable. Other relatives had owned Great Aunt Bettie's album, Virginia L. Carter first writing her name and "Richmond, Virginia" in it on March 16, 1857. "Your Absent Friends, Confederate Soldiers, C. C. Cauthorn and Major Cauthorn Jones" inscribed a blank page just after "Be Kind to the Loved Ones at Home" and "Dolly Day," in pencil writing, "To Miss Courtney, May the angels of peace ever cluster round you and guide your pathway." The other two albums contained songs published by Jas. McClure's Nashville Patriot Press, including "The Forrest Schottish Dedicated To The General And His Staff" and "Shiloh Victory Polka Dedicated To The Heroes Of The Battle At Pittsburg Landing." The Confederate Cavalryman John Morgan rode a mule away from prison and across the cover of "How Are You? John Morgan," a comic song. "John Morgan's gone," the last verse declared, "like lightning flies, / Through every State and Town; / Keep watch, and for the famous prize / Five thousand dollars down. / But he is gone, too late, too late, / His whereabouts to find, / He's gone to call on Col. Straight / Way down in Richmond town. / Upon his Mule, He's gone they say / to Dixie's promised Land, / And at no very distant day / To lead a new command." M'Clure's Collection of National Melodies included the "Oak Hill Polka" dedicated to General Ben McCulloch, the John Morgan Polka, the "Cavalry Galop" dedicated to the Texas Rangers, and dedicated to General Price, the "Lexington Quickstep." Published in New Orleans by A. E. Blackmar & Bro. and written by Harry Macarthy who also wrote "The Bonnie Blue Flag," "Missouri! Or A Voice from the South" urged Missouri to join the Confederacy. "Missouri! Missouri! bright land of the West, / Where the wayworn emigrant always found rest," the first stanza declared, "Who gave to the farmer reward for the toil, / Expended in breaking and turning the soil; / Awake to the notes of the bugle and drum! / Awake from your peace for the tyrant hath come; / And swear by your honor that your chains shall be riven, / And add your bright Star to our Flag of Eleven."

On November 4, 1864, as General John B. Hood led the Army of Tennessee out of Georgia toward Middle Tennessee in the forlorn attempt to draw Sherman out of Atlanta, Alice W., sent a letter from Nashville to Franklin, to Mary Brown, Nannie's sister. "Oh, Mary," she exclaimed, "I expect you will soon see some *sweet Rebels*, how I will envy you then, you may expect a visit from me." It is unlikely that Alice or Mary had the chance to flirt with many rebels at Franklin. Twenty-six days after Alice wrote her letter, Hood arrived at Franklin. At three o'clock that afternoon he attacked the Union forces. When the battle ended at six that night, six Confederate generals were dead or dying, and more than 6000 men, over a fifth of Hood's soldiers, were casualties.

In 1861 Innis Brown wrote Mary that he did not know where the regiment was going. "Some think to Manassa, some to Winchester, but for my part," he said, "I don't care where it goes so they get out of Vaginia." By the time of the Battle of Franklin, most of the Browns were back in Tennessee. Early in March, Tom

Brown wrote Mary from Camp Morton in Indiana, a prisoner of war camp:

> My sweet little cousin, Your Truly welcome letter of the sixth came to hand this morning. I am delighted to hear that yourself and Alice are having such nice times with the young-gents of Nashville. I truly hope that you may never know what sorrow and grief are but always walking in the *path* of *true happiness* where flowers of *eternal bliss* are continually blooming. You say Innis is flying around with the ladies and I have no doubt but what he is having quite a gay and happy time especially with one Miss Dora Davis. Well as regards the pleasure here at this place tis useless to speak of, as you have some idea as to what a prison life is (having seen the prison at Nashville). All of your acquaintances at this Camp are well and in fine Spirits at Present. Tell Alice to cheer up and not to get low-spirited.

By the Battle of Nashville, most, if not all, of the Browns were back in Tennessee. Amid the papers I found three receipts, one seemingly a duplicate of another. On December 13, 1864, "by order of Gen. J. B. Hood," ten hogs estimated to weigh 1700 pounds and worth $1190 were seized by the "The Confederate States" from Enoch Brown and were "not paid for." Two days later "The Confederate States" took 2166 pounds of tobacco worth $1624.50, these also "not paid for." Some girls did not approve of giving up the fight and in a letter to Mary, Jennie Brown, her sister, wrote, "I suppose you have heard that Cousin Joe Brown has come home and taken the oath, nearly all the first Redgment has come home. Shame on them. Tennessee is disgracing her selfe."

Disgrace seems too strong. Like William Pickering the Browns seemed rational people. When a cause is lost, the sensible man goes home and gets on with living, while the big world whirls the fervent and the unthinking into dust. Innis continued courting. Drink, however, proved his downfall. "Innis," Jennie recounted, "has ruined his fortune, he went to town in that cool weather and took too much and went by the Old Davis's, and commenct to maken love to Miss Dora before the old Folks. He has not been there since." "I am going there Friday and smooth it all over for him," Jennie concluded. Jennie must not have been successful because Innis never married.

Most men in the letters fared better with their sweethearts than Innis did with Miss Dora. "Oh why were you not at the 'Pic Nic' yesterday," William Bailey asked Nannie's sister Mary in May 1865. Although he enjoyed the afternoon, Bailey told Mary that he "would rather live in your company one hour and breathe the same air with you, than to live over a dozen such days." Later that month, he cut two lines of poetry from a newspaper and sent them to her, saying, "Please accept this 'Music' from one who, owes to you, the happiest moments of his life. And who loves you dearer than all else the world contains." "Oh! never woman charmed like thee, / And never man yet loved like me," the lines read. Bailey's letters were gentle and poetic, and that summer he and Mary married. Unfortunately he lived with her for only a year. Soon after marriage he was stricken with tuberculosis, as, I think, was Tom Brown, his infection contracted at Camp Morton.

Distant family members who leave letters behind are often more familiar than close relatives whom one knew. As a boy, I pored over the letters, searching for beginnings, middles, and often finding ends. Bailey fought for his life. Among the letters was the card of "Drs. R. & J. Hunter of New York, Physicians for the Diseases of the THROAT, LUNGS, and HEART." The doctors wrote long letters to Bailey, telling him how to use an inhaling instrument and advising him on the preparation of embrocations, gargles, and pills. Every week Bailey reported his progress to Dr. Roscoe at the City Hotel in Nashville or wrote the Hunters directly in Cincinnati. Among a group of prescriptions was a statement made after Bailey's initial examination. He was twenty-three years old and made his living as a merchant. His right lung was infected, and he had lost weight and suffered from coughs, "Hemorhage," night sweats, and shortness of breath. His liver was torpid, his bowels "costive at times," and his throat and nostrils inflamed. By spring 1866, Bailey knew he was dying, and he wrote his sister urging her to come see him. "I don't think I have long to live in this world," he wrote, "and it pains me very much to think of leaving Mary. Come—Sister and see us for I will never be able to visit you at home."

That same month he sent twenty dollars to his cousin Molly Cravens in Gainesville, Alabama. "I *do hope*, dear Cousin," she replied, "that you are mistaken with regard to your *health*. *Cheer up*, if there is any hope in the *world*, and come down and stay with us, and see if a *change* will not help you." "If, however, your fears are *reality*," she continued, "I do trust and pray that you are a *Christian*, and wait only on God's will. Life at best is but a *span* of *vanity* (Save when employed in *God's Service* it is *vanity*) and if we can only be *prepared*, it matters little when we go." That summer Bailey died. Five years later Mary Brown died of tuberculosis. Later that decade Innis came down with the disease and died.

Molly Cravens doesn't sound like someone kin to me. Her prose was smooth, but the words too glib. I attended Sunday school, but I wasn't baptized until 1951. In the initial years of Sunday school I enjoyed coloring pictures of camels and sheep. Afterward, when teachers marked attendance by sticking stars on a chart by one's name, I liked amassing constellations. Later when belief and doctrine drained the fun out of religion and turned it sinful, I drifted away. My family enjoyed church communities and served churches as Billy Pickering did, but they rarely talked about religion, thinking, if they thought about it at all, the spirit of Christianity more important than the law. Not unless the recipient of a letter wanted to hear false consolation did my family use words as embroidery, decorative and artificial, glitter attracting the eye but not the mind. Often when a person died, people said "it" was a blessing, the translation of *blessing* referring to earthly matters not heavenly, the end of physical suffering or death before medical expenses drained a bank account and deprived deserving relatives of inheritance. In sixth grade I was the only one of my Episcopal friends who refused to be an acolyte. Mother, of course, fretted about me, and in church when I mumbled prayers, she prayed louder, embarrassing me into speaking clearly. On the way out of church I paid her back and goosed her when she shook hands with the minister, invariably causing her to yip. During my childhood women wore girdles and the goose surprised more than it jabbed. Mother tried to appear irritated, but once out of the church building she always broke into laughter, saying something like "you are the damnedest boy." The truth was that she was the damnedest woman. Once when I was with her, a policeman stopped her for speeding. The policeman was impolite, or at least Mother thought so, and after exclaiming, "This is the god damnedest thing. I won't tolerate such manners," she drove away, leaving the policeman standing by the road.

A policeman has only stopped me once. My behavior was better though just as extravagant as Mother's. The result, however, was the same, no ticket. I had driven from Nashville to Hanover, Virginia, to spend Thanksgiving with Ga. We ate our Thanksgiving meal on Saturday rather than Thursday and instead of turkey had goose with friends in Louisa. The goose must have hung too long and lost its patience, for soon after lunch it began honking. By midnight I ached all over and was certain I had been poisoned. Near dawn the goose suddenly rose, circled once, and headed south. Once the goose was out of sight and body, I recovered rapidly and at nine o'clock left for Tennessee. Because I left four hours later than planned, I drove faster and near Cumberland Courthouse whipped through a radar trap eleven miles over the speed limit. Despite the goose, I was ready when the patrolman pulled me over. "Praise the Lord," I said, getting out of the car to shake the man's hand. "God's in his heaven this Sabbath." When the policeman stopped, stared at me and backed away, I knew he was as good as in the collection plate, and launched my appeal.

"Brother, do you follow Jesus?" I asked. Then before he could reply, I answered my question. "Yes," I said, "you do. From your soul the sun shines more glorious than that glowing in any earthly sky. In that bright sun, isn't there pardon for me?" "Do you think, Christian brother," I continued, stepping forward again opening my arms, fingers outspread in benediction and familiarity, "don't you think that on this the seventh day you could rest and forgive me? When your summons comes to meet the blessed Savior and you put on the Crown of Glory, no jewel will shine brighter than that of Forgiveness." At first the policeman did not speak. He glanced at his watch then as I took another step forward said hurriedly, "The Justice of the Peace has gone to church, and she won't be out for two hours, so you can go." "Hallelujah," I exclaimed, raising my hands and rolling my eyes heavenward until the whites gleamed. By the time I looked down, the policeman had gotten into his car, spun around, and was racing back along the road toward speed traps and sanity.

Amid the disease and death, life with its courtships and weddings rolled along brightly. One of the wonders, maybe bounties, of life is that almost no matter the folly or sadness, cheerful youth seems undiminished. Before the war in 1859, Tom Brown wrote a letter to his "Sweet Little Cousin" Nannie in which he described "EUDORA SOWELL," his "Goddess of Love and the Queen of Beauty."

She has a beautiful figure, a clear white complexion and with two rosey cheeks, red pouting lips, large bright eyes of a deep violent, and profusion of light brown hair as soft as silk. Her face is oval of that pure *Southern* type which fascinates many a boy and leads him to the *Asylum*. Her mischievous looking head is placed upon a swan-like neck, and inclines towards one of the prettiest shoulders you ever looked at. It is as white as alabaster. Her voice is as soft as the first stirrings of an infants dream, her footsteps light as the sylvan footed zephyr which first fanned with the wing of perfume the gable end of new born paradise.

Young Tom did not think he could do justice to Eudora, and after informing Nannie that he had studied himself into a toothache, that Innis had "quit playing the fiddle," and that "a young chap here by the name of Bailey" had written two or three letters to "a Young Lady" and had not received an *answer*, he returned to his favorite subject, writing, "Nannie, I would that my pen were dipt in the dyes of the rain bow [sic] plucked from the wings of an angel, that I might expect to paint to you *the charming girl.*"

Eleven years later Charlotte Morton wrote Nannie from White Bluff. Charlotte's letters were as gossipy and teasing as Tom Brown's were romantic. Sadness had yet to touch her, and life stretched before her, full of promise and intrigue. "Is Hugh Barry better looking than he was last winter?" she wrote.

Poor fellow, his looks will never carry him through the world. Tell Innis to look his best. I am coming up there soon to see him, if he will not come to see me. I know he will say that I must think I am something great. If Colie gets any better looking I know I will fall in love with him. I have a great many secrets to tell you when I see you.... That evening I left your house I made a certain man angry. I had *no* idea how jealous he was. I told him that evening that he was over to your house that my heart was buried; but he would not believe me.

At the end of a letter Charlotte asked Nannie, "Please look over all my mistakes as you know I am not a good scholar, and by *no means* show it to *any one* [sic]." Because Nannie was older, Charlotte realized Nannie's experiences were greater than hers. Sensing that Nannie viewed life differently than she did, she apologized, probably not so much for grammar as for tone. Having done so, she relaxed and concluded with the schoolgirlish request that Nannie keep the letter confidential. In 1860 Mary Brown ended a letter to Nannie similarly, writing, "Please please don't let any one [sic] see this *goose* letter." Although youth never vanishes, individuals age and change, and by 1868, Mary was a widow and sounded different. "You ask if I ever feel merry as we used to," she said. "I can truthfully answer that I do not. In many respects I feel like a different mortal, have learned that 'life is earnest, life is real.' Amid the changes tis comforting to know the love of true and faithful friends remains unchanged. There does'nt [sic] seem to be the same gaiety and life any place there was before the war."

I cannot explain why I took the letters from Aunt Lula's house or why I read them, even when the script had faded, reading them straining my sight and, I often thought, grinding my eyes into grit. Perhaps an innate love of story was the source of my interest. In the South in which I grew up, stories framed families. When the misbehavior of one generation repeated itself in another generation, people nodded and said it was to be expected then sketched the branches of family trees that had exploded into similar blight and canker, or into blossom—although blossoms did not lend themselves as well to tale and its consort gustatory laughter.

In 1859 Nannie gave the valedictory address at Minerva. Entitling her speech "Life's Morning Hour," she talked about the future. "In its morning hour," she said, "life is beautiful indeed and glorious as the dawn; but the moments," she warned, "are flying ever." "How," she asked, "shall we be ready for the fierce glare of noon and the cool and shaded eve and the gloom of that final night. Above us, bend the deep, deep skies of June. In robe of green and decked with coronal of pink and white and blue the queen month Summer makes rich melodies in passing. After her attendant train has passed, however, will be heard the leaden footfalls of the Autumn, tho' hushed for a time as the Indian Summer glides with angel beauty." Life was not only real and earnest, as Mary Brown quoted, but it was often short, and by the later 1860s, several of Nannie's friends had heard the heavy approach of Autumn. To be unmarried and forever dependant was dreadful, and those who thought themselves bound to tread the long *"single road of blessedness"* often wrote despondent letters. A friend wrote Nannie from Nashville in 1870 quoting "The Rime of the Ancient Mariner":

> The last young lady of my age in the neighborhood will marry within three or four months. I shall feel like 'one who treads alone.' Those who seem like children to me, are marrying every four weeks. You wish to know something of my future prospects. I have none. I am nothing more than *loose lumber* thrown about unfit for any laudable purpose. My love scrapes are nothing romantic or novel. I visit so little that I have but four gentlemen acquaintances and if one should come along green enough to propose, I feel and know I am not qualified mentally or physically to fill the place of wife.

If a man proposed, she wrote, she would be frightened out of her wits for a few minutes; then, she said, she would "reply in the negative and let them float. I know they lose nothing."

Near the end of "Life's Morning Hour," Nannie addressed her classmates directly. "Let us profit wisely by the acquisitions made here, that we may not disappoint the loved ones who watch our progress fondly." "Soon," she said, "the last words will be spoken that we may ever speak together here—let them be words of kindness and love and our memories will be held in dear esteem while blessings will still be asked from us from many true and faithful hearts. This sad hour, too quickly here, will leave from its very tears a rich deposit for affection." For me the letters became a rich deposit of the past, enhancing, as Nannie put it, "the loveliness that borders our pathway in life." I don't know what effect, if any, reading the letters had upon me. Much as I enjoyed mathematics, I liked deciphering handwritings and calculating the relationships between people, something that eventually became less important to me than the moods and tones of the letters. In school I was a good math student, but the effect of math upon me has not always been healthy. In high school, I took a math quiz every day for four years. For fifty years I've had nightmares about math, waking in the early morning covered with perspiration having dreamed I was going to class without having prepared the day's lesson.

Whatever the letters' effect, I came to like Innis, Tom, Mary, and William, and even unschooled Charlotte Morton. For Nannie I felt real affection. My great grandmother could write, and she seemed wondrously nice. Years later, after I had begun to teach, telling acquaintances that I was the first schoolmarm in my family, I rummaged through the letters again and discovered that after the war Nannie started her own school. Among the letters I found a teacher's certificate for the "Tennessee Public Schools." Scoring nine out of a possible ten points on all her examinations, Nannie was certified to teach orthography, reading, writing, mental arithmetic, written arithmetic, grammar, geography, and United States history in the public schools of Williamson County in 1874.

"It is an open path that we all are traveling though it closes in the gloom of a forest," Nannie said in her commencement speech. "To all it is more or less agreeable but the forest and the scenes we may there encounter will occasion us to pause. Happy the one who looking forward with hope and inward assurance sees glimpses beyond of green fields opening in the sunlight." By 1870 Nannie rarely wrote about sweethearts. Life's morning hour was over, and she seemed to be approaching the gloom of spinsterhood. For some time she'd had a serious suitor from Mississippi. Unfortunately his letters were prosaic and probably appealed little to the woman who'd urged schoolmates to be active in life and "possess the goodly land and gather into the storehouse of the soul true wealth, before noons intensity pours forth its wearying fervor." In one letter, the gentleman from Mississippi stated that he heard she was going to be married. She replied that she doubted that she would ever marry, reminding him that several years earlier she told him that although "I respected and esteemed you we never could marry." "I always expect to entertain for you," she added, "feelings of friendship," assuring him that "no one outside of your relations would rejoice more over your settling and success in life than myself."

Nannie was closer to marriage than she revealed or perhaps even thought. For three years she had been courted by D. F. Griffin, known to his friends as Grif and Bud to his family in Calhoun, Georgia. I could not find out much about Bud, and when I asked Father about him, he said all that he had heard was that "during the war, he had been sergeant and a martinet and that he had fought at Chickamauga." For a time I entertained myself by imagining that William Pickering and Bud Griffin fought against each other in Georgia. The Battle of Chickamauga, however, took place in September, and William Pickering was almost certainly in Carthage at the time. What is true is Pickering was a more substantial person than Griffin. Years after I first perused the letters, I discovered that Bud had been stabbed to death in Franklin in a drunken brawl, supposedly in a pool hall by an irate husband. "God, how did you find that out?" Father exclaimed when I asked him about Griffin's death. "He was a rotter, and now you will write about it."

As the old saying puts it, "he who has no scoundrels in his family was got by lightning." In any case the course of Griffin's love did not run formal as did that of the suitor from Mississippi, something that might have appealed to the romantic woman who penned a luscious graduation address. In 1871 someone sent Nannie a letter warning her against him. "A terable hush has taken posesion of my whole nature," Griffin wrote when he learned about the letter. "I cant think that you doubt my love and devotion," he declared, "but when I remember that you have some of the most serious and disgraceful charges against me, unless I can vindicate myself most *perfectly*, of these charges and establish myself a man of honor how can you respect me." Griffin suspected a doctor in Calhoun of writing Nannie, but without "positive proof," he said, he could not accuse him. The matter eventually passed, but his accusation may have been true for Griffin's life in Georgia had been tempestuous. In July 1872 he visited Calhoun and wrote Nannie.

Have seen every body [sic], believe that I *have* got some friends here, am told so, at least as well as enemies, have seen to the man that shot me, he was working with a thrasher when he saw me, he left his work and hasn't been heard of since, though I sent word to his family that I was too well pleased with Tenn—or anticipated too happy a life to ruin it by shooting him unless he was too conspicuous, but the temptation was almost too *great*—had it not been for *you* I would have shot him six times when I saw him.

In a second letter from Georgia he said,

I am about to become a politician again (as in the old times of busting up the Union Leagues). Some of the best friends I ever had are running for office in this county. I have met several & talked to them of my worst enemies, who made out charges & swore to them, carried them to Atlanta & got the Yankees after me, but it is allright *I have no feeling against them* whatsoever. It makes me feel strange to be that way. I must certainly have retrograded, lost all spirit but I don't care.

Running for office seems to have come to nothing. In any case pride ran aggressively through Griffin's letters, and he probably was tempted to shoot the man at the thresher. In 1873 he wrote Nannie asking where he stood in her affections. Instead of pleading his love, he argued it. Conscious of his honor, he declared, "It is unnecessary and out of place in this to make any protestation or assertion of my declared and known attachment because that could be construed into an entreaty or supplication."

In 1868 Mary Bailey wrote Nannie and jokingly referred to one of Nannie's suitors. "Why didn't you tell me who your sweetheart is with whom you had the quarrel?" she asked. "I think that is a good sign for the course is never straight. If he is not a good, true and noble character I shall not give my consent." By the time Griffin began courting Nannie, Mary was dead. If she had been alive, I doubt she would have consented to the marriage. Griffin was not academic and wrote poorly, albeit directly. He was difficult and quarrelsome, and he probably wasn't *true*. Still at his death one of his friends wrote Nannie, saying, "He was the noblest man I ever saw." Maybe he didn't die in a pool hall stabbed by an abused husband. I will never know, and that is all right. Enough mystery should surround distant relatives to so awaken imagination that a person half-creates his family. Be this as it may, however, when Griffin asked Nannie to marry him, she was no longer young and probably would not have had many more sweethearts. Moreover he was as colorful as the rich prose that dyed her pages purple.

Like their courtship, the course of Nannie and Bud's marriage did not run smoothly. Griffin seems to have been at odds with people in Franklin. In 1876 Nannie's friends were writing her assuring her about Bud and saying things like, "I cannot keep my tears back when I think of his troubles. I do not see how they can prove that he is a desperate man." In September, Mary Innis or Mamie, their first child, was born. By 1877 Bud had left for Texas to make a new life for Nannie and Mamie near San Saba. He liked Texas, and in writing Nannie, who had remained in Franklin with Mamie until he could earn enough money to support them, said, "[I] would do any thing [sic] in the world but leave Texas to see you and our baby.... Don't [sic] let my being among strangers trouble you, because I see a great many men here to like and none to dislike, that is a great advantage that I have here over Franklin and to tell you the truth it was about to get the best of me, my feeling towards some men there.... It soured my whole nature, and made me so ill that I did'nt [sic] care who I insulted, but I am out of all that now and I hope to heaven I will stay out of it."

Griffin's spirits rose in Texas, and he enjoyed planning a future raising cattle and writing Nannie about "the wildest country I ever saw." His letters became tough and healthy. When his jaw got infected, he wrote heartily, "I intend to have the whole bone taken out if I have to get a carpenter to do it." He was at home in a place where adventure seemed but a ride away, and now seemed to resent the fetters of domesticity. In answer to a letter from Nannie in which she chided him for neglecting Mamie's birthday and in which she had said how much she missed him, he wrote testily, "It seems to me that I am having too much anxiety from you, intend to not have so much hereafter—Yes I know when the babies birthday came, am not so hard as to forget that."

Griffin's letters were also vulgar, certainly in terms of the Brown family in Franklin. "Slept last night in a house and next room to a couple that married yesterday," he wrote, "will tell you something funny when we meet, only a thin partition between us." "Well there is one thing I will say for San Saba," he wrote on another occasion, "there is not a woman in the county of bad caracter [sic] that I have heard of and am told by every body that there is not one and there was never but one bastard child born in it, and that woman don't live here now. So," he concluded, "you need not be writing to me to be good and behave for you see I have to, but I ought not write this way to you and wont any more, only wish to tell you, so that your heart may be easy."

Nannie's letters to Griffin were filled with longing. "Honey please don't neglect to write to me for you know I cant bear suspense and trouble," she wrote after not hearing from Texas for a fortnight. "To have the blues a week nearly kills poor me. *I want to see you so bad yes so bad.*" "If you have not gotten into business I want you to come back," she wrote in almost every letter. To lure him home she described Mamie. "There is not a day nor scarcely an hour passes that I do not wish for you to see her. She is so smart and cute. Whenever she wants Emma or I to do anything she opens her little mouth and holds it up for a kiss." Mamie could say "several words, mammy, dad, daddy, kittie, tow (cow), cat, and answers when we call her."

Nannie's letters did not bring Griffin home, and eventually she and Mamie went to Texas. One of the Browns probably gave her money for the trip. Griffin was not successful in Texas, or in

Tennessee for that matter. Shortly after he left, one of Nannie's acquaintances accused him of leaving Franklin without paying a debt to her father. From Texas, Griffin importuned Nannie to borrow money from her relatives and send it to him so he could purchase cattle. Aside from a few letters written in the early 1880s the letters contained almost nothing about Nannie and Bud after they married. Once I owned a second box of letters, these consisting mostly of letters written to Nannie from Texas, but one evening Father behaved like Innis in the presence of Miss Dora's folks. After taking too much, he found the letters and threw them into the garbage.

Bud's rough language would not have appealed to Father. I never heard Father curse or say an untoward phrase. Mother's language bounced more. For a man who enjoyed lively tales, Father was very proper. For years he worked for the Travelers Insurance Company in Nashville. After his death, a woman wrote me. She wanted, she explained, to tell me how he appeared to clerical workers. She never met him outdoors, she recounted, when "he didn't remove his hat." The staff benefited from his "gentlemanly instincts," she recalled, saying, "One of the first things I ever heard about him was that he would never say anything improper to a lady or allow anyone else to," noting that "this was mighty valuable protection in the days before corporations had sexual harassment policies. He was all the protection we needed, and if you had a problem, you went to him. Some of the managers were afraid to make waves, but he wasn't." I suppose the impropriety in the letters nagged at father, and with drink providing the impetus, perhaps he decided to reduce the past to reticence. I understand the urge. I found Father's love letters to Mother in the attic. They were in a shoe box and bound with a pink ribbon. Dates on the envelopes revealed the contents. I did not read the letters. "When he comes up here," Grandma Pickering wrote describing one of my visits to Carthage, "he goes through my books, even up stairs, and brings out pictures and letters. He just lives to prowl." Prowling I did, and although I explored places inhabited by wild women and snakes, I knew that reading those love letters would have broken faith with my parents.

I had read the letters that Father threw away, but all that stuck to mind was that Nannie and Bud returned to Franklin. They had two more girls, Lula born in October 1876 and my grandmother Frances Sue, born, as a family bible records, on "Monday Morning at 3 O'clk 15th September 1879." In 1881 Bud died. Among Nannie's papers was a receipt dated March 9, 1881, and made out from Samuel Henderson to Enoch Brown, Nannie's father. On February 4, Henderson had provided Griffin's funeral clothes. Bud's suit and shroud cost $27.50; his slippers $1.50; his shirt and collar, $2; his undershirt $1.25, and his drawers $1. His socks cost 25¢ as did his cravat. Two collar buttons were 10¢; his studs, 40¢ and his sleeve buttons, 30¢. The total was $34.55.

Nannie and Bud, the Browns themselves, had only a paper attic life. I did not find a picture of any of them. Moreover they vanished almost completely after Bud's death, and my grandmother Frances Griffin quickened only after she married my grandfather at the beginning of the twentieth century. I know Coleman Brown helped the young family. In a trunk in Carthage I found a copy of a weekly newspaper the *Williamson County News*, published on February 11, 1915. In it appeared the obituary of my grandmother's younger sister Mary Innis Griffin. "When a child," the obituary stated, "she went with her widowed mother to live with her uncle Coley Brown, in the Sixth district of this county, where she grew to young womanhood, later going to Nashville to reside." Still, I have no idea how Nannie passed her widowhood and when she died or what sort of childhood my grandmother experienced. I don't know where grandmother went to school or how long she spent at Coley's. Perhaps she didn't stay with an uncle but her brother Coleman Edward Brown, or maybe with her father Enoch Brown, who had migrated from Virginia to Tennessee. Fittingly for me because I enjoy the circles of life, Enoch Brown had been born in 1807 in Prince William County, Virginia, just across the Pamunkey River from Cabin Hill, my

Grandfather Ratcliffe's farm where I spent boyhood summers. Writing to Mary Brown early in the war, Innis described an evening of sentry duty. "I had a trial of standing guard last Wednesday night," he wrote, "but as it happened I had a good night for the business. There was but one man came to my post, and I halted him, and asked for the countersign. Then he put his hand in his pocket and drew out a bottle. I touched it slightly and told him to pass on." Maybe that is all relatives do; they touch a life slightly, in this case becoming part of the imaginative, maybe intoxicating, fabric of one's days then they pass on.

Carthage Tales

My grandfather Samuel Pickering and my father Samuel Francis Pickering were born in Carthage, my grandfather spending his entire life there, Father moving away after college. Carthage appears throughout my books. At times the town is real, a small country place built high above the north bank of the Cumberland River and the seat of Smith County. At other times, the town is fictional, peopled by characters spun out of my mind and whose doings are comic, the sources of their words and activities lifted from forgotten nineteenth-century books and journals. The tales I tell are usually corny, the sort of stories I hope will make readers smile and ponder the richness of words and life itself for a moment or two. Stories furnish, and perhaps, shape the mind, and my fictional stories are grafts growing atop tales told by Father.

Often when the fret of the world nags at me, I travel to Carthage and write paragraphs that make me chuckle. Afterward I get up from my desk, and if I don't say, "God's in his Heaven, all's right with the world," at least the seasons bloom brighter, even cold bare winter. After crashing into the tool shed, Grandpa Pickering put off learning to drive for a long time, Father told me. When carriages vanished, he hired a colored man named Monk to drive him about the county when he made his rounds selling insurance. "No mule," Grandpa once said, "ever died a natural death in Smith County. Mules are the lightning rod of the animal creation." In any case storytelling has run through the Pickerings for three generations. Grandpa sold insurance to and boarded with farmers on his trips, staying up late at night, Father's brother Coleman told me, "telling big stories." Father repeated the stories to me. The stories were slow and gentle, and if hankering for the out-of-the-way was not already in my genes, the tales may have made me long for places beyond the grids of everyday life, places where words could twist about and not tumble into a pit staked with meaning and significance.

Grandpa grew strawberries, and when we drove to Carthage in berry season, I ran to the strawberry patch as soon as the car stopped. In the early fifties when Grandpa was housebound and dying of cancer, the illness concealed from me, Father apologized to Grandpa for my racing to the patch before coming inside and visiting. "For heaven's sakes, Samuel," Grandpa said, "leave the boy alone. I'd like to be out there myself." As might be expected Grandpa's tales were ripe with berries. Miss Lucy lived across the street from Grandpa. One day after picking a bucket of strawberries, Grandpa saw Miss Lucy sitting on her front porch rocking. Knowing she liked strawberries, Grandpa poured out a quart and walked across the street to give them to her. When he reached the front steps, Miss Lucy put down her fan, stopped rocking, and said, "Mr. Sam, I'm glad you came by. I've just had a nervous breakdown." "Oh, I'm so sorry," said Grandpa, "but I have brought you some strawberries." "That's nice of you, Mr. Sam, thank you," Miss Lucy said as she took the berries. After Grandpa walked back across the street, Miss Lucy went into the kitchen, washed some of the strawberries, and poured cream over them. Then she returned to the front porch and ate them. When she finished, she put the bowl down beside her chair and began to rock and fan herself again. On another occasion Mrs. Polk, a neighbor, burst into Grandpa's kitchen one morning during breakfast crying that her daughter Mary who had moved to Nashville was "ruined." "Oh, Lord," Grandpa exclaimed, "was she taken advantage of?" "Yes," Mrs. Polk answered. "She had her hair bobbed."

For the most part the stories warmed feelings and smoothed the edges of moods. Miss Dotty was the daughter of the owner of the local hardware store. She never married. An only child, she lived at home and took care of her parents until they died. Her father was not a good businessman, and at his death when the store was sold and his debts paid, Miss Dotty was left with little. Over the years the little shrank to almost nothing; yet, she did not go without. Relatives mended her roof, and neighbors brought her firewood and coal, eggs and chickens. Several nights a week at dinnertime, Miss Dotty put on her best clothes and started uptown. Townspeople watched for her, and before she walked far, someone always invited her to dinner. "Don't you look nice, Miss Dotty," a neighbor would say, "We are just sitting down to eat. We're not having anything fancy, but we'd be pleased if you'd join us."

In Nashville, Father described people he knew as a boy in Carthage. He used actual names. To protect the decent, however, I've changed the names. After Beasley Nickerson retired from the bank, he roomed with his daughter Hattie Mae and her husband in their home on Jefferson Street. Although Hattie Mae cooked, washed, and cleaned, Beasley moved in more for her sake than his. Lafayette Fisher, her husband, was charming but feckless, and sometimes when the mortgage or insurance came due, he found himself embarrassed. At such times Beasley paid the bills. The Nickersons were long-lived, however, and toward the end of his life, Beasley slipped mentally and spent much time walking about Carthage, roaming streets and a landscape that he only partly understood. No harm came to him, though, as people looked out for him and led him home to Hattie Mae before dinner. Late one day Lafayette found him outside the Walton Hotel on Main Street. He guided him home, and as they walked they talked about old times in Carthage, Beasley's memory seeming keen and clear. When they reached the little gate outside their house on Jefferson, Beasley turned to his son-in-law and said, "I've certainly enjoyed walking with you, and the talk has just been fine, but this is where I live. I'd invite you in, but I don't know if my daughter would approve of my asking a stranger to dinner."

Once during Grandpa's travels he spent the night at Chestnut Mound with Miss Fanny and Russell Hayes. The next morning when he was getting ready to leave, Miss Fanny asked Grandpa if he ever went to Difficult Creek, Tennessee, saying she heard he was quite a traveler and had been to Nashville. "Yes, ma'am," Grandpa answered. "I go there right much." "Well, the next time you go," Miss Fanny said, "please say hello to Henry McCracken; he's my brother, and I haven't seen him in over twenty years." "What!" Grandpa exclaimed. "Difficult Creek is only twelve miles away, just the other side of the Caney Fork River. Rome's Ferry will take you across in eight minutes." "Oh, Mr. Sam," Miss Fanny answered wistfully, shaking her head, "I do want to see my brother, but I just can't bring myself to cross the great Caney Fork River."

Among books I should have read during childhood was Kenneth Grahame's *The Wind in the Willows*. At the beginning of the book, Water Rat says to his new friend Mole, "there is *nothing*—absolutely nothing—half so much worth doing as simply messing about in boats." Years ago, I reached the stage of life in which I agreed with Ratty. Nothing seemed half so much worth doing as messing about. Indeed, I decided Hell was a place where everything mattered, where belief and ambition so shackled people to purpose that they spent their days bent in the hot sun, chopping and hoeing doings into significance, so ginning events that they forced themselves and others into peonage, transforming themselves into moral and intellectual sharecroppers. Not crossing the great Caney Fork River at a time when "everybody" seemed ambitious and was rushing onward and upward shouting "Excelsior" was marvelously seductive. Or so I think now. Maybe this book really is an apologia for my life, an after-the-fact justification for having slipped the bits of ambition and high seriousness.

Reams Suddaby sold Fords in Carthage. He was an inert man who spent days dozing on a bench outside the courthouse. Not even customers could stir him. If somebody wanted to look at a car, Suddaby handed him the keys to the garage and told him to poke around. Only the Ford distributor in Louisville disrupted Suddaby's calm. Fords were popular, and distributors forced dealers to take cars they didn't want. Suddaby's fights with the distributor were well-known. "This is hilly country. Don't send us any more tractors," he was once heard yelling into the telephone, "and for God's sake don't send us a Lincoln." As could be expected, outsiders were the subject of other stories. Because population tallies for Smith County changed greatly from one decade to another, or so the story went, an official from the Census Bureau in Washington came to Carthage to investigate. The first local dignitary the official called upon was the mayor. "Counting people in the hollows hereabouts is impossible," the mayor explained to the official as he took him out onto the courthouse lawn, adding as they walked that "a goodly number of folks don't want anything to do with the government, and then, of course, there is the problem of foreign language." "Foreign language," the official exclaimed, "I thought everybody in Tennessee spoke English." "Gracious me, no," the mayor said, "people in Washington often make that mistake." "See that man?" he continued, pointing to an old farmer sitting on a bench eating his lunch out of a paper sack. "Talk to him and you'll understand about foreign languages," the mayor continued, taking the official by the arm and leading him over to the bench. When the mayor reached the farmer, he stopped and said, "Whar he?" "Whar who?" responded the farmer. When my children were old enough to appreciate this shaggy dog story, I told it to them. They looked puzzled and in a chorus said, "I don't get it," a reaction that bowled me over into a squatting position and made me laugh and laugh.

In Father's and Grandpa's Carthage stories, the pompous were forever being deflated. Gainesboro, Father once began, was an out-of-the-way place. About the only people who traveled regularly to Gainesboro were drummers, and they usually traveled by horse, staying at a small hotel run by Miss Polly Gittings. One wet fall day just as Miss Polly stepped out on the porch to ring the lunch bell, a drummer splashed up, his horse caked in mud. A smart aleck, he stopped in front of Miss Polly and said, "Ma'am, could you tell me where Gainesboro, Tennessee, can be found?" Miss Polly took her hand away from the bell rope and turning around looked the drummer up and down. Then as people gathered for lunch, she said, "If you'll jump down off your horse, you'll be up to your ass in it right now."

Many of the "stories" consisted of simple statements. "My wife's relatives are gregarious and nomadic," Mr. Crittle was fond of saying each year when the Pedigrift tribe wandered through Carthage and paid him a visit. In the morning Dr. Jarrett was a fine doctor, but after lunch he drank and his diagnostic and verbal skills deteriorated. Late one afternoon a countryman brought his wife in to be examined. Dr. Jarrett took her pulse, looked into her mouth and ears, and pressed this and that. "How is she, doctor?" the farmer said, getting nervous as Dr. Jarrett sank back into his chair. "All I can say," Dr. Jarrett answered, "is that she is heading for the last roundup"—a response that exercised the farmer considerably. "The woman," Father added, "was in fine shape and lived twenty more years."

In prowling I found old Carthage newspapers. The news especially along the margin of the papers, the place that attracted me most, was brief and anecdotal, table talk that could or could not be humorous. One issue of the *Record-Democrat*, published in 1894, noted that "W.N. Adams asked us to say he will be on his round at the usual time this spring castrating colts" and "Dick Hodges lost a fine hog Sunday with cholera." "It don't take much to make a good average Methodist," the Reverend Sam P. Jones said, "Go to church once a week, give about one-tenth of what you should, and keep out of the penitentiary." In another issue, Jones said, "I wouldn't give whiskey to a man until he had been dead for three days." "When an old red-nosed politician gets so he isn't fit for anything else," Jones stated, "the Democrat Party send him to the legislature." The prose in the papers was alive, even if the subject was death. "The grim reaper of death," reported a correspondent of the *Carthage Courier* in 1915, had visited Brush Creek, "taking for its victim Mrs. Crook, the devoted wife of Tillman Crook." "We are very sorry to report that the death angel has again visited our community," began a column from Horseshoe Bend. The death angel blazed the way for commerce. On the second page of the *Courier* was an advertisement for J. P. Carter, a funeral director in Rome, Tennessee. Carter's advertisement measured three and half by four and a half inches. A horse-drawn hearse trundled across the top of the advertisement. "No trips too long, too cold or too hot," Carter declared. "Coffins, Caskets, Robes, Burial Suits from the cheapest to the best. Quarter-sawed Oak Caskets, Metallic Caskets, burglar-proof steel vaults, Cabinet-furnished outside boxes carried in stock for ready use." "In fact everything to care for the dead," Carter assured potential patrons. "I have a branch at R. A. Waggoner's in South Carthage and can have my new funeral car there within two hours. I have uptodate funeral cars, one for white and one for colored, both rubber-tired." Grandpa appeared on the same page as Carter's advertisement, shaking the hands of the quick, however. "Sam Pickering of Carthage," the correspondent from Brush Creek reported, "agent for the Home Insurance Co. was here last week writing insurance."

When newspapers described selling insurance and the loss of a hog, time moved differently than it does now. People, or family, stayed in places long enough to be known and to become characters. Earl Hodges owned a few played-out acres of land not fit for plowing. He also owned a still and made a modest living selling whiskey. Periodically the sheriff arrested him, and he had to appear before Judge Joe Russell. Earl was a master at getting off. Once he fainted in the courtroom, and the clerk took him to the doctor. Although the judge's family was distinguished and helped support the Methodist church, Judge Russell's disreputable brother, Jerry, patronized Earl and his still. On one occasion the sheriff arrested Earl while Jerry was asleep in Earl's cabin. "You've been selling whiskey again," Judge Joe said later in the courtroom. "No, sir," Earl answered. Staring intently at him, Judge Russell asked, "On such and such a day, didn't Mr. Jerry Russell come to your place, buy half a gallon of whiskey, and stay dead drunk for two days?" Earl fidgeted then said nervously, "Which Mr.—which Mr.

Russell was that?" People in the courtroom began to laugh; the case was adjourned, and Earl eventually got off.

Grandfather Ratcliffe had means, and Mother grew up at ease amid people and words. When the poor say something rough, they are guilty of bad taste. When the wealthy say the same thing, they are often thought eccentric, perhaps even charming, particularly if their money has not been tainted by ostentation. In any case Mother's language was rougher than Father's. Of course that may not have had so much to do with wealth as with the earthy nature of the Ratcliffes themselves. Among Big Ga's favorite expressions, one that reflected his knowledge of cattle, was, "Anxious enough to shit a screwworm backwards." His sister Alice was a successful schoolteacher. After her retirement a school was named for her. Later in life when I knew and loved her, she was outspoken. She was a small woman and sank out of sight into chairs, so much so she wasn't noticed and conversation flowed around her until she spoke. Even so she didn't speak until she disagreed with something. Then she said just one word, "Bullshit" erupting like an explosion from her chair. Afterward, she subsided into silence. I have much Ratcliffe in me, and my taste in stories is low. One of my favorite Carthage stories described a meeting between Miss Reba, a maiden lady who worked at the Electric Company, and Mr. Price Fisher, a pleasant but ponderously slow man. When Price came in to pay his bill, Father related, Miss Reba greeted him, saying, "Good morning, Mr. Fisher, and how are you today?" Price took the remark literally. "Oh, Miss Reba," he replied, "I'm not doing so well." "I'm sorry to hear that," Miss Reba responded. "I do hope you'll better soon." "Miss Reba, I hope so, too," Price answered. "I'm suffering from slow movement of the bowels, but I took something before coming here, and I think things will move along directly."

Of course as I grew older, Father told me broader tales. Leslie Dickenson, he recounted, once visited a country girl in her home in Una and stayed too late in the parlor. "Sister, is the company gone?" the girl's little brother called from upstairs. Embarrassed and slightly nervous, Leslie instructed the girl to tell her brother that he had gone. "Well, then," the voice came back from above, "Ma says to pee before you come upstairs. The pot's full."

Some people will think such stories are, as the old expression puts it, the last of pea time the first of frost. Vicki doesn't like my stories and refuses to listen when I mention Carthage, saying as she walks out of the room, "You were not so hokey when I married you." I assume my grandmother Frances Sue Griffin resembled Vicki and did not like the stories either. Storytellers are usually tolerant, aware of their own foibles as well as those of others. Instead of judging, they marvel, and I suspect Grandpa Pickering rarely gave people unsolicited advice. Grandma Pickering was very different, solicitous and ambitious, a parent who hovered over her offspring long after they left home. "Mother," Uncle Coleman told me, "expected too much of us." In the 1990s Coleman suffered from dementia, and I took over his affairs. He lived in Houston, and several times I flew to Texas to manage his life. In his house I found many letters from Grandma. Like Bud Griffin he had gone to Texas and, so far as I could tell, not managed well. Grandma's letters contained few stories. Instead they were tablets of advice, not the sort of thing to endear her to a middle-aged man.

After sending Coleman money to buy a new suit, preferably "a light worsted which will be useful year round," she wrote. "You must have cufflink shirts and they must extend beyond the coat sleeve. You see I notice what the well-dressed man is wearing. And you need a hat. A man should wear a hat to be well-dressed." "I would love to be there to go with you when you select your suit," she concluded. In another letter she told him to make sure all his suits fit. Fashions, she observed, had changed. Trousers were shorter and snugger than in the past. Coats, she explained, "are not as full in the back, and sleeves should show the shirt cuff when the arm is extended."

She lectured Coleman on work habits. She urged him to get to the office early and finish tasks before leaving at the end of the day. "Never be late at your work, Coleman," she wrote; "this is one of the most important items in every business. *So listen to me.* It will pay off." Grandma harped on order and appearance. "Son," she said, "*be sure* and keep your desk in good order. Every thing counts in business. *Be* careful to see that your desk is always in good order and appearance." Coleman's buying a Ford Comet provided the occasion for a lecture on car care. "Write me about your insurance now," she advised him. "Drop into a place and have the car cleaned. Keep it nice. Don't load it up with litter. Put a carton in it to hold *extras.* This carton could be kept inside on the back floor for convenience."

Grandpa's tales must have struck Grandma as pointless, providing neither morals nor guidance. I expect the richness of personality in the stories did not appeal to her. Grandma was Nannie's daughter. She was bright and would have thrived at college. As much as a fictional Carthage attracts me now, the actual town was probably too small for her then. She was strong-willed and opinionated, once confessing to me that she voted for Roosevelt "the first time." After her death I found scrapbooks in her storeroom, swollen with clippings which described the achievements of women. She was also interested in literature, and the scrapbooks contained countless poems, reviews, and articles. Most of the poems were inspirational or religious, poems which instructed, typically entitled "Symbols of Victory" and "Earth Is Not Man's Abiding Place." Occasionally, though, I found other kinds of poetry, poems for the dreamer not the moralist, poems which did not teach but which sketched moods. Pasted on the bottom of a page containing an article on "Shakespeare's Ideals of Womanhood" and a review of *For Whom the Bell Tolls* were two lines: "I've reached the land of Golden-rod, / Afar I see it wave and nod." Grandpa probably saw the goldenrod, stumbling upon it while meandering the county; Grandma probably searched for it but never found it, goldenrod being, I reckon, a happenstance sort of sight, something the disciplined often miss.

Family in Virginia

In his autobiography *The Story of My Heart* (1883), Richard Jefferies, the British naturalist, wrote, "Time has never existed, and never will; it is purely an artificial arrangement. It is eternity now, it always was eternity, and always will be…. There is no separation—no past; eternity is NOW, is continuous." Jefferies described the circling seasons, seeing beginnings in endings and endings in beginnings. Families are not so abstract; people exist in then vanish from time, their lives prolonged by scraps left clinging to the margins of passing days. Prowling turned up only a few bits of paper pertaining to the Ratcliffes, Mother's side of my family. The burning of Grandfather's house destroyed almost all records except for a family bible published in the eighteenth century. Registered in the bible were the births, marriages, and deaths of several Ratcliffes. Judson Ratcliffe, for example, married Elizabeth Baker on January 2, 1772. Norval, their son, was born on December 4, 1772. Twenty-one days later on Christmas, he died. Virginia their daughter fared better, being born in 1776 and living seventy-eight years, dying in 1853.

Other Ratcliffes appeared: Regina, Elizabeth Ann, Mary, and Gideon. Beside the dates of Archibald, a child who lived from November 16, 1824 to October 26, 1826, someone wrote, "When the icy hand of death his saber drew! / To cut down the budding rose of morn!! / He held his favorite motto full in view— / The fairest Bud must the tomb adorn!!!" Family trees, their print cankered by time, grafted the Ratcliffes to other families in Virginia: Carter, Dale, Wingfield, Armistead, and Skipwith. Not until the birth of my great grandfather Hampden Frances in 1853, however, does the family quicken into story. Until Father told me that he was named after a neighbor in Ohio, I imagined that William Pickering's middle name Blackstone celebrated the great legal scholar. In the same way I hoped and still hope that Hammy, as he was called, was named after John Hampden, the seventeenth-century English patriot. Killed on Chalgrove Field in 1643, Hampden was a Parliamentarian and one of the leaders of forces opposed to King Charles I. Thoughts about the future of the United States make me melancholy. Americans have forgotten not only their roots but also the dirt out of which all families spring. In accumulating wealth and power, too many people seem intent upon building dynasties: royalist, glittering, corrupt, and as self-serving as the divine right of kings.

Hammy was born in 1853 and died in 1934; his wife Alice Garthright died three days later. Again the Civil War seems the matter of yesterday. According to Mother, as Hammy and the maid caring for him watched the Battle of Mechanicsville, spent minie balls fell into the grass around them, buzzing like bees. Alice Garthright was from Cold Harbor, and during the battle Union troops used her house as a hospital, the blood dripping through the floors and forming pools in the basement. The home is now part of the Battlefield Memorial Park. When I was in Virginia, I found remnants of the war, Confederate money, five-, ten-, twenty-, and fifty-dollar bills, all minted in Richmond, Jefferson Davis on the fifty-dollar bill; on the ten, two teams of horses pulling a caisson and galloping toward battle, on the near side white horses with riders on their backs, on the far side black horses, on the caisson behind, three artillery men.

In my basement in Connecticut is a small sofa, on which J. E. B. Stuart supposedly slept prior to his death at the Battle of Yellow Tavern. In the sideboard are six blue and white unglazed plates nine inches in diameter and, tale tells, from the White House of the Confederacy. The surface of the plates has a bisque-like texture. A grape vine runs like a blue vein around the rim of each plate, tendrils curling in spirals down the bowl of the plate. In the center and along the right edge of the bowl lies a large grape leaf, its mid-veins blue. To the left of the leaf are two clusters of white grapes, in one cluster twenty-two grapes. Spiraling around the left and along the lip of the plate are other leaves, two more grape leaves and two sets of strawberry leaves, all blue and white; four strawberries, the small leaves at the tops of the fruit white and blue and the strawberries themselves white; and lastly four strawberry blossoms, these blue and white, beside each blossom a stem languidly dangling from the side, on the end of the stem a blue and white bud.

In a dresser I found a single letter referring to the war. "My Dearest Maggie," Mollie wrote on February 14, 1864,

> I have intended replying to your welcome affectionate letter ever since its reception but have company staying with me all the time & parties &c engrossing all time. I had rather have had a quiet time all my own in which I could have written long letters to loved friends, yet we owe certain duties to society & and when there is a gayety we generally are constantly occupied. We have had a great many parties dinners &c.... I am becoming I very much fear too dissipated. We have 8 or 10 companies of Cavalry in the county. The Regiment to which my Brother is attached is now at home, & he is with us. I was at a large dancing party, given by the Signal Corps, which is stationed a short distance from us. My Brother, a Capt. Friend from one of the R----D Howitzers & my sister accompanied me. I danced until 4-1/2 o'clock & got home just before day.

The dancing did not last. Within a month Grant assumed command of the Union forces. Leading the Army of the Potomac through the Wilderness, Spotsylvania Courthouse, Cold Harbor, and Petersburg, he drove Lee to Appomattox and surrender in April 1865. In February 1864, however, the Army of the Potomac had not crossed the Rapidan, and the dancers spun on. Mollie wrote,

The Capt. staid with us & we had many invitations out. Then I had a young lady staying here. One Saturday we went up to see a Tournament. There were eleven Knights, dressed in pretty & very becoming costumes. The cavalry had a dinner & dance on the same day & all passed pleasingly. I was invited to another party a few days since & two nice beaux came to take me but I declined. Thursday I am invited to a "grand Military Ball," given by the soldiers, several hundred invitations issued. I expect to go. Most of the girls will dress in silks. I expect a fine time. A Cousin of mine will dress in black velvet & pearls. She is a beauty & will look superbly. I will accompany her. I see some of Col. Robbins Command some times. They are stationed about 20 miles from us & have amusing dances sometimes. Mr. Tomkins looks so well. The Sargt has not yet returned & when asked by Mr. T---when he would do so, his reply was by singing "When Spring time comes gentle Annie."

Major Robinson, Mollie wrote, "is the general heart-breaker of the community. I hope I will pass unscathed." There were breaks between dances and after songs and tournaments, and Mollie was not unmarked. "Maggie dear," she concluded, "is there any appearance of peace in R------d? Do they express any hopes as to the termination of this most evil & unnatural struggle. Oh! when will we be at peace. It seems so long to look forward to—perhaps years—long weary years may escape & those most cherished will find a soldiers grave. Oh! Maggie what an awful thought! & is such a time a season for gayety—I feel condemned."

Eliza McClarin Pickering died in 1888. On New Year's Eve three years later my great-grandfather Pickering married Henrietta Haynie, the daughter of a Confederate surgeon. Father said little about Cousin Etta, as she was known. Evidently she was not popular with Eliza's children. When Eliza died, Great Grandfather buried her in the upper right portion of the family plot and asked that at his death he be buried next to her. The request did not please Cousin Etta. Instead of heeding his wishes she had him buried across the plot in the upper left hand corner, and to ensure that death would not join those whom she wanted asunder, she instructed relatives bury her in the middle of the plot between Eliza and William.

To the marriage she brought a copy of *Father Ryan's Poems*, published in 1880, writing her name Miss Etta Haynie on one of the front pages, the tops of her letters swirling up and tumbling over like small waves breaking on a placid shore. Ryan was once famous, the poet of the Confederacy, "whose spirit," it was said, "shall keep watch over the Stars and Bars until the morning of the Resurrection." A Vincentian Father who taught at Niagara University in Niagara, New York, then later at the diocesan seminary in Cape Girardeau, Missouri, Ryan joined the "Confederate service as a freelance chaplain" in 1862. "Until the Conquered Banner was furled," Ryan "shrived the dying on the battlefield and carried wounded to safety." His contemporaries said that "of himself he had no thought and of death he had no fear." After the war he served as a priest throughout the South, in Biloxi, Nashville, Knoxville, Clarksville, Macon, and Mobile. He made frequent lecture tours, donating his fees to "victims of recurrent plagues" and to the widows and orphans of Confederate soldiers. When smallpox erupted in Gratiot Prison in New Orleans and the chaplain decamped, Ryan was the only divine who ministered to the sick.

In contrast to a life quick with incident, Ryan's poetry is slow and melancholy. Suns set in the west. Vesper bells rang. Nights were starless, and valleys shadowed. Shrouds of grass covered graves, and icicles of woe hung in sorrow's vale. Despite—no, maybe because of its gloom, Ryan's poetry was popular. "The Conquered Banner" and "The Sword of Robert E. Lee," an historian wrote, "were long sung in households and schools of the Southland." "The Prayer of the South" begins, "My brow is bent beneath a heavy rod! / My face is wan and white with many woes! / But I will lift my poor chained hands to God, / And for my children pray, and for my foes." "The Land We Love" had become a "Land where the victor's flag waves, / Where only the dead are the free!" In "The Conquered Banner," Ryan urged, "Furl that Banner, softly, slowly! / Treat it gently—it is holy— / For it droops above the dead. / Touch it not—unfold it never, / Let it droop there, furled forever, / For its people's hopes are dead!"

"When falls the soldier brave, / Dead at the feet of wrong, / The poet sings and guards his grave / With sentinels of song," Ryan declared in "Sentinel Songs." In "A Land without Ruins," Ryan asked to be given a land "where the ruins are spread, / And the living tread light on the hearts of the dead." He wanted to live in a land "blest by the dust" and "bright with the deeds of the down-trodden just," a land "that hath legends and lays" and "memories of long vanished days." He asked for "story and song" of "wreck and the tomb," for there was "grandeur in graves" and "glory in gloom." "For out of the gloom future brightness is born, / As after the night comes the sunrise of morn."

The Civil War materials interested me, but ultimately they weighed heavily, especially the Southern mementoes. When I was a boy in the 1950s, people talked about the war in Ryan's terms, almost as a fortunate fall. Defeat, so the argument ran, enriched white Southerners intellectually and spiritually, making them aware of aspects of life Northerners could not imagine. No other part of the nation had lost a war; consequently people in other regions of the country were soft and glib, given to superficial sociological formulations and practically incapable of looking into the recesses of the human heart. Defeat made the birth of Southerners privileged, raising them above the simple material things which corrupted the rest of the nation and initiating them into the possibility of profound insight. On the other hand such arguments did not affect actual living. Alight with the natural energy of youth, I went to dancing classes at Fortnightly, square dances at Mrs. Brown's, and skating parties at the Hippodrome.

Frequently I heard people mulling missed opportunities, Bragg at Chickamauga, Lee at Gettysburg, "what ifs" punctuating sentences—what if Stonewall Jackson had not been shot by his own troops? In later years I was glad that Great Grandfather Pickering fought for the Union. He freed me from Southern hagiography of the sort promulgated by Ryan. I grew up during the last years of segregation, a time when it seemed no Southerner could do the right thing, at least in the opinion of "outsiders," as they were called. A bunker mentality developed, fortified by romanticizing the Lost Cause and turning the idea of a gentleman almost into a cult. Although I read family letters and saved memorabilia, I longed to escape the South, its legends, lays, and sins, all things that appealed to me. At times I longed for anonymity and the loss of identity. Of course I may simply have wanted to escape history itself, all those stories and words that pin one to place and character like an insect on a specimen board. In any case I suspected the cult of the gentleman, often epitomized by Robert E. Lee, a man whom I eventually decided made a terrible decision and fought for the wrong side with murderous results. Still, wraiths of family and place attracted and perhaps shaped me. Maybe they were partly responsible for my settling far from Tennessee in the northeast. For a child from my background at my time and in my place, the Civil War was initially alluring but ultimately inescapable and oppressive, staining the imagination. My children's lives have been different. They have not heard of Longstreet and Forrest. "Tell Hill he must come up" means nothing to them. They don't know the names of battlefields. Their ignorance frees them to know other things. Instead of pondering distorting history, they mull the present, asking their "what if's" of the future, not of the past.

If I had not discovered Nannie's letters, the war would not have been so big a part of my growing up. In 1943 Mother had a tubal pregnancy. She almost died when a fallopian tube ruptured. She did not know she was carrying another child. Three days later she lost the second child. As a result she was no longer able to have children. If the twins had been born, my life would have been different. Perhaps Father would have felt pressure to become more corporate and would have courted promotion in order to increase his salary. We might have left Nashville. There might have been less to spend on my education, and pleasure. If money had been hard to come by, perhaps I would not have dreamed about travel and would have married and settled in Nashville.

What fear Mother must have experienced when I was sick. In the first letter Ga wrote after she learned of my birth, she asked Mother, "How many more do you want?" Reading that letter now stops thought, as does another letter in which Ga said she was willing to wait for her namesake. In fact I did not learn about Mother's tubal pregnancy until I was over forty. I was oblivious to such matters and was wondrously happy as an only child, though once or twice I hankered for a sibling. In great part I amused myself by reading and by prowling. If I'd had brothers and sisters, I might not have become a prowler, an activity that comes naturally to an only child.

Hindsight is only hindsight and probably inaccurate more often than not. What the man sees, the boy probably didn't notice. Maybe I am only imagining the cult of the gentleman. The gap between words and deeds is vast. From small towns in and around Middle Tennessee, the fathers and grandfathers of my friends didn't rock their lives away in graceful patrician idleness. They did not want school to turn their sons into cultists devoted to an old order. Perhaps the gentleman was an ideal to which people had grown accustomed to praising, so much so they actually believed in its existence, albeit it did not influence daily life. Out of custom, platitudinous and reflexive, Nashvilleans regularly declared that shaping a gentleman was the purpose of a good education while in truth making money counted for more, as in fact it always will in a mobile society.

In the attics I discovered little about the family of Ga or Grandmother Ratcliffe. An obituary of Grandmother's sister, Aunt Lucille, reported that she had been born in Abingdon, Virginia and attended Stonewall Jackson High School. I don't know whether or not Ga went to the same high school. Once I heard that Ga wanted to attend Hollins College but that her father would not let her.

Amid scrapbooks I found pictures of Benjamin Rodapil Catlin, her father. In one he held me as a baby. In another, he himself was a child, posed at the Foster Studio in Richmond. He stood on the seat of an ornate Victorian chair, woodwork running in curlicues around the frame. He wore velvet shorts, leather hook and ring shoes that reached above the ankle, dark socks, and a lacy blouse. He had a page boy haircut, and his left arm was crooked outward, his hand on his hip. He held up his right arm; in his hand was a bouquet of seven large artificial black-eyed Susans, the petals probably yellow, and the centers black or midnight purple. In a third photograph he was old and stood in an alley of big trees, sunlight dappling him. He was elegant and wore a double-breasted white suit, the cut smooth and perfect, the coat hanging without wrinkles. Three weeks after I was born, he sent Mother a small check, saying, "God may see fit to take me out of this world before that great grandson gets large enough to know me, but I do want to start him off with a little bank account." My grandmother's mother was Hattie Horne; in a photograph taken in Richmond at Richmond Photo at 827 1/2 Broad Street, she stood in a heavy glossy Victorian dress, a wave of thick ribbons pouring out of the back in a stomacher. She rested her hands in front of her on a rug tossed over the back of a chair. She had a round face, a straight mouth, and short hair hanging down over her brow. In another picture of the family taken years later, the fat had vanished from her face and her cheeks had sunk, almost as if she had lost her teeth. In the picture nine family members, including Ga before marriage, sat on the front steps on a house. Behind them stood two colored servants. My grandmother's hair was thick and dark and brushed around her face, framing it in an oval. She looked beautiful.

In the envelope in which I found the picture of Hattie was another picture mounted on thick cardboard, time having gnawed the edges. Gables, cupolas, and balconies decorated a wooden Victorian house. Standing on and along the front porch were ten people, the two on the right colored servants, handkerchiefs over their heads and wearing long white aprons. Three of the people in the picture were children, two of them barefoot. In front of the house ran a wooden picket fence decorated with finials; behind the house loomed a building, probably a barn, gray and sliding out of definition. The people in the photograph could have been Hornes or Catlins, or Powells, Faulkners, or Starkes, other names I ran across on bits of paper. Much as the picture had faded and the identities of the people were part of the "gone past," so I know almost nothing about Ga's family. Indeed Ga herself only comes alive on October 4, 1911, the day she married my grandfather John Leigh Ratcliffe. She was nineteen years old, and he was twenty-five. On July 23, the next year, my mother Katherine Winston Ratcliffe was born.

Grandparents and Cabin Hill

Hampden and Alice Garthright Ratcliffe lived at Cedar Hill in Henrico County. They had nine children. The Ratcliffes were clannish and clung together. My great aunts and great uncle, Alice, Betty, and Harold, didn't marry and lived together in Henrico in a big brick house, a few acres of farm land ruffling about them. By my childhood Richmond had spread, and blocks of small houses had mushroomed around the farm. At the edge of the farm, great uncle Wilbur lived with his wife Aunt Elizabeth. Wilbur was the youngest of the nine children and was only twelve years older than Mother, his niece, and she, he, and I were close. He was a dentist, and I enjoyed going to his office and visiting him and his nurse Mrs. Lane. Never did I just enter; I always burst in, usually when Uncle Wilbur was grinding on a patient, her mouth cranked open and stuffed with bales of cotton. "Dr. Ratcliffe," I once exclaimed before he could greet me, "it's good to see you almost sober for a change." I'd like to imagine that on hearing me the patient's knuckles whitened, but I doubt that. Only a jackass would be unnerved by the doings of a small boy. Of course in my and Mother's world, donkeys brayed everywhere. One New Year's Eve, Mother and Father hired a new sitter, a prissy old woman who, she said, had to have her coffee made "the right way." Sometime during the evening, I told her I was going to cut her throat. When the woman took me seriously, I got a butcher knife from the kitchen and chased her through the house, shrieking and having a whale of a good time. The woman barricaded herself in Mother and Father's bedroom and, telephoning them at the party, screamed that I was trying to kill her. They rushed home and found me asleep on the living room sofa, the butcher knife on the coffee table. "That goddamn old fool," Mother said. "Sammy's a good boy. If she had asked him for the knife, he would have given it to her. What a jackass!"

Uncle Wilbur took me for rides on his tractor, and Aunt Elizabeth doused me with cake when I visited. He also told me stories about lions and bears, and he became part of my imaginative life. Years later I was a camp counselor in Maine, and when I told stories I sat on a low stool in the middle of the cabin and wore a flying cap which I bought at an army surplus store. In the cap I wrote "Wilbur Ratcliffe" and told campers that it belonged to a great uncle. He had worn it during the First World War. He was an ace, I said, and had shot down the Red Baron but had been too modest to correct history. Like all the Ratcliffes, Uncle Wilbur had a sound, earthy sense of humor. Once, he told me, a man woke up late on Sunday morning. He ran down the street toward church and seeing a crowd outside asked a woman, "Is mass out?" "No," the woman answered, "but your hat's on crooked."

Walter, another of Big Ga's brothers, lived in Philadelphia and had two children, Jane being the only name I remember. Some summers we spent a week at his cottage on a hill above the Tappahannock River. Cows grazed around the cottage, and once a cow chased me through a field and into the river up to my chest. Big Ga's cows were easy to avoid. A quick step to the side, and they went crashing past. This cow had the muzzle if not the nose of a hound and followed my every zig and zag. Down the hill and to the right of the cottage was a marsh, pocked by mud holes and tufts of tussock grass. Often I explored the marsh, thrusting my hand into the holes and scooping up turtles. During one of my little game expeditions an animal bit me between the thumb and index finger on my right hand. The bite left two small holes and stung, my hand swelling slightly. At the time I thought a baby water moccasin bit me, but since the swelling did not go past my hand, I didn't tell anyone.

Sam Pickering

Visits to the Ratcliffes fattened me as not only Aunt Elizabeth, but also Osceola, Aunt Betty and Aunt Allie's maid, baked sweets for me. The house was a balanced 1920s Georgian, two windows on each side of the front door, five windows on the second story, three in the attic projecting from the roof, and a screened porch on the right side. In front of the house stood big locust trees. During summer nights I lay on my side, an ear to the ground. I could hear cicadas digging through the soil, and I caught them as they crawled through the grass toward trees. I took them back to my room at Cabin Hill where I kept a stump. I put the "locusts" as I called them on the stump and stayed up all night watching them push through their shells, first appearing silver then turning light green and finally black as their wings unfolded and hardened. In the morning I turned them loose. Sometimes locusts could not escape their shells, and at Cabin Hill I found them immobile on trees bent into black humps their wings folded into hard packages, ants scurrying around them.

Aunt Betty was an accountant. She almost married and had once run off with a man from Philadelphia. The family didn't think the man suitable and had the train in which they were riding shunted onto a siding in northern Virginia where they removed Betty, discouraging her beau at pistol point and suggesting he continue on to Philadelphia. He stayed in Pennsylvania and married there, not before suing the family for alienation of affection, a suit settled out of court by Big Ga, who despite not being involved in the railway incident, was the only family member with means. Uncle Harold became a lawyer and was eventually commonwealth attorney for Henrico County. He was Big Ga's executor, and in the early 50s suddenly sold off most of the land in Grandfather's estate for a pittance of its value. Mother and Father drove all night to Richmond to stop his selling the last plot and impoverishing Ga, a remnant of the money for which the land eventually sold paying my children's college fees. Shortly after Mother and Father's trip to Richmond doctors discovered that Uncle Harold had a brain tumor.

Accounts of fortunes missed speckle family histories. Not a tumor but a malignant growth of integrity stripped me of my inheritance. For twenty years Father managed the affairs of Aunt Lula, Grandmother Pickering's widowed sister. Father was Lula's nearest relative, and Lula called upon him whenever anything went wrong. For three summers running Aunt Lula fell ill during Father's two-week vacation, and he rushed back to Nashville in order to put her in the hospital. Aunt Lula owned a farm, 750 acres of land just outside Nashville in Williamson County. The farm had been in the family for generations, and during vacations from college, I roamed it, hunting rabbits. Aunt Lula did not have a will and when Father's closest friend, a lawyer, learned this, he urged Father to let him draw one up for her. "For God's sakes, Sam," he said, "you have nursed her for years. She would want you to have the farm. I will make out the will tonight and you have her sign it tomorrow." Father demurred, and when Aunt Lula died, two relatives who'd never met her shared the estate. Father put the land up for sale and received a bid of $75,000. "Borrow the money," Mother advised, "and buy the land yourself. Nashville is growing by leaps and bounds, and the farm is worth much more." "That would not be right," Father answered, and the land was sold. A decade later it sold again, this time for over a million dollars. One generation's patterns of behavior are visited upon the next. For years I managed Uncle Coleman's affairs, never paying myself for the hours I spent, this despite an accountant's urging, "You are entitled to something. After all you have done, you'd be foolish not to take it."

The Ratcliffes were peculiar and a little reclusive, but they had rich imaginative lives. Big Ga knew just the tonic for sickness when he wrote me in 1947 after I had been ill, saying that he "was going to the farm to a kill a few wildcats. I hope I don't meet too many," adding "I'm thinking about dashing down to Nashville. The firemen here in Richmond promised to loan me a wagon and engine and boy when I hit the road, look out for I'll be coming round the corner when I come." I had been so sick that I practically boarded in the children's ward at Vanderbilt. My fever climbed to 105, and doctors warned Mother that I might die. I don't know what ailment I had, probably some variety of meningitis. In any case penicillin saved my life, but I was weak for a longish time, and waiting for Big Ga behind the wheel of a fire engine loaded with wild cats invigorated me. "Every time a truck turned into the Sulgrave," Mother said, "you ran to the window to see if Big Ga had arrived." Uncle Harold sent me $5, asking "What in the world are you doing sick! Here, I have been waiting all the winter for you to finish school and come up and take over my sheep. I am sending you $5.00 advance payment on your wages and am expecting you here just as soon as school is over, so don't you let me down."

How different these letters were from those Grandma Pickering sent. Touching and heartfelt her letters were, but they did not make me rush to the window and look outside. Not until I was much older did they affect me. On my first birthday, she sent a present and a letter. Ostensibly the letter was written to me, but in fact Grandma wrote for the future and a scrapbook in which I might someday discover her letter. She wrote,

> You are just a beautiful and innocent bundle of sweetness to us and we would, were it feasible, keep you always as you are today. But God's plan is different so we can only hope to see you hurdle many of life's barriers in safety and security. Today, looking ahead through the years, we visualize our baby in noble manhood, yet we can see you, even then, our precious one, as you are now. Gifts should always be expressions of love and this one from us to you is a pitiful display of the greatness of our devotion to you—our muchly beloved "Sammy."

Big Ga was a florist with huge greenhouses in Dumbarton and a store on the corner of Fifth and Grace Streets in Richmond. He opened his first store in 1911 starting with almost no money except a loan for $5000. During the twenties he had been very successful, opening stores in several cities and buying farms. He even owned a construction company. The Depression battered him, and he lost almost everything. By the time I appeared he had the single store in Richmond, the greenhouses, assorted plots of land, and in Hanover and King William counties two farms totaling 2200 acres, Cabin Hill and Etna Mills. He had a knack for success, and he tried to persuade Father to join him in the florist business. He also offered to set Father up with his own insurance agency. On both occasions Father demurred. "I suppose I erred," Father said later in life. From the standpoint of his life Father did not err. At times, though, I wish Father had joined Big Ga in the florist business, flowers being one of the loves of my life. I have one picture of Big Ga when he was young. Taken in 1892, the picture showed all the pupils in a one-room school in Mechanicsville, Virginia. Big Ga was the youngest and smallest of the twenty-three children. He was barefoot and wore trousers that gathered and buttoned just below the knee. He sat on a bench at the end of the front row. Between him and the next boy was a space, the only space between pupils in the picture. In his hands he held a clump of flowers, foreshadowing the future.

In 1947 Big Ga gave a talk at the Country Club of Virginia, entitled "Flowers and Their Relationship to the Happiness of Man." "The love of land and garden," he declared, ran through "the blood of every southern man and woman." "I once asked a surgeon what he thought was the best thing for a patient after an operation, and the surgeon replied, 'flowers,' not," Big Ga continued, "because the patient would be dead, but because flowers produce a mental picture which lifts a person out of suffering and appealing to one's love of the beautiful makes him temporarily forget himself." For my part, at my funeral I want flowers strewn everywhere, flowers that will wilt like life itself but which for a moment will spread color and sweetness, distracting people from grief or perhaps celebration. Throughout my summers at Cabin Hill a platter creamy with magnolia blossoms sat on the sideboard in the dining room. I loved white water lilies, and Big Ga kept a dish of them in my bedroom. Before falling asleep at night I smelled them. Nowadays when I see lilies blooming near the edge of a pond, I will trudge into the water, mud filling my shoes and water sloshing up to my knees, in order to smell the flowers, the fragrance never failing to bring to mind my bed at Cabin Hill, in the room of mother's brother Uncle Buster, on the dresser athletic trophies he won at St. Christopher's School in Richmond for football and track. In afternoons I lay in bed, read, and waited for the inevitable thunderstorm to blow up along the Pamunkey River and crackle over Cabin Hill. Storms frightened Big Ga, and if he were home during a storm, he grabbed me, and we sat on the basement stairs, halfway between the basement and the pantry. Cabin Hill was perched on a knob of land, and lightning ricocheted around the house. Often it struck the locusts in the front yard, tossing splinters into boxwood. Once, Mother recalled, "a ball" of lightning came down the chimney and bowled through the living room, making Ga screech and lift her legs off the floor. Big thunderstorms did not agree with Mother either, and they occasionally drove her to bed. Once she answered the phone during a storm and was knocked across the room when lightning struck the wire. In later years circuit breakers prevented that from happening, but Mother refused to answer the telephone during a storm. Once on her answering the phone when, as she put it, "the old master was rolling his potatoes," I picked up the other receiver in the house and made a loud buzzing sound, at which Mother screamed "Jesus" and tossed her phone across the room.

Big Ga seemed inordinately frightened of lightning, but then his house in Richmond had burned to the ground. Because lead had been used on the roofing, he prohibited people from trying to save furnishings. Some workmen did enter the house, but instead of removing paintings, they seized the grand piano and blocked the front door. Big Ga's house in Richmond was big, and his garage was larger than the house in which I now live. Arched windows opened rooms to the sun, and a long columned porch ran along the front and one side of the house like an entrance to a Greek temple. Big Ga loved flowers and Italy, and every spring went to Italy to see the flowers. He also decided to furnish the house with furniture from Europe, buying paintings and tapestries, whatever appealed to him. Just when his furnishing was complete, the house burned, the fire also destroying the manuscript of a novel he had finished and an entire room of Civil War artifacts, including uniforms and boxes of letters collected by Uncle Buster from veterans in the old soldiers' home in Richmond.

Big Ga had a round cherubic face and brown, almost puckered smiling eyes. But he was resilient, not soft, in great part because he had to be, as other people's happiness depended upon him, both that of his family and his employees. Ga was not at home when the fire started, and he prevented her from returning and seeing the destruction. In 1942 builders finished his house at Cabin Hill, twenty miles outside or Richmond along route 301 and at the time a country place. When compared to the home in Richmond, Cabin Hill was modest. It was a classically balanced two-story wooden house with a basement and an attic, four dormers in this last, three rounded in the front and decorative. At each end of the house were two brick chimneys. The foundation was brick as was the front stoop. On the first floor across the front were a door and six windows, three on each side of the door. On the floor above were seven windows. At each end of the house were side porches, one screened and facing fields where cattle grazed, the other open to the driveway.

In back of the house a screened porch opened off the kitchen. Upstairs were five bedrooms and a dressing room for Ga, as well as two bathrooms. Downstairs the door opened into an entrance hall that served as a sitting room. Behind it stairs climbed upward through two levels to the second floor. Along the back of the house were the kitchen, two pantries, and a sitting room. Along the front were the dining and living rooms. The house itself was twenty-eight feet wide and fifty-five feet long without the porches; the porches added another 22 feet to the house. Behind the house was a three-car garage, part of which had been turned into a chicken house. The sound of chickens made me happy, and I enjoyed feeding the chickens tossing them grain from a pan. Also in the garage were dirt dauber nests. Dirt daubers sting spiders, paralyzing them. They store the spiders in nests that resemble clay fingers and lay an egg in each finger. When the larva hatches, it feeds on the spiders until it pupates. Sometimes I knocked down the nests and counted the kinds of spiders I found. The number of black widows amazed me because no matter how carefully I hunted for them outside I couldn't find many.

Because I lived in an apartment during the school year, Cabin Hill was my Treasure Island. At Cabin Hill Big Ga had planted, Mother said, 25,000 boxwood, and many of the boxwood at Williamsburg came from him. When I was small, Big Ga wrote me about the house. "This beautiful picture on the back of your letter," he said, "I will hang up in my new house that I am having fixed, and I do not want any little boys to pull off any of the paper off the wall, and if they do, it is no telling what will happen to them." "I am fixing everything as nice as I know how," he continued; "I am working my finger nails [sic] to the bone to get food for you and your Mother when you get here." Breaking me of stripping wallpaper off the wall took imagination. When small, I stood in my crib and dug my nails into the wall nearest me. One summer in Hanover, Daddy warned me against pulling the paper off, saying the Wallpaper Wolf would get me. The next night as I dug my fingers into the wall, the Wolf burst into the room and roared, Daddy having bought a wolf mask and perfected his roar, this last probably far from the house as the sound was impressive. I never pulled wallpaper again. Later I hoped my children would prove to be wallpaper pullers, but none of them, alas, ever stripped the walls and I missed the great pleasure of buying a wolf mask, though I bought other masks. When Francis was little, I put two folding chairs near the road in the front yard. We put on idiot masks covered with rails of bushy hair, and we sat by the road and waved at cars.

Cabin Hill was beautiful, blooming through my days like an album of pictures. A long gravel road ran up to and curved behind the house. Planted on either side of the road was a lane of boxwood, behind the box, dogwood alternating between white and pink. In back of the dogwood was a whitewashed rail fence. At the top of the drive stood tall magnolias. The front yard consisted of two circles of box, one inside the other; within the circles were dogwood and locust trees. Big box grew shrubby around the house itself. I chewed boxwood leaves, in summers keeping a handful of leaves in my mouth like a wad of tobacco. The taste was woody and astringent—country cultivated. In a field to the left of the house were pecan trees, behind the house persimmon and mimosa. One of the mimosas was my climbing tree, and I spent hours perched in the tree smelling the puffy pink flowers and searching for tree frogs after rain. Across a pasture were apple and pear trees, the last always hard and green in the summer but just the thing for a growing, healthy boy, and I was always healthy in the country, the only thing bedeviling me being poison ivy to which I was horrendously allergic. Eventually Mother discovered Neoxyen, a remedy not sold today. The bottle came with a handful of tongue depressors. These I used to scrap the welts of poison ivy until they bled; then I sloshed on the Neoxyen, which dried the sores. Remedies that worked in the country did not work in the city. On warts I put Apinol, almost turpentine. Three weeks of Apinol, and warts vanished.

Big Ga was an individual. He always went to Europe alone, in part because Ga did not want to make the long trip, and later after Buster's death, because she did not feel up to it. Big Ga always sailed, and "once," Mother said, "when Ga and I were talking about him, he walked through the front door. He had arrived in Southhampton with a cold, and thinking he was dying, he walked down the docks and that afternoon boarded a liner bound for New York because he did not want to die away from home." Hospitals frightened him, and he thought if he ever entered one, he would catch an illness and never come out. When Ga came down with a terrible mastoid infection, one doctors were not sure could be cured, he did not visit her in the hospital. They were staying at the

Jefferson Hotel at the time, and he sent her to the hospital in a cab. Every day he sent baskets of flowers to her room, but he did not appear. Ga had long dark hair which Big Ga "loved." To operate, doctors shaved Ga's head. When she returned home, Big Ga never mentioned her hair, and "that hurt me," she said. Germs also frightened him and not once during their married life did he kiss Ga, something with which I sympathize. When I was in high school, I disliked New Year's Eve parties, and, as I phrased it, "their oral promiscuity."

Big Ga was also superstitious. Once when I was driving with him to Etna Mills, a black cat ran across the road, and he turned the car around and drove back to Cabin Hill. He was also generous, and he supervised the parties he gave because "Ga was a little stingy." For guests he bought favors, usually a piece of silver. Once when I became ill, he tried to charter a plane to fly me to Nashville so I could be treated by doctors who knew me. Mother stopped him, and I recovered. I enjoyed being in the car with him; something always happened. Once we stopped to let a skunk and her kits cross the road. When we went fishing at Etna Mills, we spotted snakes swimming across the pond. On another occasion a chain gang was working on route 614. The men were colored, and Big Ga knew them and the deputy who watched them. The men wore striped uniforms and were chained together. When we stopped, the deputy brought the men over, and after Big Ga spoke to them, they serenaded us, singing hymns. Once he took me to watch gypsies dance, real gypsies who traveled about in wagons. He let them stay in an old house he owned just on the Hanover side of Norman Bridge's because he said, "If I don't let them, they will burn the place down." I suspect, however, he let them stay because he liked them. I remember the dancing, and the skirts swirling red and yellow around the women. Occasionally he stopped when we were going someplace, and he talked to the families of displaced persons, usually Latvians or Lithuanians who had been settled in Virginia after the war. In their countries they had often been bankers and lawyers, and Big Ga thought the government should have done better by them, finding them jobs more appropriate than farm laborers. He should not have worried. Once they got small stakes, they moved, usually to Chicago and did well. For a while I had a crush on Rasma. But then she left. Later I heard that she graduated from college and eventually married a college professor in Rochester or Ithaca, New York, the truth concerning appearances and disappearances of people often being vague. Cars also made him nervous, and each year before Mother married, he bought her, Ga, and himself a new car, saying, "no one but a damn fool would drive a car longer than a year." Learning to drive took Ga time. Turning around was especially difficult for her, and for a while John, a huge colored man, accompanied her, sitting on the back seat. John was fabulously strong, and when Ga could not turn the car, he lifted the back of the car and turned it. Once when Mother was in the car with Big Ga, robbers blocked the road with mules. "Hold on Katherine," he said pressing down the accelerator, "if we stop they'll cut our throats." The mules scattered.

Big Ga was marvelously tolerant of the right sort of foolishness, that is, the kind that was harmless and exaggerated enough to delight. Mother was a day student at St. Catherine's School in Richmond, graduating in 1930. She drove to and from school, in the afternoon often carrying a carload of girls. Streetcar tracks ran down the middle of the road in front of St. Catherine's. Passing a slow car was easy, however. The road was wide, and if a person drove on the right side of the lane, cars behind could pass without approaching the tracks. One afternoon, Mother recounted,

I got behind an old fool poking along in a beat-up jalopy. Every time I tried to pass he drifted to the left and pushed me against the tracks. Finally I decided to show the nincompoop. I pulled wide and bounced over then along the tracks on the opposite side of the street until I got alongside then I whipped back in front of him. I turned a little too soon though, and my back bumper hooked his front bumper. The moron blew his horn, so I stepped on the gas and jerked his bumper right off. I sped away down the street and was still chuckling when father came home from the store that night and said, "Katherine, have you ever heard of license plates. Even an ignoramus can sometimes read one, especially when cars are hooked together."

Big Ga was more the subject of stories than a teller of tales. One year he became convinced that bananas sold in groceries were dirty and dangerous, so he decided to grow bananas in the greenhouses at Dumbarton. He bought some small banana trees and took great care of them until they produced fruit. Mother was at the breakfast table with him when he was served his first homegrown banana. He took a single bite then spat the banana out, screaming, "Great God, I'm poisoned. Cut the trees down." On another occasion he decided to grow grapes and make his own wine. He flew an expert down from New York to supervise planting the vines. Later when the time came to harvest grapes and make wine, he imported another expert. The wine was poured into wooden casks that he had sent to him from France and stored in the wine cellar he had built in the basement. After the wine had aged for what he had been told was an appropriate period, he opened a cask. He took only one sip. "Hell's bells," he shouted blowing the wine out of his mouth. "Vinegar. Vinegar. This will kill us all." The next morning farm workers carried the casks off, throwing into a deep gully in the woods where they tossed dead cows. "My God," he said, "fumes from that wine could pollute all the milk in the dairy. If someone drank a glass of it, he would be paralyzed or go blind. Then I could be sued for everything, and we would end up in the poorhouse."

Like all small places, Hanover was an anthology of stories. Many mornings Ga drove Big Ga to the Hanover station where he took a train to Richmond. In the afternoon she picked him up. Apple's store was across the road from the station; in the corner of the store was the post office. The store was a country place with barrels and cats everywhere, and late in the afternoon before the train from Richmond arrived, women bought groceries, mailed letters, and visited with one another. Children ate nickel cups of ice cream using small wooden spoons shaped like paddles. Mr. Apple, the owner, referred to his wife as Little Bitty Bird. Mrs. Apple enjoyed shifting the furniture around in her house. One night after Mr. Apple had drunk a little too much at a lodge meeting and returned home late when all the lights were out, he crept upstairs. His pajamas hung in his closet, so he undressed in front of the closet and after hanging his clothes up, silently slipped into his pajamas. He then turned and walking to the side of the room leaned over what he thought was the bed. Unfortunately Mrs. Apple had shifted the bed to another part of the room and as he reached to pull back the covers, he fell to the floor with a loud thump, whereupon he cried out, "Oh, Little Bitty Bird, what have you done?"

I liked going to the station and watching the trains come and go. One morning a work engine was on a siding, and the engineer took me for a ride up and down the line. I was always barefooted, and that morning I had painted my toenails red. I was so embarrassed that I tried to curl up the tips of my toes under the pads of my feet so the engineer wouldn't notice the paint.

Not far from the station was St. Paul's Episcopal Church. Built in a grove of pine trees in the nineteenth century, St. Paul's was a small clapboard building. A Sunday school wing, probably added in the twenties jutted out into the graveyard. Beyond the graveyard was a field where picnics were held and on the Fourth of July the yearly Donkey Softball game. One evening I won a raffle and had a choice of many prizes, among others a Coleman lantern and a trunk of firecrackers. I chose the firecrackers and spent the rest of the summer having firecracker fights with the Johnsons who lived at Cabin Hill. We also had Roman candle fights, holding the candles close to our sides and shooting fireballs at each other, the most serious injury being a singed sweater.

St. Paul's was small and comfortable. Everyone knew everybody else, and after church gathered in the parking lot to chat. A red carpet ran down the middle aisle and worn gold cushions covered the pews. On the walls were plaques in memory of parishioners who had served the church well. In summer the minister put fans out on the pews. Donated by an undertaker in Ashland, the fans resembled spades. On them beside the undertaker's name and telephone number were pictures of Christ performing miracles: walking on water, healing the lame, and, appropriately enough, raising Lazarus from the dead.

Not until Big Ga died in 1948 did we attend St. Paul's regularly; at least I did not attend in the summer. Afterward we went more often, especially when Ga married a second time. Then we sometimes drove up from Nashville for Christmas, the drive taking sixteen hours and Mother getting us up at two in the morning to start. The day before she packed a lunch, but twice, at least, she forgot it. At Christmas the service did not follow the prayer book. Inspired by the season and eggnog, the congregation came to sing, not to pray. Bourbon was in the air, and when the alter boy lit the candles, it seemed a miracle that the first spark did not send us to heaven in a blue flame. One Christmas, candles circled the inside of the church in L's, starting on both sides of the front door, the foot of each *L* running to the side of the church where the letter turned in a right angle to the leg. While Father parked the car, the rest of us sat in the second pew. Father was going "pretty good," as tipplers say, and when he entered the church he staggered first to the right then to the left, hitting the candles on both sides and starting a double domino effect, all the candles eventually toppling over to Mother's embarrassment and my wonder.

One church story stuck in my mind, and years later I wrote it up, some of the details license but the story itself true. Easter was a joyous time at St. Paul's, and women blossomed in bonnets, some ordering hats not simply from Richmond but Philadelphia. Across the railway tracks lived Miss Kitty and Miss Jo Winston whom I liked to visit because guineas ran cackling about their yard and sometimes they would shake letters out of a pillowcase and show me letters written by Thomas Jefferson and Robert E. Lee. They always asked me if I wanted any of the letters, but I knew enough to say no, realizing that distant members of the family coveted them and felt entitled to them. One Easter Miss Kitty purchased a bouquet of artificial flowers and turned her bonnet into a garden. Daffodils, Zinnais, and black-eyed Susans hung yellow and red around the brim of her hat while in the middle flourished a magnificent red peony. In all his glory Solomon could not have matched Miss Kitty's bonnet. The congregation could not take its eyes off it; even the minister had trouble concentrating on his sermon. After the last hymn everybody hurried out of the church, eager to get a better look at Miss Kitty's hat. As she came out, the altar boy began ringing the bell. The noise frightened pigeons who had recently begun to nest, and they shot out of the steeple. The congregation scattered, but the flowers on Miss Kitty's bonnet hung over her eyes, and she did not see the pigeons until it was too late and the peony was spoiled.

Miss Kitty acted like nothing had happened. She greeted people and asked about their health and the heath of absent family members. People tried not to look at her hat but were not successful. For two Sundays, Miss Kitty's "accident" was the subject of after-church conversation then it was forgotten for almost a year. But as Easter approached again, people remembered the hat. They wondered about what Miss Kitty would wear to church. Some parishioners speculated that she wouldn't attend Easter service. Even the minister had doubts. To reassure Miss Kitty, he and his sons borrowed ladders two weeks before Easter and climbing to the top of the steeple, chased the pigeons away and sealed off their nesting place with chicken wire.

Easter Sunday seem to confirm the fears of those who doubted Miss Kitty would appear. The choir assembled in the rear of the church without her. Half-heartedly the congregation sang the processional hymn, "Hail Thee, Festival Day." Miss Kitty's absence had taken something bright away from the day, and as people sat down after singing, Easter seemed sadly ordinary. The congregation was of little faith. Just as the minister reached the altar and turned to face the worshippers, there was a stir at the back of the church. Silently the minister raised his right hand and pointed toward the door. Miss Kitty had arrived. She was wearing the same hat she wore the year before; only the peony was missing. In its place was a wonderful sunflower; from one side hung a black and yellow garden spider building a web while fluttering above was a mourning cloak, black wings dotted with blue and a yellow border skirting the edges. Hearts leaped up, and at the end of the service people in Richmond could have heard the congregation singing "Christ the Lord Is Risen Today."

Cabin Hill Summers

Mother and I took the train from Nashville to Richmond at the beginning of summer. Sometimes we flew, my first flight being on June 14, 1943 on an American Airlines DC-3. Father drove up and spent his two-week vacation with us in August after which we drove back to Nashville together. I missed Father and wrote him during summers, my prose that of a small boy. "When are you comeing?" I wrote one summer on note paper, four inches tall and two and a half wide. "We want to see you. I hope you are comeing soon. I had lots of fun to day with Boys. I love you a lot. Thank you for the $1. Mother eats a lot of ice cream. love and kisses. Sammy." At the bottom of the letter, I drew three hearts, a bow with an arrow knocked in place pointing at them.

In part we went to Cabin Hill because Mother wanted to be with her parents, especially after Buster died, and because she loved country things. In greater part we went because of my health. In Nashville I was sickly, my tonsils becoming infected and having to be removed, and my sinuses forever being drained, Doctor Manus instructing me to say "Kaa" while he vacuumed out mucus. One winter Mother took me to West Palm Beach where we stayed two weeks with friends in hopes that sun and water would buck me up. Because of my sinuses I missed fifty-six days in first grade. Nashville sat in a basin, and since many people burned soft coal, the air was terribly polluted. Soot covered walls and floors, and I could taste it in the morning. In Hanover the air smelled like boxwood and pine, and I thrived, gaining weight and energy.

Polio also contributed to Mother's taking me to the country. Polio burned through cities in the summer, and isolated, deep in the country I was relatively safe. One summer there was an outbreak of polio in August. Wytheville, Virginia, was particularly hard hit. The road from Nashville to Hanover ran through Wytheville. Before reaching Wytheville on the way north to fetch us, Father rolled up his car windows. Somehow, though, as he drove through town a June bug got into the car. Once beyond Wytheville, Father lowered his windows and shooed the bug out the window. When Mother heard about the bug, however, she would not let me get into the car until after the interior had been scrubbed then wiped down with alcohol.

Of course I didn't remain sequestered at Cabin Hill the entire summer. On Fridays Mother, Ga, and I drove to Richmond. We always visited great aunt Lucille, Ga's sister, who lived at 4114 Crestwood, a one-story white house with small gardens bracketing the side and backyards. While I explored the gardens sniffing flowers and studying insects, the women sat on a screened porch and drank ice tea. One night during a dinner with Aunt Lucille and her husband Uncle Frank, Uncle Frank ate one of his teeth, swallowing it in a mouthful of mashed potatoes. At the time the incident was laughable, but now the event does not rise quite so quickly to the funny bone. Two years ago I munched three teeth in the space of eleven months. Aunt Lucille and I were close, as close as two people so far apart in age can be, and I wrote her until she died. The penultimate time she came home from the hospital, her cleaning woman greeted her and after making her comfortable said, "You don't know how I envy you." "Why?" Aunt Lucille asked. "Because," the woman said, "you are going to see Jesus before I do."

On trips to Richmond we occasionally stopped by the Jefferson Hotel. Early in the summer we took Ga's furs to storage. Generally we fit in visits to Uncle Wilbur or saw Uncle Harold, Aunt Allie, and Aunt Betty. Often we ate lunch at Miller & Rhoads Department Store, usually deviled crabs in the tearoom while a man played the piano. I liked riding the store's escalator. Once the tip of my right tennis shoe became caught between two steps, and the teeth at the top of the stairs chewed the end off my shoe, causing a woman behind me to scream. I had pulled my toes in, and when I uncurled them they stuck over the ragged tip of the shoe. Terrified that I had broken the escalator, I did not tell anyone until after we were driving back to Hanover. The next week Miller & Rhoads gave me a new pair of shoes.

Miller & Rhoads was close to Big Ga's store, a place I could have stayed all day. Built out of rectangular white stones, the building resembled a shoebox, a door and three large picture windows facing Grace then around the corner on Fifth another door and window. On the roof boxwood and flowering shrubs grew in long planters while ferns and ornate Italian vases overflowing with flowers filled the windows. Inside, the floor was sanded stone. Bowls and pots of ferns and flowers sat atop wrought-iron tables or on stone benches. At one end of the store under the business office, from the windows of which ferns draped in luscious green falls, was the refrigerator. The refrigerator was the first place I visited. I closed the door and sat inside. A fan always twirled, and I separated the breeze into cool, clean strands of fragrance. Afterward I talked to Big Ga, his secretary Mrs. Bass, and Charlie, his flower arranger. Charlie's life was erratic. He missed work, and sometimes his appearance was scruffy as he showed up sporting bruises and black eyes, marks from fights with his lover. Charlie arranged flowers superbly, and Big Ga refused to fire him. Once I asked Mother about Charlie's black eyes. "Charlie's friend is excitable," she said, adding that "a lot of people are excitable." Germs disturbed Big Ga, but people did not. Before milking machines became widespread, farm hands milked his cows. One morning someone hexed the barn, scattering beetles over the concrete floor, and the hands refused to enter the diary. As a result Big Ga had to visit the local voodoo man. For $10, a fortune at the time, he bought jar containing a dead snake. As soon as he put the jar in the barn, the hands returned to work.

Big Ga died from a heart attack in 1948 when he was sixty-one years old. He suffered from high blood pressure, an ailment plaguing the Ratcliffes. I missed him. He was lively, and when he walked into a room words swirled. Every day when Big Ga was in Hanover, his herdsman Pallinda came to the house and described the mood of the herd. When Big Ga went out of town, Pallinda wrote him letters. Once after breakfast at the old Ritz in New York, Big Ga went to the main desk to fetch his letter. "Yes, sir, Mr. Ratcliffe, there is something for you," the clerk said and started to hand Big Ga an envelope. Suddenly concern spread over the clerk's face, and he said, "Oh, dear, I am so sorry." Big Ga was puzzled until he saw the letter. Under the address in big, clear letters, Pallinda had written, "P. S. Grandma slipped last night." Although the clerk did not know it, Grandma was not my grandfather's wife or mother. She was an old cow, and the night before she had not fallen on the stairs or in the hall, but in the language of the dairy, had lost her calf. Although I could not have expressed or even felt it at the time, when Big Ga died, a wonderful, sometimes unpredictable but paradoxically always dependable richness vanished from my life.

Ga was nice, but she was not as lively as Big Ga or Mother. In part Buster's death battered her, writing Mother that "this world is a terrible mix up for me." In public she was more formal that Big Ga, and in pictures taken of her when she was eighteen, she sits posed wearing big hats wrapped in ostrich feathers. She wrote me regularly, though, telling me about new lambs or in 1946 "that the white mamma cat brought four little kittens here Sunday night," adding for Mother's benefit the question referring to the kittens, "what will I do?" In the early 50s when she married Bob Gwathmey, he convinced her over Mother's wishes to move into his house and sell Cabin Hill. Shortly thereafter Virginia slipped from my life. Bob's house was small. Trips to Hanover shrank to a week, and my wanderings practically stopped. Bob's yard was modest, and if I wanted to explore all I could do was walk down to the train tracks that ran below the property and amble along the rails. "Keep your eyes peeled," Mealy, Big Ga's cook, repeatedly advised me, usually before warning me about copperheads in the woodshed. I don't know a better recommendation for improving life, and I have followed Mealy's advice for sixty years. In any case once or twice I saw sights along the tracks that made my heart leap: off the right of way a cloud of tiger swallowtail butterflies swarming around milkweed. Hanging on the plants and looking like leaves were myriads of praying mantises, and whenever a butterfly lit, a mantis seized it and ate the body, letting the wings fall to the ground. For a hundred yards yellow wings streaked with black covered the ground like snow, and I ran beside the milkweed, kicking my feet through the wings and tossing yellow flakes above my head. About a half mile from Bob's house at the edge of pine woods was a box turtle crossing, a place where box turtles scraped gravel from beneath the rails and burrowed under the tracks in order reach a wetland on the far side of the right of way. Long slow freights don't seem to have bothered the turtles, but faster passenger trains flipped the turtles and rolled them, and when I went to the crossing I often found thirty dead turtles. Sometimes I found live turtles. I picked these up and after carrying them across tracks freed them in the wetland. I took a sack with me on turtle walks and brought a selection of empty shells back to Bob's. Nubs of flesh usually clung to the inside of the shells, so I scrapped them then let them age outside. I carted some shells back to Tennessee, always in the trunk of the car because they were fragrant, a perfume that bothered Father. I thought the shells good luck charms. In 1957 I put a shell under the front seat of the first car my parents bought me, and since then I have put a shell under the front seat of every car I've owned.

Ga spent her last years living with Mother and Father and me in Tennessee. Father added a combination sitting and bedroom with a bathroom onto the house. Ga lived to eighty-nine, wearing out a pacemaker in the process. She was sweet and kind, but like many old people she sentimentalized the past and often told Mother that she wished she were back in Virginia, imagining herself young and surrounded by friends. Ga's remarks hurt Mother, who, along with Father, had given up independence in order to care for her. Toward the end of her life Ga had many ailments, and Mother almost wore herself out getting up throughout the night to watch over her. Mother was so exhausted that I worried that she would die, and I considered smothering Ga in order to relieve Mother and Father. Ga died soon after I had such thoughts and was buried in the Ratcliffe plot in Hollywood Cemetery in Richmond.

Mother arranged for Ga's body to be flown to Richmond. A local undertaker whom we did not know picked her up at the airport, and by the time Mother and I arrived, he'd laid her out in an open coffin under a huge acrylic painting of Jesus standing open-armed on the edge of a luminous gold and purple sea. The woman who washed and set Ga's hair for years in Nashville insisted upon preparing her hair for the funeral, and when Ga left Nashville, every lock was glued in place. "My god," Mother said, "I couldn't turn the woman down. She meant well." By the time Ga arrived in Virginia, a few strands of hair had slipped loose, tumbling across her forehead and right cheekbone. Seeing them, Mother strode over to the casket and, brushing the hair back, turned to Father and me and said, "It must have been a goddamn rough flight." With that she slammed the lid of casket down, glared silently at the undertaker, and strode out of the funeral home, her shoes whacking the floor like a jackhammer. Mother incidentally did not tiptoe through days. Her step was fast and hard. Once when I was small, a cyst developed and broke deep in my left hip, and I was hospitalized for a week. My room was at the end of a long corridor, but I always knew when Mother was approaching. As soon as she swung into the hall, I heard her footsteps, the hard familiar banging, reassuring and comforting.

Of course I am probably wrong about Ga. She may have been lively all the way through her sixties. Her last years may have colored my memory. I watched her grow feeble and become a burden. Big Ga died before he aged into the time, as a friend put it, "of patch, patch, patch," and I remember him only as energetic and playful. In any case before Big Ga died and until Ga sold Cabin

Hill, the going in Hanover was good. I picked fox grapes off the bank bordering the road in front of the house, and Ga made jelly. In the red barn, I built forts out of bales of hay. A man who lived along the road running in front of Cabin Hill collected lightning rods, and every summer I counted them usually discovering he had added one or two more to his roof. Although only thirteen, the man's son smoked cigars. I was told to avoid him if I saw him. He wasn't trustworthy and in his middle teens spent time at the Hanover School for Boys, as it is now known. In the 50s, it was simply the reform school. In a field I stood and watched buzzards devour a litter of drowned kittens, there being no spaying or SPCA in the country and drowning being the usual and an efficient way of disposing of unwanted pets. I churned milk and watched Mealy chop the heads off chickens, after which the chickens ran about in a fluster. Then I helped her pluck the feathers after we stuffed the birds in tub of hot water.

Not everything was perfect, though it seemed so at the time. My friends and I made a sliding hill down a bank at the edge of a pine woods. One day when we were ten or eleven some strange boys fourteen years old or so appeared in the woods and while we were playing on the hill took off their clothes and demonstrated "cornholing." They invited us to join them, but after closely scrutinizing one boy's bottom I demurred and, so to speak, low-tailed it out of the woods. Today the experience or the lack thereof would probably be thought formative. In 1950s such matters had little significance. Three years later when boys in Nashville spent Friday or Saturday nights at a buddy's house, they occasionally subjected a friend's "red eye" to close examination, to see, as one boy put it, "what was stored up there." Friday night comparative anatomy did not progress beyond looking to touch and was harmless. In fact sleep-overs most likely stirred the physician latent in many boys, for the first time making them dream of attending medical school. Indeed I suspect a goodly portion of the best Southern surgeons of my generation would have been bankers or lawyers had it not been for the interest awakened by weekend anatomy classes.

Frequently I accompanied Mother and Ga to Cross's grocery in Ashland six miles away. Usually we had to stop at least once so I could rescue a box turtle from the road. Train tracks ran through the center of Ashland, and while Mother and Ga shopped, I sat on the curb in front of the store and watched trains rumble through the town. Names painted on the boxcars intrigued me, and I imagined traveling to Louisville, Sante Fe, and Rock Island. In Nashville, Father and I often walked along the tracks not far from the Sulgrave. He read me the names on passing cars, and I collected spikes that had worked their ways out of the sleepers. For Christmas in 1949 my parents gave me a Lionel train. The engine was numbered 2026 and was a 2-6-2, that is, it had two wheels behind the cow catcher, then six, followed by two near the tender, a whistling tender. Beside the engine and tender, the train consisted of a red caboose, an orange boxcar, a flat car, and a silver tanker with Sunoco on the side. The train might not have carried much cargo but it covered untold miles, steaming nonstop around a board, whistle blowing and smokestack puffing.

Most afternoons in Hanover the family sat on the screen porch and drank iced tea, this being before air conditioning. Wallace was the only son of a widow living in Hanover. He was retarded and couldn't speak, but he could moo like a cow. Often as the cows began to trail through the pasture on the way to the dairy to be milked, he appeared suddenly, walking around the side of the house. When he reached the fence that separated the yard from the pasture, he stopped and mooed. Usually the cows answered him, something I could never make them do though I tried repeatedly.

Some nights we drove to Caroline County and ate at a family-style restaurant run by Mr. and Mrs. Beasley and noted for fried chicken, homemade pies, and, as it turned out, Mr. Beasley's conversation. Once when we entered the restaurant, Mrs. Beasley wasn't in her accustomed place behind the counter. Mr. Beasley, though, was wiping tables. "Good evening, Mr. Beasley. How are you?" Mother said as we sat down. Then looking around she added in passing, "I don't see Mrs. Beasley. I hope she's not sick." "Oh, no," Mr. Beasley said, putting down his rag. "She's not sick. She's in the bathroom and will be out directly."

I thought goings-on in Hanover normal. By sixth grade I was a child of the suburbs living in West Nashville, three streets way from the Belle Meade Country Club, an area Father affectionately dubbed a "Republican ghetto." At the beginning of the school year, my teacher asked us to write two pages on our summer vacation. I wrote about Hanover. The next day the teacher accused me of making everything up and made me read parts of my piece aloud to the class. She then told me rewrite my account and tell the truth. I gave her the truth she wanted. That night I crafted a normal summer vacation at a summer camp listing and celebrating activities like swimming and archery. "Now, that's more like it," she said the next day. "Being creative is fun, but you must always tell the truth."

During my first years at Cabin Hill, my closest playmate was my first cousin—my only first cousin—Sherry, sixteen months older than I. Sherry stayed in Hanover for a week or two, but we formed a friendship that lasted for decades until the multifarious responsibilities of family life loosened the ties. Even now we call each other three or four times a year and laugh, the details of summers at Cabin Hill forgotten but the remembrance of moods past cheering us. Because Sherry was Buster's daughter, Ga felt sorry for Sherry. The fact that Sherry's mother was Catholic and was raising Sherry as a Catholic exacerbated Ga's sorrow. Often she lamented that Sherry was not allowed to attend St. Paul's with her but instead had to be driven to the Catholic church in Ashland. Today my children cannot imagine the rifts that religion caused. I remember my parents discussing the daughter of good friends and saying how sad it was that no one would marry her because she was Catholic. If a person married a Catholic, he had to sign the "White Paper," an agreement that all the children of the marriage would be raised Catholic, a matter probably more of social rather than spiritual significance. Times change, but maybe not so much as people believe. I've told my children that the race of their spouses does not matter, but I have advised them not to marry a believer of any denominational stripe—Catholic, Protestant, Jewish, or ersatz.

Sherry herself enjoys tales. Many years ago, the *Richmond Times Dispatch* quizzed her about me and the family. "On hot nights when the family ate on the screened porch," she recounted, my mother wore only a white sheet. When fried chicken was served, she asked Father "to pass the bosoms" whereupon he replied, "Say chicken breasts, Katherine." The story almost sounds true. Undermining it, though, is *breasts*. Mother would have used another of her favorite words, *tits*. The last time I heard Mother use the word, in the singular in this case, was at a hospital check-in desk. A clerk asked her what she was being admitted for. "To have my left tit chopped off," she said. "It hasn't been useful in years, so you can toss it out the window afterward." When the clerk looked startled, Mother added, "Some hungry dog might make a meal of it." Mother was diabetic, and after the operation she had a heart attack and died.

In any case in the *Dispatch* interview Sherry turned me into pedophile, saying that I met Vicki when I was a graduate student at Princeton and her father head of the English Department. "Vicki was thirteen when she first met Sam," the paper stated. "Thirteen years later when she was twenty-six they married." "Once a Ratcliffe, always a Ratcliffe," I thought on reading the piece. "Thank goodness."

Chickens figured high in Sherry's and my play. I had a pet rooster named Sammy rooster. Sammy was a one-boy bird who disliked girls. One afternoon when Sherry and I were on swings near the screened porch, and when as always, Sherry was irritating me by swinging higher than I, Sammy came tearing around the house. Ignoring me, he sprang into the air and attacked Sherry. Sherry screamed, leaped off the swing, and ran around the corner of the house, Sammy scurrying after her. I thought the performance fine. I was, alas, the only family member who applauded Sammy.

That night we had fried chicken for dinner. Halfway through a drumstick, a terrible truth dawned. "Is this Sammy rooster?" I asked. "Yes," Big Ga answered, and for a moment emotion welled. But then I smelled the chicken in my hand. Sammy had never been sweeter. I dried my penchant for tears and reaching across the table, grabbed the other drumstick and said, "He was my pet, and I ought to be able to eat most of him." Once after I dumped a handful of beetles in a sandbox in which she was playing, Sherry baked me a chocolate cake, using a mix and adding kernels of chicken "do" for seasoning. I ate a slice and thought it fine, neither the taste nor the fragrance of droppings being things that have ever bothered me. Times, as I have said, change. Almost all the children I teach have grown up in cities, and although I ask each class, I have yet to run across a single child who has spent even one afternoon in a good manure fight, tossing cow patties at his, or her, best friends.

Sometimes in Hanover, Mother picked up items at Willie Marshall's store on the shoulder of 301. Bare feet had blackened the floor, and the store was ramshackle and congenial. People, both colored and white, met friends in the store and greeted them enthusiastically, the confined space somehow raising their voices. My only memory of World War II is sitting on the steps of the store and watching troop convoys streaming up the road toward Richmond, highway trains, I thought them. Once Sherry bought a Coca Cola at Marshall's. The day was hot, and the drink was in a hard glass bottle. When Sherry stepped outside the store, the bottle exploded like a grenade. No fragment touched Sherry, but I was sitting on the steps eating ice cream, and pellets sliced into the back of my head. Blood spurted and streamed down the back of my shirt. The explosion caused some commotion in the store, but I wasn't hurt. In fact I was proud of the bloody shirt and didn't want Mother to wash it. At Cabin Hill I lived a healthy life and bled a lot, turning my hide into map of cuts and scratches. When blood really streamed, I spread it across my face and went on the warpath, something I continued to do when my children were little, stamping and hollering, tripping a heavy fantastic toe.

Bees stung me scores of times, as they still do. I stepped on honeybees every week and while playing games ran into the nests of paper wasps hidden in boxwood. Discovery of a nest led to bravado and welts. Sometimes I tried to knock the nest out of the box with a bamboo pole, this chopped down from a forest of bamboo at the edge of a field, the longest I ever "lumbered" over forty feet tall. Other times I threw hot water on the nest, this last riskier and more fun because it was almost dangerous. Once I knocked a nest down and the wasps abandoned the area, I studied the nest, opening sealed cells and examining pupae. A wood hornet whacked me with my worst sting. A group of boys were throwing rocks at a hornet's nest in a fence post. I warned them they were going to get stung then turned away to walk back up a dirt road. Just then a hornet hit me on the right upper arm. The sting hurt more than the shot I received each June to prevent Rocky Mountain Fever. Ticks spread the fever, and over the summer Mother plucked clusters out of my head. Ticks are especially fond of boys' scrotums. Mother, and I, missed these, and sometimes they swelled bloated to the size of small grapes before I discovered them. If they were big enough, I clamped them between my thumb and index finger, and squeezing my fingers together, popped them, shooting the black blood a foot or so. The best ticks for shooting were on dogs, often in their ears, some as big around as nickels, in my exaggerated memory at least.

Ga was intermittently religious, which probably means she was agnostic. On her deathbed she called me into her room to tell me something "important." I had long left the eighth grade behind and having aged into crassness, I expected her to describe a gift left to me in her will. Instead she said, "Don't forget your God." The remark from someone who rarely mentioned religion, except to lament Sherry's Catholicism, startled me, besides, of course, disappointing me. To a degree, Sherry, or the way Ga described her reaction to her father's death, was responsible for her faith. Sherry was three when her father died. She did not attend his funeral and visited Hollywood cemetery for the first time ten days after the burial. She and Ga went together. No one told Sherry, Ga said, where they were going, though Sherry must have overheard snatches of conversation. Be that as it may, as soon as the car stopped and the doors were open, Sherry ran across the grass and winding through the headstones went directly to her father's grave. "Daddy's here," she said, repeating herself, "Daddy's here." Shaken by Sherry's words, six months passed before Ga took Sherry to the graveyard again. Once more, when the car doors opened, Sherry ran to her father's grave. This time, she stopped as soon as she reached the plot and turning her head to face Ga, said, "Daddy's not here anymore."

Sherry and I were great pals through the Cabin Hill years. Only a great good friend would bake a chicken-shit cake for a person. Sherry seemed everything a boy could want in a buddy except she preferred caramel to chocolate cake. Despite my protests during Sherry's visits Ga baked caramel cakes, all of which I refused to eat. Sherry and I wrote and sent cards to each other for twenty years. In 1947 when I went into the hospital just after Christmas, she wrote, "Dear Sammy, I hope you feel find. I feel find. Are you having fun in the Hospital? I am having fun with your Christmas present. Are you wearing my Christmas present? I like your present." Later she wrote me in Florida, in the letter writing "I love you" eight times and "kiss" thirty-five times.

Sherry's and my playmate, and minder, at Cabin Hill was Lizzie, a colored girl probably three years older than Sherry, say ten, when Sherry was seven. Lizzie was tall and skinny and nice and in hide and seek could twist herself so that she fit into cavernous places. Lizzie and I also wrote for years. In 1946 when I was sick she wrote, "I hope you get well. When you get well, you must kiss your mother and father. I will kiss my mother." "I hope you are a good boy," she continued, "but I no you is a good boy." At the end of the letter she drew five figures: a girl named Hattie with frizzy hair and wearing a red dress, Brad a boy in bulbous blue trousers, "my dag name spot," a ball red on the ends and green in the middle, and finally a brown paper sack shaped like a shoe.

Photographs of colored people fill my scrapbooks and memory, William bigger than myth, his enormous arms wrapped protectingly around mine, Mealy cradling me in her arms and standing beside the woodshed at Cabin Hill, and Marie sitting on a blanket in Nashville, supporting me while I struggled to walk. I was born with a knobby head, and when another servant in the Sulgrave Apartments told Marie I had bumps on my head, Marie answered, "My baby ain't got bumps. My baby's head is smooth." "You had," Mother said, "the bumpiest head I have ever seen." When I was little, Mother used to run her hand across my head and say the old rhyme, "Da, da, da, bumpsiree, I got bumps all over me. Da, da, da bumpseroo, you got bumps all over you."

During my childhood, colored and white people lived side by side and word by word despite segregation. After a white preacher substituted at her church when the regular minister was ill, Mealy reported that the sermon "didn't have no gravy." In Nashville when a cousin of Rosie who worked for Mother and Father had a nervous breakdown and Mother got her an appointment with a psychiatrist at Vanderbilt, the cousin explained that her mind was "scattered," a phrase which mystified the German-born psychiatrist but which Mother thought the best word imaginable. In later years, long after we stopped going to Hanover, colored people telephoned Mother, both to talk about the old days and to seek her help, frequently, with legal or medical problems. Once I found Mother sitting at the kitchen table, leaning over, her hands pressed against the sides of her face. "Colored people are killing me," she said in despair. Later that morning she telephoned Richmond and convinced a lawyer into handling the case of the person who called for free. In Nashville once she visited the sick relative of a woman who worked for us. While in the relative's house, Mother discovered that the woman had been buying a chair on time for over twenty years. The next day Mother drove to the merchant's store. When she finished talking, the woman's debt had been erased, and that afternoon a truck left the merchant's carrying another chair and a sofa to the woman. "Gifts," Mother said sarcastically.

Mother knew she had a duty to the people who worked for her or her family, a hangover from being the daughter of a comparatively wealthy man and from spending much of her life in the country, a place that not only forced but taught a person to be more democratic than did life in the city. And maybe niceness was naturally part of her being, though the word *genes* was not mentioned when I was a child. During the early 1980s she saw Mr. Leasor to the grave, making sure he had a place to live and plenty of food in his old age. Mr. Leasor mowed our yard occasionally. He was from the hill country of Kentucky and was as angular as a ridge of the Pine Mountains. Mr. Leasor worked only when he felt like working, and Father wanted to get rid of him, saying he'd never be reliable. Mother disagreed and said simply, "wait." And wait Father did until one day when Mr. Leasor knocked on the back door and said, "Mrs. Pickering, I'm going home. There is no sense in raking these leaves. The squirrels chew up so many hickory nuts that the rake catches on the ground." "That bothers you, does it, Mr. Leasor?" Mother said. "Yes ma'am," he answered in a contrary and irritated tone. "Well, I'll take care of that," Mother said and went to the bedroom and got her shotgun out of the closet. "Mrs. Pickering, what are you going to do," Mr. Leasor said when he saw the gun. "I'm going to get you meat for Brunswick stew," she replied, handing him a sack. "You can't shoot that gun in the city," he said. "Who is going to stop me?" Mother answered going out the door. "Not you. Come along." Mr. Leasor followed silently and that evening after he finished raking and after Mother poured him two-thirds of a drinking glass of bourbon, he carried home eight squirrels. He was not late to or absent from work again, and whenever I saw him in later years, even on his deathbed, he said, "Sammy, I've never seen a woman shoot like your mother. Right in the city—eight shots and eight squirrels and some of them in Mr. Knox's yard."

Colored people wandered through my childhood, cooking, cleaning, and working one way or another. They were as much a part of my life as relatives. We saw each other every day. We did not go to school together, but as a boy I didn't think about or maybe didn't even notice that. At times I winced: when I visited a maid's house and saw my picture in the middle of the mantle or when a seventy-five-year-old man called me "Mr. Sammy." But I didn't ponder such matters. I was a typically busy, thoughtless boy, wandering about catching the creeping and crawling generations and prowling attics and drawers. We gave each other presents, from colored people, fried chicken, turnip greens, and love, real affection not flim-flam to fool "Whitey" or "Old Master," and from us furniture and clothes, lamps, chairs, china, linen, toys, mahogany coffee tables, beds, the furnishings of kitchens, and real love, too, this blended with paternalism, but love nonetheless. Our lives twisted together, and we gave each other stories, often from today's narrow point of view racist, but stories that made us chuckle and somehow warmed hearts undermining the hard crust of racism. In the late 1950s, William, the oldest son of Feenie, who worked for Big Ga, left Virginia for New York where he became a successful undertaker. Toward the end of their lives Feenie and Mother called each other two or three times a year, old Hanover and family being the subjects of conversation. "Oh, Miss Katherine, William is doing just fine," Feenie replied when Mother asked about William. "He's so light skinned that people think he's a spaniel."

After Ga moved away from Cabin Hill, I never saw Lizzie again. Once I asked Mother about her, and I think Mother said she had had a baby "very young." Segregation limited Lizzie's opportunities for worldly success, a success that seems as I approach the noose end of my years not worth the sacrifices made to attain it. Of course only the privileged, the comfortable like me, have the leisure to indulge in such speculation. In any case Lizzie may have enjoyed a wonderful life. I certainly hope so, a life rich beyond my imagination. People should not forget that the Civil War was fought to end slavery, an evil that smudges the high-flown language of the "Founding Fathers."

Amid Nannie Brown's letters lay the will of Philip Leland written in Williamson County, Tennessee in 1845. All I can gleam about Leland from the will is that his daughter Frances married Enoch Brown, the uncle of the Enoch Brown some of whose Civil War letters were in Nannie's possession. The length of the will gives it a dark power, the sort of power that does not, as sentimentalists would have one believe, bring the light but instead makes a person shake his head and say, "Fuck."

Leland first directed that his executor settle his debts and pay his funeral expenses.

Secondly I give and direct to my beloved wife Susan during her natural life all my real estate. Thirdly I give and bequeath to my said wife during her natural [life] all my personal property of every description except the specific legacies hereinafter named to wit, 1st I give and bequeath to Frederick Ezell in trust for the sole and separate use of my daughter Matilda Ezell during her natural life and at her death to be equally divided among her children the following negroes, to wit, Wiley and Evaline [Periods inserted to make reading easier]. 2nd I give and bequeath to my son Elderidge Leland Amy. Thirdly I give and bequeath to my son William Leland a negro boy named Joe. 4th I give and bequeath to my son Francis N Leland a negro boy Anthony and a negro girl Phillis. 5th I give and bequeath to Enoch Brown in trust for the use and support of my son Philip W Leland his wife and children [Phillis and her children?] during the lifetime of said Philip W and at his death to be equally divided between the children of the said Philip W the following negroes to wit Clarissa and Matilda. 6th I give and bequeath to Alexander Brown in trust for the sole and separate use of my daughter Charlotte Brown during her life and at her death to be equally divided between the children of said Charlotte the following slaves, to wit, Caroline and William. 7th I give and bequeath to Enoch Brown in trust for the sole and separate use of my daughter Frances during her natural life and at her death to be equally divided between the children of said Frances the following negroes to wit Sandy and Sarah. 8th I give and bequeath to George Morris in trust for the sole and separate use of my daughter Susan Morris and at her death to be equally divided between the children of said Susan the following slaves Martha and Felise. The most of which slaves are now in the possession as a loan of said legatees the intention of the above trusts is that the husbands of my said daughters shall jointly enjoy the use of said property with my said daughters but that the same shall not be liable for the debts contracted and wills of their husbands. It is also my will and desire that any increase of the above mentioned slaves may hereafter also shall be considered and taken as being bequeathed with their mothers. It is my will and desire that at the death of my wife Susan all the property above described and bequeathed to her for life is sold and of the proceeds seven hundred dollars to be equally divided between the children of my son James Leland deceased and should any of said children die before my death [to] their children should they have any living to have the same portion such deceased child would have received if living.

The will continued for another page, listing individual monetary bequests to be paid after all Leland's "property" was sold. The will was probated on April 30, 1845, after Leland's death. His property must have been extensive because the court required Susan Leland to give a bond of $5000 "conditioned for the faithful discharge of the trust reposed in her" along with several others mentioned in the will. In 1885, a relative in Kentucky sent Nannie a letter in which she discussed the Civil War. "It may be that Providence," she wrote, "was working out a great problem, the freedom of the negro race—which no doubt in the End, will be the best thing for us, both as a People & as a Nation!" The wheels of Providence have turned very, very slowly.

Grandparents in Tennessee

A person never knows his grandparents or parents. Indeed one has several sets of parents, each pair disappearing and becoming a new pair as a person ages. Time strips away one's youthful and middle-aged parents, ultimately leaving him with clearest memories of an aged, often diminished couple. When I look at pictures of Grandma and Grandpa Pickering, I wonder if I really know anything about them. A person can speculate, but life is composed of such disparate elements that any whole woven out of speculations will be fictional. If following the injunction "know thyself" is impossible, how can a person know others? Although Grandma's letters to Coleman were tablets of worldly advice, pictures of her as a girl were romantic, in part reflecting the genre but in part her personality. As a little girl of four or so years, she sits legs akimbo on a prop, a stone wall with a column at the end, fake ivy scrolling over it. She wears a frilly white dress and dark stockings. Hitched to her left arm at the elbow is a small wicker basket, and if her expression were not so solemnly thoughtful she would seem ready to skip off singing, "A tisket, a tasket." In a photograph taken when she was eighteen, her hair is pulled back over her forehead and her head is tilted slightly to the right, a single earring visible in her left ear, making her resemble a gipsy. Her blouse is lacy and flies up around her shoulders and behind her neck in wings. Her expression is solemn but knowing and sensuous. In a third picture she wears a long, layered white dress loose as cirrus clouds. On her left stands Father; on her right Coleman leans into her resting his hand on her lap. Both boys are dressed in white: white shorts, white socks that reach halfway up the calf, and white blouses with black belts. They are wearing black sandal-like shoes, open at the top and with a strap around the ankle. Coleman is five and Father two years older. The boys' hair is blond while Grandmother's is graying. By twenty-seven her hair was completely white.

In a tribute to her after her death, Grandma was quoted as saying, "people grow old by deserting their ideals," not a statement Grandpa Pickering or Father would have made. They were more comfortable with the mixed nature of life. Indeed, much as life abounds in the tattered hedgerows around a field, not in the field itself, so perhaps real living occurs beyond margins, not within crafted lines running across a page. Grandma also said, "You are as young as your faith, as old as your doubt, as young as your self-confidence, as old as your fears, and as young as your hopes, as old as your despair." Grandma tried to straighten the crooked ways of living, something that must have led to frustration even if one were confident and hopeful. Once I heard that Grandpa drank and on occasion disappeared into the hills around Carthage for two or so days with cronies. The story may be false. During the last decade of his life when I knew him, he was a teetotaler, as was Coleman during his entire life. In any case Grandma dressed her sons well, better than other parents dressed children in Carthage. In a picture, two teachers and forty-two students stood on the steps at the front of the elementary school in Carthage. The children were young, most appearing under nine. The girls had bangs and wore sack-like dresses cut from checkered cloth. Their shoes were scuffed, and some of the dresses were soiled. Father stood on the edge of the third step. He was the best-dressed boy in the photograph. He had a page-boy haircut and wore knickers that spread yeasty at the knee. His coat looked like it was velvet. Over the shoulders of the coat, a white collar spilled out in a ruff.

Some years ago Houston McGinness who knew my grandparents and Father and Uncle Coleman sent me a letter filled with memories. One spring day my grandmother showed Mr. McGinness a nest of baby cardinals in a vine outside her kitchen window. "Those were the first baby birds I ever saw," Mr. McGiness wrote, "and probably contributed to my favorite hobby, birdwatching." Grandma liked animals and once resuscitated a baby pig using artificial respiration, a success picked up by newspapers around the country. Unlike many of their classmates, Father and Uncle Coleman wore "proper clothes to school—short pants, stockings held up by fasteners on the underwear, and billed caps." "Once I got to the third grade," Mr. McGinness recounted, "Mother said it was time for knickers, just like the Pickering boys had worn." Not until eighth grade did Mr. McGinness wear long trousers. "But," he added, "I never held your father or Coleman responsible for my sartorial suffering, thinking that they, too, perhaps had been uncomfortable." Father and Coleman spoke impeccable English. "Mother often pointed out that Samuel and Coleman never used slang or bad grammar," Mr. McGinness said, adding that his mother urged him to copy "the speech of the Pickering boys." For one year in high school Father attended Kentucky Military Academy. All he ever said about it was, "A child should never be sent to a military school." For years I assumed he was sent to the academy because he found the Carthage High School too easy. I was wrong. "Samuel read so much," Coleman told me, "that he stooped. Mother sent him to correct his posture. All he learned was how to cuss."

Still, I know little about Grandma. I don't know the date she and Grandpa married, not that such things matter, for I cannot recall the day I married Vicki—either the 26th or 27th of June in 1978 or 1979. I found part of a clipping from the *Tennessean* describing Grandma's wedding, however:

> The parlor, reception hall, library and dining room were thrown together and beautifully decorated. Luxuriant palms and ferns were used through the room and in the parlor a wealth of bride's roses were used while in the library LaFrance roses were employed in decoration. The ceremony, which was performed by Rev. C. A. Moore was proceeded by a musical

program given by Mrs. James Buchanan at the piano and Miss Jennie Farnsworth on the violin.... The bride wore a becoming gown of champagne silk and she carried a chatelaine bouquet of brides roses and ferns.

A reception followed the ceremony at which Mrs. Griffin [Nannie] was assisted in receiving by Misses Daisy Jarratt, Annette Hill, and Mrs. Edwin Jackson. Frappe was served by little Miss Mary Wikle. Mrs. Griffin wore a handsome black gown of net and lace.... Mr. and Mrs. Pickering left on the afternoon train for Carthage, where they will reside.... Among the out-of-town guests were: Mr. William B. Pickering of Carthage, Mr. and Mrs. John Stiles of Lebanon, Mr. and Mrs. Nelson Fisher of Carthage, Messrs. W. E. Myer, H. B. McGinness, E. S. Hart and E. R. Reynolds of Carthage, Mr. and Mrs. Douglas Wikle of Franklin, Misses Frances and Daisy Jarratt of Smyrna, and Mr. C. E. Brown of Franklin.... Many costly wedding gifts were received. Mr. C. E. Brown [Coley] presented a chest of silver and handsome china was given by the groom's family. Many handsome pieces of furniture, cut-glass and silver were received.

The names of the people and the presents lurk in the hedgerows bordering, perhaps confining, life. The wedding doesn't matter in any great sense; yet, to a prowling boy, the clipping was treasure, providing glimpses of the past, not simply of names and things but of words also.

Grandpa's house was on Main Street in Carthage. Grandma may have owned it as she bought it on November 5, 1909, for $4,000. She sold in it 1952 for $15,500. Huge sugar maples grew in the front yard. In a picture taken in 1915 the maples were small, and Father and Coleman stood in the front yard in playsuits. The house was a white clapboard, two-story Victorian with a tin roof. When I slept upstairs, I loved hearing the rain pattering across the tin. A porch rose over the front door and ran around the left side of the house. At one corner the porch lifted up into a cupola topped by a weathervane. In the picture, a rocking horse and swing were on the porch. Beside a small screen porch outside the kitchen was a well with a rusty iron pump on top looking like a bedraggled crow. Behind the house were sheds, fields, a tobacco barn, and then a long slope down to the river. When I was young, Mother and Father took me to Carthage several times a year. Rows of iris trailed down the side yard, deep blue iris and blue and orangy-brown iris, creamy with fragrance. Rolling up before the foundation were thick bushes white with snowball hydrangea. Grandma liked flowers and collected flower catalogues, and after I gathered strawberries, I thumbed through her flower magazines. Later I walked down the back lane beside a long trellis to the tobacco barn. Sometimes I wandered through the rows of tobacco searching for hornworms. Grandpa only grew a little tobacco. Grandpa was popular, however, and buyers who attended the market in South Carthage across the river, or Russia, as it was known, always paid more, Father told me, for his tobacco than it was worth.

Inside the front door in the hall was a grand piano, though I never heard Grandma play. A sidewalk ran past Grandpa's house to downtown, 300 yards away. Father and Coleman rollerskated on the sidewalk, and every morning Grandpa walked uptown and had coffee with friends, after which he walked back home and Bessie the maid prepared breakfast for him. When Grandma's roses bloomed, Grandma would put a rose on the table beside his plate. Grandma always had cats—Scarlett, named after Scarlett O'Hara, being the cat of my childhood. Scarlett was a large orange tabby, and when she died, I cried more than when Grandpa died. One year I took a kitten back to the Sulgrave Apartments as a pet. Winkie was a big orange male. Once he ran up our Christmas tree and toppled it. I took Winkie outside on a leash, but often he got loose. When he did so, I unwound a ball of twine and walked through the alley behind the apartment building dragging the twine. Inevitably Winkie scampered out from the garbage bins and plucked at the twine, not before I had peeked over gates into backyard gardens hoping to get a glimpse of my favorite spider, the black and yellow Argiope, the "Queen of the Garden," hanging like a hand in her web, a train trailing silver above her.

In pictures taken when Grandpa was young, he looks serious, the only hint of playfulness being full lips, puckered, ready to tell a tale. In all his pictures he wears a suit, even when Mother, Father, Grandma, and he are sitting outside in Adirondack chairs, watching me play. Usually his elbow rests on the arm of the chair and his hand is pressed against his cheek, his expression quizzical. The stories surrounding him are the ones he told. He enjoyed words, though, and for some time, Father said, he edited the *Smith County News*. Although he could knot paragraphs together, Grandpa was not mechanical. Neither was Father in whose hands a hammer was inadvertently a weapon. I inherited the Pickerings' lack of mechanical ability. At Cabin Hill during the summer of my fifth year, I burst in on Big Ga who was napping. "Big Ga, get me an ax," I shouted. "Why?" Big Ga answered. "To cut off these hands of mine; they are no damn good," I said.

Bessie, Grandpa's maid, made the best strawberry shortcake I've eaten and if berries were in season, she served it when I came to Carthage, along with a cup of sweet coffee. Bessie's husband, however, ran around, and one evening when he returned home after a night of gallivanting, she shot him, not killing him but removing one of his legs below the knee. Today in America a person is, as the saying puts it, innocent until his money runs out. The law was more personal in the past. Bessie didn't spend a night in jail. After Grandpa pled that she was the best cook in Smith County, she was released into his custody. Later she received a suspended sentence. Bessie's husband limped out of town, and eventually Bessie married again, this time a preacher. She moved to Nashville and lived happily ever after, as family account puts it. Occasionally Bessie helped out when Mother planned a large dinner. One Christmas Bessie and Bertha, another maid who had worked for Mother and Father when I was a child, came to the house Christmas Eve, Bessie to cook and Bertha to serve. After they appeared and before guests arrived, Mother and Father went to a neighbor's house for a cup of Christmas cheer.

Wrapped in a gray suit and decorated with a blue and red striped necktie, I stayed home with nothing to do. Before me stretched an evening in which I'd sit straight, not swing my legs like, as Father put it, "someone with the St. Vitus Dance," and would endlessly say, "Yes, ma'am"; "no, ma'am"; "yes, sir"; and "no, sir." Just after Mother and Father left, Bessie asked me a question, "Mr. Sammy, do you still catch snakes like you used to?" Bright, happy, Christmas chaos suddenly flickered. "Oh, yes, Bessie," I answered. "I've got the biggest copperhead you ever saw down in the basement. Let me go get him." Before Bessie could answer I scooted down the basement steps and balling up sheets of old newspaper crammed them and a piece of wood into a washtub. "I've got him, Bessie," I hollered and started back up the stairs. The basement was dark; the only light was behind me near the furnace, and the stairs themselves curved down from the kitchen. As a result people standing on the landing and looking down from the kitchen could not see well. Bessie and Bertha appeared at the top of the stairs, leaning forward and peering apprehensively into the dark. As I started up the stairs, I shook the tub about making noise. As I drew close, they backed away, and as soon as I was sure they saw me, I shouted, "Look here." Simultaneously I began to beat the stick about in the paper, the noise sounding like a big snake thrashing about. "Oh, Lord," I yelled, "he's getting loose. I can't hold him." "Here Bessie," I screamed, "you take him." And with that, hollering loud as I could, I gave the paper an almighty beating then tossed the tub up the steps. "Jesus!" Bessie screamed and slammed the basement door. By the time I opened it, Bertha and Bessie were in the backyard and that is where they stayed until Mother and Father came home, my importuning not moving them. Because much of the meal was not cooked, dinner was late. The men seized the occasion to have more drinks than usual, and the women swilled eggnog. Formality unraveled into informality and hearty Christmas cheer, alive and green and red with story and affection.

When I was a child, the natural world entranced me. I caught all sorts of creatures, studiously trying not to harm them. Often I played little tricks with them, my parents being sensible people comfortable enough with themselves to laugh. On evenings when people came for dinner, I stuck cicada shells to the undersides of armrests and wound snake skins through bowls of flowers. *Jesus*, incidentally, was a word often used in my house, especially by Mother. Snakes frightened her, and in summers in Virginia I unpeeled newly killed snakes from the road outside Big Ga's farm. Because the road was soft dirt, the bodies were not messy. Sometimes Mother went upstairs and napped after lunch, and when she did, I stretched snakes out in the hall outside her door then, of course, decamped and waited for the yells that always came. One day in Nashville while roaming after school, I caught a big king snake. I put the snake down my shirt, and when I walked into the house said, "Momma, I've got a pain in my stomach. Let me show you where." When Mother bent over to look at my belly, I unbuttoned my shirt. The snake jabbed its head out, and Mother high-tailed it into the bedroom and shut the door. The antics of the boy, alas, sometimes influence those of the man. I am still a snake handler, though for social not spiritual reasons. When my daughter Eliza was small, I caught a red-bellied snake, and after blocking off my throat because no one wants a snake wriggling in his lung or stomach, I put the snake in my mouth. Of course the snake pooped in defense, but I have tasted things off stoves a lot worse than snake droppings and so I didn't react. Anyway I mumbled, "Eliza, honey, come here, and let your daddy give you a kiss." When Eliza turned her face up to mine, I opened my mouth and the snake dropped over her eyes onto her nose, an event that so delighted her that she wanted to try the trick on Vicki, something that I forbade.

Bessie, incidentally, was not alone in having the law applied to her in a reasonable, personal way. The law was applied personally to both white and colored people. In Virginia Big Ga's herdsman Pallinda occasionally drank too much. A night in the Hanover jail, Big Ga decided, might do him good, so Big Ga called the sheriff. The next morning while the family was eating breakfast, Pallinda telephoned. "Mr. Ratcliffe," he said, "come and get me out of this jail. The coffee is no good and the cream is sour." Mother told many stories about Pallinda. He was English and good with the cows, but his knowledge of geography was rudimentary. Early one morning during the Second World War, not long after the Germans attacked Egypt, Pallinda knocked on the kitchen door and asked to speak to Big Ga. "Mr. Ratcliffe," he said, "the Germans are getting mighty close. I heard they bombed Alexandria last night. Shouldn't we move the cows?" Pallinda's amorous life was the subject of table talk and admiration. He had several "wives," none of whom he divorced, or, for that matter, married, and all of whom he met through lonely hearts magazines. "They came, stayed, and went," Mother said.

I have only one sample of Grandpa Pickerking's handwriting, fitting, I suppose, for a story-teller. Scribbled on the front page of *Familiar Scenes; or, The Scientific Explanation of Common Things* was "Sam Pickering began this book in Mr. Morris's School." On the back binding he listed nine children attending the school: himself, Ada Salter, Josie Myer, Charles McClarin, Ernest and Julian Fisher, and the three Sanders children, Ed, Bettie, and Alex. At the top of page five he wrote, "If how to be rich / You wish to find / look on page 109." Scratched across the top of 109 was "*mind your business.*" At other places in the book he practiced his penmanship, writing in blue ink "do you know?" and "S. Pickering Dec 3, 1885." The only other book of Grandpa's I found was a copy of Aesop's fables, inscribed "To Sammy Pickering who won the prize in his Sunday School Class this Book is Presented by W. D. Gold."

Grandpa Pickering does not seem to have been a reading man, at least not like my Father whose reading must have pleased Grandma despite her concerns over his posture. I remember only one story describing Grandpa's education. In the 1870s and early 80s the Carthage elementary school was small. Rumor swirled about Mr. Bradshaw, the man who taught Grandfather. He had come to Carthage, children believed, from the Indian Territory that later became Oklahoma. Children thought he had killed a man in the territory and had fled to Carthage to escape the hangman. In any case Mr. Bradshaw treated students harshly and was fond of switching boys. When a boy misbehaved, Mr. Bradshaw sent another student outside to cut switches. Selecting switches was difficult. If a student cut thin, weak switches, Mr. Bradshaw got mad. If the switches were too thick and strong, the boy being punished became angry. One day Henry Fisher misbehaved, and Mr. Bradshaw sent Grandpa outside to fetch switches. When Grandpa returned to the classroom, Mr. Bradshaw fondled the switches lovingly, turning them over and over in his hands. "Sammy," he eventually said, "these are the best switches I have ever seen, much too good for the likes of Henry Fisher, but just right for a good boy like you." "Whereupon," Grandpa recounted, shaking his head and laughing, "Mr. Bradshaw whaled the tar out of me and made my legs bleed, even though I had done nothing wrong."

The split in ages between Father and Coleman was two years. Other differences ran deeper. Father was never without a book. He carried a book to work with him at the Travelers and slipped it into the top drawer of his desk to read throughout the day, closing the drawer when he needed to solve a problem. He got along well with folks and solving problems was easy for him. "Your father could make things fly even when they did not have wings," a man told me. "I think I have just been fired," an office worker told Father's secretary, "but Mr. Pickering was so nice I think I'm glad I was fired." Coleman was more irascible, more a Griffin, than Father, and I wonder how well they got along as boys. Later when Coleman moved to Texas, he bundled himself in and out of good corporate jobs, leaving, it seems, because of imaginary slights. Eventually he became a postman, the rounds enabling him to chat with people but preventing him from knowing anyone well enough to become angry at him.

Coleman did well in school and was valedictorian of his class in Carthage. But he wasn't an omnivorous reader like Father. Unlike Father who tottered when he walked, Coleman was a good athlete. Among things I found in Houston was a box containing medals and a picture of Coleman taken when he was a member of the Vanderbilt track team. His legs were slender and bowed, muscle wrapping his calves in sinewy bundles. He looked as if he could run forever. The medals were for running: three for winning the "Intramural Cross Country" at Vanderbilt, two dated, 1929 and 1930; another for being part of the championship mile relay team at the "Southern Conference Meet," and another for being a member of the winning four-mile relay team at the Southern Relays held at Georgia Tech in 1930.

Coleman had much promise. He was vice-president of his class at Vanderbilt and could, Father said, "have done almost anything in Nashville." Instead he went to Texas sometime after he married in 1939. In Texas he distanced himself from family. I remember Father repeatedly telephoning him and entreating him to call their mother. On the few times he did call, Grandma immediately informed Father, bursting with happiness and affection for Coleman, never knowing that getting Coleman to telephone took innumerable calls from Nashville. In a sense Father was the dutiful responsible son while Coleman was the prodigal son who did no wrong because he did nothing. Only rarely did Coleman write Father, something Grandma wrote him about. "I *do* wish you would write him," Grandma wrote, speaking about Father. "It hurts him that you seemingly don't care to write him. And he has always loved you so much and really wants news of you. He asked me Sunday, as he always does, if I had heard from you." When close relatives died, Coleman neglected to write notes of condolence. When a relative married, he did not send a present. "Have you ever written Sammy a thank you note for your gifts on Christmas?" Grandma asked, speaking of me. "Please do that. Your *gifts* were reminders that he was thinking of you and loved you. It is an unpardonable lapse of decent courtesy to ignore a kindness and among friends often strains a deep and long lasting relationship. Somehow, I just can't let my appreciation go unexpressed."

After Coleman's wife Amanda died and he drifted into dementia, I became Father and Grandma. Although I had not seen Coleman in three decades, I managed his affairs for several years. Ironically I spent more time nursing an uncle who didn't care much for family, certainly not on the surface and surface may be all there was or is, than I spent caring for Father. But to sound like Grandma, perhaps duty elevates us out of selfishness and is responsible for whatever moral stature a person achieves. Coleman died one summer when Vicki and the children and I were on our farm in Nova Scotia. I arranged his burial on the telephone. "Mario," I said to the director of the funeral home, "can we put this on my charge card?" "And what card would that be, sir?" Mario asked. "MasterCard," I said. "That's fine," Mario answered. "You should have charged everything on Visa," Vicki said later. "Coleman is traveling to a new country."

Grandma was always dutiful. When Mother and Father became engaged, she wrote Mother a long letter welcoming her into the family. The letter was warm-hearted, but the prose was formal and still, deadening when it meant to be quickening. "When our son told us a few days ago that he and you were to be married he duly confirmed our expectations," the letter began. Good wishes filled the pages. "We are such a small family that we feel the need of a daughter to make our little circle complete and all of us shall try to make you very happy among us." After saying that she knew Mother's mother would miss her, Grandma wrote, "I hope she will find consolation in the knowledge that Samuel is a young man of exemplary habits and conscientious almost to a fault. He has the qualifications that should meet her wishes and above all, I am sure, will be kind and unselfish with you at all times. All this his mother desires him to be."

To quibble because kind thoughts are expressed in a stilted way is petty. And in truth it is responsibility that does tedious chores such as stuffing scrapbooks and shaping family history, something that may influence later generations as they pour over the books and imagine seeing traces of themselves. Grandma kept Father's baby teeth in an envelope labeled "Samuel's first Teeth Shed, June 1915, Age 6 Years, 11 Months." In another envelope supplied by "The City Barber Shop. Sam King. Proprietor. North Side Public Square. Carthage Tennessee Box 201" was a lock from "Samuel's first hair cut—just before his first school day in fall of 1915." Father's hair was silvery blond and the lock seven and a quarter inches long. In Lena Douglas's first grade class Father's grades in the final four marking periods averaged, 99 1/3, 98 5/8, 99 7/8, and 99 7/8. In language he made all *E*'s, and in deportment made 100 in the last two marking periods. During the year he was absent six days. At Vanderbilt, Father lost hours and quality credits each semester for "excessive absences." During his four years he made two *B+*'s and no *A*'s. He made ten *D*'s, two *E*'s (Passing, 50-59), and one F, this in gym and in my view not a regrettable mark but an honor. When I discovered his grades, I read them out loud at dinner on more than one occasion.

The truth was Father had skipped two grades in Carthage and was sixteen when he entered Vanderbilt, "too young," he told me, adding that the Carthage schools were "not too good." Part of the reason that he lost quality credits and hours is that he worked his way through school, often holding down three jobs, for example, managing the Beta Theta Pi fraternity house, serving as business manager of the school yearbook and selling advertisements on commission, and then repossessing cars. Grades don't measure much. Many years later, a prominent woman in Nashville told me Father was the smartest man she ever met. When I started publishing essays, some people believed Father wrote them. "Do you know Grace Cheney?" a friend wrote after reading one of my books. "She told me how much she enjoyed reading your essays.

She said she didn't know whether you or your father had written them, but she suspected it was your father because he is so witty."

Of course Grandma was not as stiff as her letters make her seem. She was very bright, and she loved me dearly. Ironically she worried that I was too competitive, probably thinking I was undermining my health, and she wrote Father advising him not to repeat praises he had heard of my academic success. She was active in reading groups in Carthage and in the Eastern Star, becoming Worthy Grand Matron of the State of Tennessee in 1927. After Grandpa died, she spent Christmases with us in Nashville. Mother made eggnog that, she said, would "knock the ass off a mule." Although she was a teetotaler, Grandmother swilled the brew after Mother told her it was Christmas tonic. Among the first record albums I owned was a collection of gospel songs, among others, "In the Garden," "Just as I Am," "Old Rugged Cross," and "Love Lifted Me." When Grandma heard the songs, she cried. Consequently during the holidays I played the album soon after she arrived. On coming home from the office, Father invariably found his mother tearful. "Damn it, Sammy, not again," he always said, laughter and exasperation mixed in his voice. Of course, the again occurred again.

Grandma was stubborn. A lesser person would not have sent Coleman so many signatures of advice. For my part I admired her resilient obstinacy. She should have stopped driving years before she finally stopped, but because she refused to do so, I associate her with a rusting red Studebaker. Whenever she left Carthage for Nashville, the Carthage sheriff radioed ahead to the highway patrol, warning, "Mrs. Pickering's on the road." Along the way patrolmen watched out for her, and when she reached Lebanon, one telephoned Father. Then he and Mother and I drove out to the Stuckey's near the city limits and waited. After what seemed forever, she appeared, inevitably with scores of cars stacked up behind her. At Stuckey's Father took over the wheel of the Studebaker, and Mother drove me home in our car.

While I was a student at Cambridge in 1963, Grandma had a heart attack. She recovered nicely in the hospital, appearing so well that visitors were allowed to see her. So many friends came to see her that she became exhausted and had a second heart attack and died. What a nice way to peg out—full of years and amid bouquets of good will and affection. In a picture taken in 1944 she was holding my hand while we followed Scarlett the cat down a lane. I wore a loose, checkered sweater, blue jeans, and black basketball shoes with white laces. Grandma was happy, but her hair was white and she looked old. I wish that I had not found the letters she wrote Coleman. Written words don't simply haunt the present; they determine it. Betty Key who wrote a tribute to her for the Eastern Star recalled her laughter and praised her wisdom, saying she "could speak the words that served as 'oil on troubled waters.'" I remember her affection, and I know she was smart and sensible, but of her laughter I have no recollection. For my first two months at Cambridge I wrote her every week, sometimes twice a week, because, as her grandson, that was what I should have done. She did not reply. I became irked and at the end of November stopped writing her. A month later she was dead. "Sammy, Mother really enjoyed your letters," Father said when I visited Tennessee that summer. "She wrote you many times, but the poor thing got the address mixed up, and all the letters were returned to Carthage." Father continued, handing me a packet of letters, "I thought you would like them, so I saved them for you." "Oh, no. Shit," I thought, the last word a sign of guilt and emotion.

Writing an account of one's early years, even wildly happy years, is sad. Looking at pictures and reading letters makes a person aware of the fallings from him, often of people whom he never knew and of the many people his relatives were before he met them. Yesterday I looked at a photograph of Father or "Sammie," taken, a note on the back said, when he was three years and eight months old. Father sat sideways and tentatively on the armrest of a wicker couch. On his head was a round black hat with a brim and a black ribbon around the crown. The hat tilted to the left, and his

Sam Pickering

blond hair hung down over his ears. On his feet were leather shoes,
his legs covered by leggings that resembled spats but rose and
blanketed his knees. Six snaps ran up the outside of the leggings,
and at the top were two buckles. He was also wearing a gray coat
buttoned across the chest; on the left sleeve was a child's military
insignia, transforming him into a playground sergeant. His hands
and cheeks were chubby, and he looked apprehensively at the
camera. The picture made me wish Sammie were my grandson. We
could have such fun together. I'd put him into shorts, a loose shirt,
and sneakers. I'd tell him stories about mountain lions and
cannibals with ten legs and red mouths big as basements, snakes
thick as plaque wrapping their teeth. We'd roam the woods in
Storrs, following Penny and Bert, my dogs, holding hands and
talking, just seeing what we could see. Sam Pickering was a
wonderful father, and I owe Sammie weeks and years of happy
times. I'd play catch with him, and I'd teach him how to ride a
bicycle as he taught me, running alongside and catching me when I
tumbled over.

The point is that when emotions must be reduced to words a
memoir dissatisfies the writer as much as it pleases. I don't want a
closer walk with thee as the gospel song puts it; I want something
really impossible—closer walks with family members fallen from
me. But as Father said many times, "Don't fret; conditions will
ultimately adjust themselves," after which he would tell another
Carthage story, one touched by fiction as all stories are.

Abraham Oldacre was a successful, small town businessman.
Among his employees was Monroe Dowd. A migrant countryman
from Difficult Creek, Dowd marveled at his employer's success,
something he trumpeted to every drummer who came through
town. Dowd told strangers that Oldacre had arrived in Carthage
thirty years earlier as a Jewish peddler, carrying pots and pans and a
different last name. Now, he owned, Monroe liked to point out, a
row of buildings. One day a drummer thinking a good marriage
must have laid the foundation of Oldacre's rise asked Dowd about
his employer's marriage. "Did he marry a gentile?" the drummer

asked. "On, no," Monroe answered. "Oh, no, I don't know any Gentiles, at least not here in Smith County. He married a Ferguson."

Father

"The more I see of old people," Father wrote near the end of his life, "the greater my feeling is that the bulk of them should be destroyed." "Not you," I thought, "at least not yet." In the letter Father said that he and Mother disagreed about the past. "I tell her," he wrote, "that her recollections remarkable, albeit not necessarily accurate." My memories of Father are neither accurate nor remarkable, but they are the bricks and mortar of a good childhood. Photographs are the source of some of my memories. In one picture Father is bent over building a snowman. I stand behind him wearing a playsuit and leaning the opposite direction so that we look like a pair of oddly matched punctuation marks, one font large the other minute. Other memories come from the mind's graying eye not that of the camera, Father's talking with his mouth full or late at night after a party stuffing a glass with bread and pouring milk over it. I remember that Mother liked chocolate, and whenever Father was given a box of chocolate he hid it in his closet so Mother could not find and munch through it. The closet was dark, and as he grew older and his sight failed Father kept a flashlight in a shoebox.

Father's eyes were big and brown like his mother's, and when he was bemused the left side of his mouth turned up as did hers. Occasionally Grandma Pickering took him and Coleman to Nashville to visit Aunt Lula. In a photograph Father and Coleman sat on a white pony, Father appearing to be five years old and Coleman three. In front of the pony stood Aunt Lula's son, Cousin Jerdan. He looked six or seven and was dressed in a double-breasted jacket with a velvet collar, on his head a pie-shaped hat, a ribbon encircling it and tied in a bow. Coleman wore a dark sweater, white leggings, and a stocking cap. Father wore a short coat and a sailor cap with the brim turned down. Grandmother must have been careful with money and bought clothes to last and be let out because I'd seen the coat before, in a picture taken when Father was three years and eight months old. As a boy Father had an Airedale named Jerry who sometimes rode uptown on the running board of Grandfather's car. Jerry was the best fighter in Carthage, and once tangled with Jimmy Fisher's dog Jack and whipped him.

One never knows much about another person. Not long ago I looked across the dinner table at Vicki and wondered, "Who is that woman sitting there eating rhubarb pie?" "How did she get into the house?" I asked myself, and "what does she think about?" The children themselves seemed strangers who mysteriously wandered into my life and had remained mysteries for a quarter of a century. Pondering such matters is momentarily good for the waist because it causes the fork to pause in mid-air. In the long run, puzzlement increases girth as one eats more in hopes of swallowing his way out of doubt and thought into doziness. I know that Grandpa had a horse named Donald and that Father occasionally rode him, not at Mother's rail-breaking pace but as Donald walked into the pasture. For a couple of years Father played the piano but eventually quit because he had, as Coleman put it, "no musical sense." Not having musical sense did not stop him, however, from listening to opera on the radio, being especially fond of Verdi, none of whose works he ever saw, the second act of *La Traviata* with its "Di Provenza il mar, il suol chi dal cor ti cancellò" being Father's favorite act in opera.

Father told me that one afternoon he almost stepped on a huge rattlesnake while exploring Battery Hill just beyond Carthage. Once he almost died after eating homemade ice cream at a birthday party. Indeed, Lucy, the talented little girl who lived next door, died from trichinosis. In the summer of his sixteenth birthday and just before entering Vanderbilt, Father worked on the highway as a water boy. The spring was a mile from the construction and as soon as he brought water up to the road he had to turn around and fetch more. He carried two buckets, for white men one with a green stripe on the outside and for black men one with a red stripe. Everyone worked ten hours a day and was paid twenty-one cents an hour, except men who were paid a bit more because they furnished teams of mules.

Occasionally, Father told me, The Mighty Haag circus came through Carthage. The circus was puny rather than mighty, and some of the best performances were shaggy and clownish. One year the "big" event was a badger fight. Tied to a stake driven into the ground was an old dog, rough and bony with long yellow teeth. Nearby sat a large wooden box; sticking out from under it was a thick rope, at the end of which was, supposedly, the badger. A circus employee held the rope in order to control the badger so the dog wasn't killed right away. As soon as the box was lifted, the man was to jerk the rope toward himself and pull the badger into the fray. Preliminaries to the fight took some time, and while the man held the rope and two other circus employees sat atop the box to keep the badger from digging free, members of the audience bet on how long the dog would last. Finally, however, the tent grew quiet after which Haag himself appeared, dressed in red and gold and carrying a trumpet, looking as if he were marching through Georgia. He blew a long fanfare—sounding, Father said, like a cross between a cattle call and the "William Tell Overture," after which the two men jumped down from the box, and grabbing handles at both ends, lifted it as the other man jerked the rope, pulling toward himself not a badger but a chamber pot.

Sometimes I think heredity more a matter of family story than genes. Not only does a person repeat tales, probably adding to them in the process, but tales trigger inclination. Every year in my essays, Hollis Hunnewell leads a carnival through Carthage. All the exhibits smack of country humor. One year I varied the routine by adding a "Home Going Parade" to doings in Carthage, all the exhibits being floats, and religious, as might be expected in contrast to a "Home Coming Parade." Unlike Father's tales, my stories smack of the bawdy and the "questionable" as Grandma Pickering once described the language of a retarded boy whose mind ran "to calling girls." The most popular float in the Home Going Parade was Bathsheba Bathing, sponsored by the Toodle Ranch on Highway 70. A wrangler at the ranch, Betty Lou Gamphasante, posed as Bathsheba. Betty Lou stretched out in a tin tub shaped like policeman's cap. She wrapped a thick terry cloth towel around her legs, binding it together at her waist. She also wore a veil and a cowboy hat, a white rose stuck in the band. In her left she held a louver sponge. Her right hand she waved at the crowd. Like Bathsheba when she flourished as the apple in David's eye, Betty Lou was naked from waist to veil. Because of the veil and hat, she was not easy to recognize, only being recognized when Hopp Watrous noticed the tattoo "Viva La Amish" curving beneath her left breast. "She got that on a spread in Pennsylvania," Hopp explained, adding, "Amish Catholics really impressed Berry Lou." "She's also got a tattoo of a horse-drawn carriage," Hopp said, "but it's mushed, and you can't see it now. She's a little ashamed of it, and the first time I was a dude at the ranch she didn't want to show it to me. But I told her, 'You can't conceal a tattoo from God, so why hide it from man?' That did the trick. She's got a way of moving so the horse gallops and the carriage, praise King Jesus, bounces up and down just like it was traveling on washed out road deep in the country."

The Sulgrave Apartments where I lived for eight years have vanished. So has Ransom School, which I entered when I was five. For the first months of school, Father walked all the way to Ransom with me: along West End; across Fairfax, where Mr. Underwood the policeman waved at us; and from there to Ransom crossing three small residential streets that no longer exist. Slowly, as I grew surer, Father walked less of the distance with me. Eventually he left me at the corner of Fairfax under the watchful eye of Mr. Underwood. Most of what a person knows about his childhood comes from stories told to him by parents and relatives. One day as Father and I sat on the stone wall in front of the

Sulgrave, a man and his sweetheart walked by spooning, arm in arm. "Daddy," I said pointing, "look at that man's big ears. They sure are funny." The trouble, Father recounted later, was that the man's ears were big and that he was too in love to have a sense of humor.

Many of the shards I unearthed about Father's life had to do with his days at Vanderbilt, universities being addicted to records, including grades the most insignificant of all records, Father, by the by, making *D*'s in all three courses he took in psychology during the academic year 1927-28, marks that reflect well on his common sense. In 1927 Father skipped so many classes that the dean called him in for a conference. Story had it that if the dean got out of his chair and put his arm around a student's shoulders, the student was certain to be dismissed from school. Midway through the interview, the dean rose and approached Father. Quickly Father got up and walked around the desk, and thereafter the conversation proceeded in circular fashion, with the dean lecturing and pursuing and Father explaining and running. The result was probation not expulsion. It was a wonder Father had enough energy to elude the dean because he rarely attended gym class, a required course, albeit like most required courses silly. Not attending gym classes almost prevented Father from graduating. But before graduation one of Father's physician friends wrote a letter, urging the suspension of the requirement in Father's case, explaining, "Pickering has a lameness in his back." After reading the letter, the dean said in exasperation, "No more lies, Pickering; out of my office." Father left silently and graduated.

Although Father majored in English during the great years of Vanderbilt's English Department—the years of the Fugitives and Agrarians—his college experiences were personal, not intellectual. From Carthage he brought with him the small-town world of particulars and familial relationships. For him, as for me, reality was apparent and truth clear, and he had little interest in hidden structure or ornate reasoning, making *D*'s in philosophy as well as psychology. He was not religious, but he genuflected to social niceties. As was proper he attended church with Mother, but I never heard him speak about religion, either to praise or criticize. Neither religious faith nor doctrine played any part in his life. Hypocrisy or, to put it better, genteel behavior costs little and often smoothes the lives of others. For Mother's sake, I acted like Father and had all three of my children christened. Our first child was christened in St. George's Episcopal Church in Nashville. When we arrived at the church, the minister drew me aside. "Sam," he said, "I knew you would not want the new service used in the christening of your son, so I rummaged through the church and found eleven old prayer books." Strangely enough, in light, or dark of my absence of belief, the minister was right. I would rather listen to a reading from the *Red Cross Water Safety Instructor's Manual* than one from the new Episcopal prayer book.

In later years Father only talked about classroom matters if there was a story attached. When John Crowe Ransom assigned two poems to be written, Father exhausted his interest and ability on the first after which he asked his roommate who had some lyrical talent to write the other. A week after Father turned the poems in, Mr. Ransom read Father's poems aloud, finishing by saying, "Mr. Pickering, it is inconceivable to me that the same person could have written these two poems." "A matter of mood and inspiration, Mr. Ransom," Father replied, and he was right. Whose mood and inspiration seem beside the point when the nonpoetic have to write verse. In any case how much better for me that Father followed biblical injunction and bringing his skills to bear adapted the assignment to his talent instead of burying his head in his hands and doing nothing. As a result I have a story that makes me smile and appreciate life, a story that is a cure-all for drudgery, one that enables me to delight in, if not openly celebrate the creative doings of my own students. "It's an imperfect world," Randall Stewart, the chairman of the Vanderbilt English Department, once said after he hired an assistant professor without consulting other members of his department. Thank goodness, for in imperfection lies the source of joy and perhaps of decency itself.

I inherited Father's poetic skills, and in fifth grade when I was assigned a poem, I turned to him, and he wrote, "The Zoo," a poem not up to Mr. Ransom's expectations but all right for an eleven-year-old.

I like to go to see a zoo
As boys like me so often do,
It's lots of fun to spend the day,
To walk and watch the animals play.

All sorts of beasts are there to see
With names that start from A to Z;
The monkey, tiger, kangaroo,
The zebra, snakes and crocodiles, too.

I learned from Father, and in sixth grade when forced to write a poem for an in-school contest, I wrote "The Garbage Truck," in which rhymes came easily, this being before recycling when everything went into the garbage, not simply tomato, potato, but chair, hair, and underwear. Students selected a poem to represent the class, and over the teacher's tactfully wondering if "this was the right sort of poem," "The Garbage Truck" carried the day, hay, and map to show the way.

Despite his lack of composing talent, Father read poetry and throughout his life quoted verse. The poems were always old but good standbys like Browning's "Rabbi Ben Ezra," Thomas Gray's "Elegy Written in a Country Churchyard," and Oliver Goldsmith's "The Deserted Village," "Sweet Auburn, loveliest village of the plain," especially clear when recollected amid bourbon. Father quoted Tennyson, it sometimes seemed by the hour. He enjoyed the sound of Tennyson's verse, and in every recitation, he included "The Splendour Falls." On my bookshelf between copies of Kipling's and Browning's verses that I read at college sits *Poems of Tennyson*, the edition Father studied in English his freshman year at Vanderbilt. Inside the front cover Father wrote "Samuel F.

Pickering 359 Kissam Hall 1925," and on page 272, Father wrote the name of his poetic roommate, "L. Huxley Roberts."

Father's favorite poet was Byron, and the dying gladiator from *Childe Harold* was a companion of my childhood while the Coliseum seemed not to stand far away and crumbling in Rome but on the bookshelf in the living room, somehow forever fresh and green, stars always twinkling "through the loops of time." College may have had something to do with Father's enjoyment of Byron, but the source was probably closer to home. On a shelf I found *The Works of Lord Byron in Verse and Prose*, published in Hartford in 1840 by Silus Andrus and Son. The book was inscribed "Wm. B. Pickering from his Father. Over the inscription a child wrote, "Sammie F. Pickering." Under that in a firm youthful handwriting was written, "Samuel Pickering, Beta House, Vanderbilt University, 1926."

In 1915 in the *Carthage Courier* appeared an advertisement for Tabler's Buckeye Ointment, "Cures Nothing but Piles." At Vanderbilt during the 1920s literary criticism was shifting from the personal and anecdotal to the intellectual and ultimately to the abstract. Instead of explaining ordinary life, it began to create an extraordinary world of thought far from piles. For Father I suspect the shift led to boredom and the conviction that although literary criticism entertained some people, it was insignificant. In the eighty years that have passed since Father entered college, criticism has become more rarefied, with the result, as a friend put it, "We write books that even our mothers won't read." Carthage influenced more than schoolwork. It probably determined the course of his career, although *career* was not a word used so often then. After graduating from Vanderbilt, Father went to work in the personnel department of the Travelers Insurance Company. Years later he told me he had erred. "I did what my father did," he said. "I should have done something different, even run off to sea." An old man's thoughts often wander far from the path happily trod by the young man, and running away to sea is only accomplished in books and dreamed about when the house is quiet and children asleep.

Writing a memoir, even one that stops at eighth grade, provokes dreamy thoughts of what-might-have-been. In 1963 I sailed on the *United States* to Britain in order to study at Cambridge. Sitting at my dinner table was an older woman, probably 35 or so it seems from hindsight. "Don't go to Cambridge," she said. "I own land in Kenya. Come to Kenya and live with me." Only now does the offer tempt me. What in the world, I wonder, what I was thinking, or not thinking, in 1963? How different my life would have been had I accompanied the woman to Kenya.

Father was not ambitious. After being transferred to Nashville, he refused further promotion, not something easy to do when one is young. He was home, however, and in his way did not hanker to cross the "Great Caney Fork River." He made enough money to live on, and with Mother's small bit, more than enough. The wild growth of wealth that changed the topography of everyday life had not yet occurred, as it did during the 1960s and afterward. A son can only view a father through his own distorting vision. But as I scampered away from positions the world thought important in order to shape my days insofar as was possible in society, so Father did the same. Still, I think Father was in the wrong profession. He would have been a good college teacher, one who could have made people enjoy books and as a result perhaps appreciate living more. He read through libraries and wrote well. When I broached the subject of teaching, he hesitated to answer. Eventually he said, "I might have enjoyed teaching. But who knows? Anyway I had to work my way through school and couldn't make good grades." Because a lot of money did not matter to Father is not to imply that he thought money and power unimportant, especially for other people. Once in a while, but not often, he urged me to make the most of my chances, citing Coleman as a warning. Coleman, he said, could have succeeded in almost anything; yet, he refused to grasp opportunities.

After school, the thoughtful realize life is a maze of inconsistencies, the greatest perhaps being the discrepancy between principles and deeds. From infancy through school people are taught the value of general truths or principles, the sanctity, for example, of honor and truth itself. As a person ages and attempts to apply principles to real people, one learns that rules are cruelly narrow and, instead of bettering life, often lead to unhappiness. The sense of principle or belief in general or accepted truths is so deeply ingrained, however, that one repudiates it with difficulty. Instead one continues to pay lip service to it and may actually believe it while in actuality jettisoning it and never applying it to individuals. Thus during the turmoil over integration in Nashville in the 1950s and 60s, Father sounded conservative. One day, though, while he, Mother, and I were walking along Church Street, we came upon four white toughs or hoods, as they were then called, harassing a colored woman. "You, there," Father bellowed, all 136 pounds of him, he having gained six pounds since marriage, "Who do you think you are?" Then as Mother and I slunk into a doorway, he grabbed the biggest tough and shaking him, "Apologize to this lady. This is Tennessee, and people behave here." "Yes, sir, yes, sir," the man responded meekly and apologized. Father then turned to the woman and while the toughs scurried away, took off his hat, and said, "Ma'am, I'm sorry for what happened. You were probably walking to the bus stop. If you don't mind, my wife and I and our son would like to walk with you."

Although Father occasionally waxed unfeeling and expounded political and moral generalities during the comparative isolation of dinner, he did not apply them to people's lives. He delighted in people too much to categorize and thus limit his appreciation of them. Not long after the incident on Church Street, Father was invited to join the Klan. Around eleven every morning, a man brought a cart to the Travelers building and sold doughnuts and sweet rolls. Father usually bought a doughnut and a cup of coffee and chatted a bit with the man. On this occasion, the man said, "Mr. Pickering, I've known you for some time, and you seem a right thinking man. This Friday there is going to be a meeting of the Klan at Nolensville, and I'd like for you to attend and become a member." "That's mighty nice of you to invite me," Father replied, "but I believe I will just continue to vote Republican."

Father knew all sorts of people, something that paid off in many ways, including the literal. One year the IRS scheduled him for an audit. Father told me he was frightened that his taxes were wrong, and he'd be fined a fortune. "Sam," the man who was in charge of Father's audit exclaimed when Father walked in the door. "I didn't realize I was auditing you." The man was from Smith County. "Sam," the man continued, "why don't you just give me twenty dollars. That will make things right. Let's forget all these numbers and spend the hour talking about Carthage."

Father believed in justice, but not book justice. Once he made justice prevail when he served as foreman of a jury. A cook at the Maxwell House Hotel in Nashville made a batch of apple pies. To cool the pies the cook set them on window ledges. Unfortunately when she was bringing the pies back inside, she knocked one pie off the ledge. The pie fell on the head of a woman walking along Church Street. The woman sued the Maxwell House claiming the pie damaged her brain, making it impossible for her to stop blinking. "She had the worst case of blinking imaginable," Father said. "In the courtroom she blinked nonstop."

The trail began late in the morning, and after a time the judge recessed the court for lunch. Father did not want to eat downtown, so he drove to a restaurant on the Nolensville Road. "I had just started eating," Father said, "when I glanced across the dining room and saw the woman eating lunch with her lawyer. She wasn't blinking." Not once while Father watched her did the woman blink. Father bolted his food and left the restaurant. He knew that what he saw was privileged information and not admissible in court. He realized that if he told the judge he would be excused from the jury. An alternate would replace him, and the woman, and her lawyer, would win a big sum of money. "So I did what any decent person would do," Father said. "I kept quiet, and when the jury reconvened after lunch, I took charge and spoke first." "This is a clear case of neglect," Father said. "The pie caused this woman to blink terribly, and I think we should award the poor soul a lot of money to prevent this kind of accident from happening again. I suggest we give her $250." The rest of the jury agreed with Father, and the award affected a miraculous cure, so startling the woman that she stopped blinking.

"Your mother," Father often said, "does not appreciate my sense of humor." That was a loss because laughing was important to both Father and Mother, and for much of his life he played harmless, albeit sometimes highly wrought practical jokes. Such jokes are almost an implicit recognition of the foolishness of man's endeavors. Involving actual individuals rather than comparative abstractions like word play, for example, such humor flourishes in stable communities in which people's positions remain relatively constant and defined. Money undermines community and thus practical jokes, by making people more mobile and changing the terms by which position is defined. As people become financial or other accomplishments, not neighbors, cousins, sons, and daughters, they generally take themselves more seriously. When people determine what they are rather than being defined by a web of relationships over which they have comparatively little control, their own actions grow increasingly important and laughter that was once fond and benign is often thought mocking, anti-social rather than a reflection of social life. Once we visited Mother and Father's good friends, the Dearborns, shortly after they had bought a new rug for their living room. The rug was big, expensive, and blue. Before going to the Dearborns', Father went to a fun store and bought an empty bottle of ink, the glass inside the bottle painted dark. Accompany the bottle was a lobed piece of shiny metal, also painted black and looking an ink spill. When Bill Dearborn went into the kitchen to prepare drinks, Father stayed in the living room to, as he said, to admire the rug. While Bill was out of the room, he arranged the props, placing the bottle of ink on its side on a low desk and the spill on the floor below. Then he shouted, "Oh, damn, not the rug. Bill, come quick." Bill rushed out of the kitchen, saw the rug, and said, "No, no, no." Then he swiveled about to get cleaner from under the sink, shouting for his wife Lee to come help him.

In rummaging through my attic, I found traces of Father's humor. In a drawer was a copy of a letter Father wrote in 1948. That October he and Mother and Dewiss Tate, a friend from Nashville, drove to Sea Island, Georgia, and spent a long weekend at the Cloister. While there they met the Brellsfords, a couple from Richmond, stopping at Sea Island for a few days while on their way to Florida. The Brellsfords, Mother and Father, and Dewiss made a gay fivesome and during their last evening together drinking heavily, so much so that the next day Tate remembered little that occurred. "My God, Dewiss," Father said, seizing the chance to enliven the tedious drive back to Nashville, "my God, man, don't you recall flirting with Grace Brellsford, whispering something to her then leaving the table? She followed soon after, and Lyndon Brellsford was furious." When Dewiss said he could not remember anything about the evening but assured Father that he was not the sort to fool around with another man's wife, Father grunted and said, "Well, we shall see. Truth will out."

Back in Nashville, Father wrote a letter and sent it to a friend in Richmond, instructing him to mail it to Tate:

> Dear sir, no doubt you will be surprised to receive this communication from me and to learn that I have canceled my trip and returned to Richmond. Furthermore, you will be interested to know that I left my wife in Florida and I am now making arrangements for a divorce. While my reasons have been cumulative over the months, the events of Monday evening, October 11, were the final straw. As best I could I tried to forgive and overlook the happenings at the table. After all I hoped what transpired had been induced by alcohol and though objectionable and disgraceful was not necessarily vicious. However, after my wife left the room for a rendezvous I could stand no more. Through the medium of the hotel staff I found whom she met and where. Need I say more?

"Mr. Tate," Father's letter concluded, "you may wonder why I have troubled myself to write you. It is simply that I am extending you the courtesy of forewarning you so that you may be prepared—which incidentally is more than you did for me. You may expect to hear from me in a more formal and legal vein within a very few days—when the papers are served. Yours, very truly, L. W. Brellsford." Soon, Dewiss, who worked in his uncle's law firm, rushed to see Father: "I am ruined. If Uncle Horace finds out about this, I'm ruined. Sam, what can I do?" Dewiss moaned. "Perhaps," Father suggested, "some sort of financial remuneration would allay Lyndon's anger. Would you like me to serve as a mediator? Katherine has many friends in Richmond." Dewiss accepted Father's offer, wringing his hand and thanking him enthusiastically, thereby letting the fox into the hen house and extending his suffering for another ten days.

Very little learned in classrooms sticks to the mind, except in classes devoted to mechanical matters, say medical classes on anatomy. If potential doctors did not learn the difference in functions and locations of the heart and the colon, bypasses, not to mention colonoscopies, would become extremely interesting, perhaps even poetic. Matter discovered in an attic is more adhesive, binding itself to a person and sticking tight even into serene age. I am afraid I have written a folder of jocular letters, following Father's sentences down the page. To give but one example—some years ago my son Edward played on the town twelve-and-under soccer team. On Memorial Day the team participated in a tournament near Danbury. The referee of the first game was poor. Rarely did he shift his position from mid-field, and only occasionally did he look at the line judges. Near the end of the second half the father of one of Edward's teammates stepped onto the field and called the referee a turkey. The referee overreacted and awarded the other team a penalty kick. As an artist, the father was a mild man, and the referee's action provoked laughter, not exasperation.

Three days later I sent a letter to the father of Edward's teammate. My older son Francis created a letterhead for me on the computer: a black and white soccer ball three and a half inches in diameter. Circling the ball in bold black letters were the words "Connecticut Soccer Association." Supposedly the writer of the letter was Annette D. Barcombaker Worthy Grand Matron of the "CSAss" and a resident of 476 Post Hole Road in Darien:

Dear Mr. Zinsser,

This morning I received a litter from Mr. R. F. (Fred) Jaggerson, director of the Newtown Kick-Off Tournament. Fred informs me that during this past weekend you used fowl language on the athletic field, calling a referee a turkey. Actually I understand that the phrase used was more personal and that you said, "you turkey" to Mr. Igot Highballs, one of our most respected officials. The use of such language is reprehensible. If you had called Mr. Highballs a coxcomb, we at the Association would be more understanding. But to give a man of his distinguished appearance the bird is shocking. By the way did you hear about the sick man whose doctor advised him to eat a piece of pullet? The man refused, saying it might lay on his stomach. Ha! Ha! We at the Association are a lively flock. There are no flies on our giblets.

I can only assume that hormones triggered your behavior. Are you middle-aged, Mr. Zinsser? Many soccer fathers your age experience problems with testosterone. I recall that on one occasion a former All-American football player and father of a lovely blood child aged twelve started growing breasts after he passed thirty-eight. From this distance I do not presume to analyze the effects of hormones upon you, but I do advise you to seek professional help. Fred tells me that not only did you call the official a turkey but that you stepped upon the field to do so. Only once before has one of our fathers violated a field to address an official. That happened, as I recollect, in 1986 during the first half of a game between the Greenwich Bandits and Milford Darlings. Like you the man was an artist. He encroached upon the field not to criticize but because he was overcome with passion. The official that day was Mr. Billy Capon, a man with the most divine buns and who played the organ at All Saints' Episcopal Church in Woodbridge.

The father couldn't control his lust, and he embraced Mr. Billy near the thirty-yard marker, disrupting a breakaway. All ended happily, however. He and Mr. Billy eloped the next day. They now own an antique shop in Westport. As I recall the man behaved a great deal like you, calling Mr. Billy "my itsy-bitsy turkey gobbler." Mr. Zinsser, examine your motives for stepping on to the field. Did desire master reason? I leave the probing of your parts to you alone. I must now stop to prepare Cornish hen for my beloved spouse. But I want to stress that all of us in the Connecticut Soccer Ass. are praying for you. We think of you as a member of our extended family.

Only after two days and six readings did my recipient conclude the letter was a joke.

Father's humor was rarely as bawdy as mine. I, of course, had a different mother, one looser of tongue than Grandma Pickering. The jokes Father told were usually gentle tales about foolishness. My favorite was the old story called "Edgar the Cat." Two bachelor brothers, Herbert and James, lived with their mother and James's cat Edgar in a little town not unlike Carthage. James was extraordinarily attached to Edgar, and when he had to spend several days in Nashville having work done on his teeth, he left Herbert meticulous instructions about Edgar. At the end of the first day away from home, James telephoned Herbert. "Herbert," he said, "how is Edgar?"

"Edgar is dead," Herbert answered immediately. There was a pause then James said, "Herbert, you are terribly insensitive. You know how close I was to Edgar, and you should have broken the news to me slowly." "How?" Herbert said. "Well," James said, "when I asked about Edgar tonight, you should have said, 'Edgar's on the roof, but I have called the fire department to get him down.'" "Is that so?" said Herbert. "Yes," James answered, "and tomorrow when I called, you could have said the firemen were having trouble getting Edgar down but you were hopeful they would succeed. Then when I called the third time you could have told me that the firemen had done their best but unfortunately Edgar had fallen off the roof and was at the veterinarian's, where he was receiving fine treatment. Then when I called the last time you could have said that although everything felinely possible had been done for Edgar he had died. That's the way a sensitive man would have told me about Edgar. And, oh, before I forget," James added, "how is mother? "Uh," Herbert said, pausing, "she's on the roof."

Among the bits of Father's life I found was a small four by six inch "Vanderbilt Notebook Student Series," which Father took to class. On the cover Father wrote his name several times in blue ink and then drew scores of whirling attached circles, shaped like Slinkies. Inside he jotted down remarks about Thoreau, Emerson, Whitman, Melville, Twain, Lanier, and Poe. His teacher spent much time discussing Puritanism and things Southern, and Father's notes often referred to H. L. Mencken and Stuart Sherman. Of Mark Twain, Father wrote, "Dangerous to carry humor too far in dealing with great subjects." For my part I am not sure what the great subjects are, and whenever I hear the word *great* used to celebrate or as a compliment, I become suspicious, thinking the speaker has designs upon my thought.

With the exception of the Civil War, the struggles of the nation have not touched my family. Coming of age between battles, the last three generations of Pickerings have not probed the dark side of man's heart. Perhaps because of this, we laugh a lot and are soft, and in our desires, conscious or subconscious, to remain free, have become evasive. Few matters are simple, though, and this very evasiveness may be a sign of a shrewd and even tough vitality, one that has little use for high murderous words like honor and patriotism. Aware that those who respond to challenges and fight for causes or worldly success are often destroyed, we have learned to live unobtrusively and, like weeds, blossom low to the ground. Even when a Pickering does answer a call, it's usually not for him. In 1942 the Navy rejected Father's application for officers' training school because he was too thin. In 1944 Father was drafted; two days before he was slated to leave for training camp and after a series of farewell parties, he received a telegram instructing him not to report, explaining that he was too thin. For his part Coleman joined the Quartermaster Corps, and because he majored in French at Vanderbilt was packed off to France where far from the sound of guns he ran a bread factory staffed by German prisoners. "The best bread factory" in France, Father said.

The letters I found at Aunt Lula's house intrigued me because they were the voices of relatives and were not written for public perusal. When I was a boy, people, not family members, gave me the books of Bruce Catton and Douglas Southall Freeman as birthday and Christmas presents with the intention of, I suppose, in some vague way making me a devotee of the Old South, as Romantics painted it. At school I learned about Sam Davis, Middle Tennessee's Nathan Hale. Caught delivering messages for the Confederacy, Davis refused to betray his comrades and although a "boy" was hanged, his nobility supposedly moving his Yankee captors to tears. Attitudes toward Davis's "martyrdom" mirrored attitudes toward matters Southern in Nashville in the 1950s. Davis's life was held up as an exemplar of integrity, patriotism, and devotion to duty. When it came to actual living, however, I suspected few parents wanted their sons to behave like Davis. In any case I, as a sensible Pickering, thought the celebration of Davis wrongheaded. If he had not been a spy, I told a friend, he would not have been executed. If I had to choose between life and betraying a source of information, I told friends, I'd choose life. The phrase "I'd rather be dead than red," fashionable in some asinine patriotic time, struck me as absurd, for I would rather be red, orange, purple, pink, or measled with polka dots than dead.

While at Vanderbilt, Father bought an old car. On a trip to Carthage, the car broke down, and having to hurry back to

Nashville to take an examination, one of the few times he attended class, Father left the car in Carthage and took the train. For a modest fee, George Jackson, a colored man, agreed to drive the car to Nashville once it was repaired. Father wrote out careful instructions and drew a map detailing the way to the Beta house at Vanderbilt. Alas, George lost both, but this did not deter him. On reaching Nashville, he stopped a residential area, went up to a house, and asked where "young Mr. Samuel Pickering" lived. Amazingly the people in the house knew Father. They gave George clear directions, and he delivered the car. When Father learned that the map had gone astray and George had lost his way, he asked him how he knew whom to ask for instructions. "Mister Sam," George answered quickly, "everybody knows you."

In the Vanderbilt notebook, Father listed six items under "Things Associated with the South by People." The first was sentiment, of which Father noted, "Passes too often into Sentimentalism." For me Sentimentalism is the fifth cardinal virtue, expansive and loving and far superior to narrow temperance and prudence, less dangerous than fortitude, and certainly less suspect than justice as administered by any society. In "Rabbi Ben Ezra," Browning began, writing, "Grow old along with me! / The best is yet to be, / The last of life, for which the first was made." Father and Mother grew old, but they did not live long enough for me to know them when they were young, perhaps even to know them at all. No matter, I was fortunate to have had such parents, and whenever I think about them sentiment courses red, and alive, not dead, through my heart.

Mother

Last year my cousin Kathryn Ottarson described a day she spent many years ago with Mother. They drove downtown to shop, and Mother was searching for a parking place when she turned a corner and saw a man kicking a horse. The horse was old and had collapsed between the shafts attached to a wagon. "Katherine slammed on the brakes and jumping out of the car grabbed the man by the shoulder and spun him around. 'What do you think you are doing?' Katherine said. 'Stop or I'll have the police on you.' When your mother spoke," Kathryn Ottarson continued, "people listened. The man took one look at your mother and immediately backed away from the horse. 'Now,' Katherine ordered, 'get down and help that horse up.' 'Yes, ma'am,' the man said and bent over to help the horse. 'I'll be watching you from now on,' Katherine said staring at the man. 'If you mistreat that horse, I'll know, and you'll be in trouble. Do you understand?' 'Yes, ma'am,' the man answered. 'I'm sorry.' 'You better be,' your mother said." Mother was impressive looking. She had dark brown hair, a nose straight as an aqueduct, high cheekbones, and icy-blue eyes. She was five feet ten inches tall. Her waist was narrow, and her back and shoulders were broad and athletic.

Mother's childhood burned when fire destroyed Big Ga's house. Between her birth certificate and her high school annual in 1930, the papers of her life are blank. I know a story or two, but I have no records, letters, or pictures. In 1930 when she was eighteen, she graduated from a girls' school, St. Catherine's School in Richmond. She was one of thirty-three graduates and had attended St. Catherine's for three years. She lived in Dumbarton in a house Big Ga owned near the greenhouses. The house was large, two-storied, and white and brown with plaster and dark wood bracketing the windows like mascara. The original house seems to have been a country farmhouse with a low roof along the lower story sliding out over a porch. Built onto the right front and side of the house were two wings. Behind the house was a horse barn. Mother loved to ride and had an assortment of horses, among others, Nellie, Dick, Sam (who would go to sleep standing up and would often fall over on his side), Arab, Trixie, and Dodie, a pony. She and Buster also had dogs, generally English setters, some named after characters in Kipling, for example, Kim and Danny, this last named for Danny Deever although Mother also called him Danny Boy after the Irish song.

Although Mother was a superb rider, she did not join the riding club at St. Catherine's. In fact she did not join a single organization, hold an elective office, or play a sport. No activity was listed under her name in the yearbook, and no picture aside from that of her as a senior appeared in the *Quair*, the school annual. She was different from me. To my present embarrassment, I studiously piled lines of activities up under my name in the high school yearbook, nine lines in all. I also decided to get my picture in the annual more than anyone else in the school. Although I could not sing a note, I joined the glee club for sake of another picture. I succeeded beating my close friend Lionel by one picture. Under Mother's name appeared a quotation from Fernan Caballero, "If common sense has not the brilliancy of the sun, it has the fixity of the stars." I grew into common sense later than Mother as the quotation under my name was "I came, I saw, I conquered."

The photographer forbade smiles, and Mother stared whimsically at the camera. Her hair was plastered in curls down her right brow, and she looked formidable but fun. The sketch under her picture reads,

On an average of four days a week, a little Ford chugs up to school, and Katherine alights in the matter of fact way that she does everything. We have come to rely a great deal on her common sense and level head, too much perhaps for her own peace. But just try to tell Katherine to do something she doesn't want to, and see how far you get! We have learned by experience just what having 'a will of her own' means and we've almost given up trying to intrude on her independence. No one makes a better friend than Katherine, and no one can be funnier. Her dry humor keeps us chuckling continually, and we judge from repeated rumors that it has an irresistible appeal for certain M.D.s. Hush! Do we hear wedding bells in the distance?

The wedding bells were nine years off, though a classroom of beaus appears in Mother's scrapbooks, not so many as horses and dogs but still a goodly number. Sappy as I may sound, the first part of the sketch makes me proud. Humor and independence are not always the consort of a level head. Moreover today when students turn themselves in sandwich boards of achievements in order to get into college, not participating in a single organized activity but instead going one's own way seems remarkably appealing, just the independence colleges should celebrate but never do, in great part because colleges have also turned themselves into sandwich boards. Of course the danger with common sense is that at first it is soothing and makes a person remarkably comfortable in the world. Later, though, common sense makes a person uncomfortable and distances him from the world as he begins to see the absurdity of things, words, and deeds—something that has happened to me but never happened to Mother, maybe because she never lost the capacity to love.

Mother did not attend college. She applied to a couple and was admitted, Byrn Mawr perhaps being one. Admission in 1930 consisted mostly of simply writing one's name and being able to pay fees and tuition. "I didn't like studying," Mother told me, "and going to college would have wasted everybody's time, mine and that of the college." Closer to the truth was a later statement. Big Ga suffered in the stock market crash. "Money was scarce," Mother said, "and I didn't want to burden Daddy more. He had enough worries." Mother did not linger around the house like the last corsage of high school, however. Sometime in the 1930s, she spent two months in the west riding and shooting, much of it at Castle Hot Springs in Arizona. In jeans and chaps with her hair tied up around her ears in muffs, she looked tough and fit, at home in the barren landscape of low bush and rocky dusty hills. In one picture she sat on Blondie backwards; in another Curly a cowboy had his arm around her. Before marriage her life was full, among other things, shooting quail and sora, coon hunting, one of the hunts organized by Big Ga at, as the *Times-Dispatch* phrased it, Cabin Hill "the John Ratcliffes' Country Place," and attending the Morris and Essex dog show with Ada McCrae and showing dalmatians. In a picture taken before she left for Fancy Dress at Washington and Lee College she sat on the ground in front of the house at Dumbarton, her skirt spread like a pool wide about her, her bonnet round and framing her face, turning her head into a daisy. In another picture she stood with a beau on a beach in Darien, Connecticut, she told me, being a place in which fox hunting was not fun because the participants were too formal. On the steps at Carters Grove she leaned back smiling in the sunlight. She shot skeet at Bayside on Long Island and picnicked with friends on the way to the Maryland Cup, sitting on a plaid blanket, big leather hampers and silver flasks piled like booty around her. In another picture was Billy's Rolls, boxy and white-walled with headlamps bigger than the eyes of dragonflies. In a box I found an address book kept by Mother before marriage. In the book were addresses of both people and stores. At DiPinna, Miss Cahill waited on Mother while Madame Pettijean waited on her at Bergdorf-Goodman, Mr. Sidney at Robinson Shoe-Shop, and Miss Rain at Jane Engle.

When I was young, Mother tried to teach me to shoot accurately, but I was too uncoordinated to learn. She enrolled me in a horseback riding class, but I was frightened, and the horses controlled me, not I the horses. Learning the crawl stroke took me years. Her scrapbooks awakened a soupcon of envy, in part because I could not do the things she did and also because the glitter of what I imagined her life to have been seduced me into longing. For a time I dreamed of riding in a Rolls. Incidentally I never have puttered about in a Rolls, something that appeals to me now about as much as an attack of piles, the veins thicker and more clamorous than a nest of tent caterpillars. Mother was remarkably level-headed, more so than the man I became. Once she married Father, she rarely talked about the high doings of her spinster days. Sometimes, though, she became impatient when visitors from the head office of the Travelers in Hartford came to Nashville and ate dinner at the house. To her, I suspect, the men appeared dull and hidebound. Once when I sat beside her on the couch across the room from a long-winded bore to whom Father was listening, if not intently, she drew an arrow on the slipcover. The arrow pointed at the man; beneath it she wrote "turd." Other times when visitors swelled pompous, she deflated the evening by volunteering that she had an appointment the next day to see the "tooth-dentist." On another occasion she was "imprisoned" on one end of a couch in the living room listening an older woman at the other end who, as she put it, could "bore the ass, and trunk, off an elephant." "I thought only Death could free me," she said, "but then an expression of disgust appeared on the woman's face." For a moment Mother was puzzled, but then a horrific odor swept down the couch and over her. "Heinzie [our dog] had farted beneath the couch." When I asked Mother if she explained the source of the smell to the woman, she said, "Of course not. The fart was a blessing, just the thing to drive a prissy person out of the house."

Despite Mother's playfulness, she was very practical. As a young woman, she attended the horse races at Hialeah and always made money on her bets, getting tips from grooms and touts whose language she could speak. In Nashville, she, not Father, played the stock market getting tips from friends. Because shares of Martha White Self-Rising Flour rose, I was able to attend Cambridge University.

Only when I found a cache of pictures of Father when he was young did I realize why she married him. He was six feet two inches tall and weighed 130 pounds, but he was handsome. He held himself well, and his eyes glittered and burned. When the Travelers transferred him to the company's Richmond office, one of Mother's friends arranged a date with him for her, saying, "Katherine, he's god's gift to woman." "God's gift," Mother snorted, "I thought him the goddamnedest little pissant I'd ever met." Many beaus appeared in Mother's pictures. Ernest had been her best beau for a time. His expression was bland and had none of the bright seductive power of Father's expression in the 1930s. Ernest looked certain to be disappointed in love, and I traced his courtship up to the telegram he sent on the eve of Mother's wedding, apologizing for not attending. "TERRIBLY DIS-APPOINTED," it read; "BUSINESS ENGAGEMENTS PRE-VENT BEING THERE STOP MY SINCEREST BEST WISHES ERNEST."

Mother and Father were married at 6:30 in the evening at Centenary Methodist Church in Richmond. Mother had three bridemaids, two of whom were classmates at St. Catherine's and whom in later years we visited during summers, Virginia Keen and Adelaide Rawls. Adelaide lived longer than Mother, and once when I telephoned her and in the conversation mentioned that Eliza, my child, was doing well in school, Adelaide responded, "Of course she is; she is Katherine's grand-daughter." Mother's wedding dress spilled down and around her like thick cream, the train long enough to reach to Hanover, or so it seemed. Her gown, the newspaper reported, was "ivory slipper satin," her veil Brussels lace held in place by orange blossoms. In her arms she carried a bouquet of white orchids. When she carried the bouquet at her waist, it rose in a bank of white above her breasts and trailed below her knees falling like white water. In tails and a top hat, Father looked gleeful like a tall boy. Big Ga decorated the church. Ferns and palms spilled out of pots. Calla lilies rose like tapers, and candelabras burned with candles, seventy-six so far as I could count. The reception was held at Cabin Hill. Most men wore white ties, and the bars sagged under the weight of cases of whiskey. Mother and Father received 435 wedding presents.

They spent their first night together in the Jefferson Hotel in Richmond. The next morning they started for Nashville in Father's Ford coupe. On the outskirts of Richmond, they stopped for gas, and Mother bought a paper in order to look at the wedding pictures. She spread the paper across the front seat of the car and was looking at the pictures with Father when the man who was cleaning the windshield spoke up, saying, "It's a pity about that wedding. I feel so sorry for the girl." "What do you mean?" Father asked, jumping in before Mother could respond. "Well," the man said, "she didn't marry the man she wanted to. She was in love with a poor insurance man, but her father made her marry a rich fellow." "Who told you that?" Father asked. "Oh," the man said, "a colored preacher who comes through here told me all about it. He preaches up in Hanover, and some of the members of his congregation work on her father's farm." "Hmmm," Father said, "I hate to ruin your story, but look at the picture of the groom and then look at me." This," he said gesturing toward Mother after the man had had a good look, "is that unfortunate girl, and I am the poor insurance man. The preacher was wrong; sometimes in life poor folks carry off the prizes."

Words are frail and inexact. Only rarely can a person dissect a moment. Certainly words are not adequate to describe a marriage or the workings of family. From my point of view, Mother and Father ambled happily through the years, almost never bruising each other. When Mother became exasperated at Father, she often said, "If you don't behave, I'm going to chop your you-know-what off." At least once a month, usually after a drink or two and late at night, Father went into the pantry and for fun began shifting pots and pans about. The clatter brought Mother running. Before she spoke, Father always said, laughter bubbling beneath his words, "Katherine, I am doing you a favor and trying to establish order in these cabinets." Such small things are the big bricks of a good marriage. In this chapter, I have written comparatively little about Mother; yet, her presence, not that of Father, colored my days. She drove me to and from school, took me to the doctor and to visit friends. She stitched the threads of my days so sensibly and lovingly that heartache and disappointment never caused me to unravel.

She also entertained me. At the beginning of my freshman or sophomore year in high school, I owned a James Dean jacket, red on the outside and white and as full as cotton candy on the inside. One Friday night I accompanied friends to the Richland Country Club. I was dressed poorly in the jacket and blue jeans. The next morning I left the house early. Greeting me on my return was a smoldering fire in the middle of the driveway. In my absence Mother had learned about my appearance at the club and had burned my jacket and jeans. "Oh, Lord," I thought as I looked at the pile in the drive. Later when Mother lectured me on manners and appropriate dress, all I could think was, relying on one of her expressions, "If this doesn't take all dog. What an astonishing experience, one for the scrapbook." When I describe the "conflagration" to people, they look concerned and usually ask, "How did that affect you?" The fire did not affect me except to make me realize, yet again, that I had the most wonderful, wonderful mother.

End of the Summers

After Big Ga's death, Ga sold Etna Mills and Cabin Hill's cattle and farmland, keeping only the house and twenty-five acres. A hundred yards behind and below the big house was a small frame caretaker's cottage, consisting of a living room, kitchen, a bath, two bedrooms, a back porch, and a covered front stoop. Because Cabin Hill was relatively isolated and Ga disliked living alone, she let the Johnsons move into the cottage. Mr. Johnson was a gifted carpenter, and the Johnsons lived rent free in exchange for Mr. Johnson's doing small chores on weekends, the presence of the family also providing security. The Johnson family eventually consisted of five boys, two of whom became my playmates, Johnny, my age, and Hank, a year younger.

For a moment life was idyllic. We roamed wood and field like a small gang of characters from a Booth Tarkington novel. Along a back road leading to the red barn, Mr. Johnson helped us build a hut, papering an A-frame made from two-by-fours with tar paper. Next to the main room, we built two small teepee-like rooms, each with separate entrances. We connected the rooms together with bamboo speaking tubes, although the rooms were so close together a person could hear others whispering no matter which room they were in. Around the hut we dug traps for wild women. We filled the traps with thorns and disguised them by spreading meshes of twigs over the top. We climbed trees, each of us having a special tree, mine a mimosa near the kitchen. We played games, Steal the Pig in the afternoon and at night, every night it seemed, No Bears. The game was simple, but it was the best game I have ever played. One of us was the Bear, and he hid not far from the Johnsons' house, usually in a lane of fat yellow cedars that Big Ga had planted years before. The Johnsons' front stoop was the base; over it hung a weak light bulb. Once the bear vanished into the dark, the rest of us—sometimes the third Johnson, Jeff, joined us—strode off the porch in different directions chanting, "No bears are out tonight; no bears are out tonight." When one of us approached too near the bear, he broke cover, screaming and yelling, always terrifying us, and either tagged one of us or chased us back to the safety of the porch. We played Steal the Pig in front of the cinder-block housing covering the pump for the well. The pig was a short stick, and the object of the game was to grab the pig from under the watchful eye of the farmer who guarded it and to run back across a safe line. If one made it back across the line without being tagged, he received a point. While the farmer hovered over the pig, the rest of us darted back and forth, trying to grab it. Usually one of us approached too close and the farmer tagged him. When the farmer tagged him, someone else grabbed the pig. The game rewarded caution and led to arguments, the discussion running like this, "Why don't you try to get the pig some time and distract the farmer. All you do is hang back while I take all the risks. It isn't fair for you to get all the points."

Snaggletoothed, shoeless, in shorts or ratty jeans and t-shirts with broad stripes running horizontal across the front, we were motley and happy, only our imaginations limiting days. Since the outside was so various, imagination thrived. We caught dragonflies and June bugs, the emerald color of these last shining in memory as the brightest green I have ever seen. Some afternoons we played Monopoly on the screened porch. Except when Sherry played and the game went on so long that we stopped and called it a tie, I always won, something that became a burden. In fact, before I was out of my teens, I stopped playing games with friends except games so dependant upon chance that winning was arbitrary. Of course I played Hearts and Dirty Eights with my children, invariably trying to rig the results so they won. But as a boy I always won, and that somehow made playing too intense. I played Canasta with

Grandmother Pickering and never lost. Father never beat me in Scrabble. While he spread long words across the board, I poked about finding cracks I could plug with one or two letters and for which I'd receive double or triple points, say, placing an *X* on a triple letter score forming *ax* and *ox*, thus making the triple letter count twice. I have always shunned competition and stopped playing tennis and golf because of my dislike of competing. On the other hand, people are not always as they see themselves. My friend Roger in the English Department once told me that I was the most competitive person he had ever met. "In what?" I asked. Roger just shook his head and said nothing.

Off the board, winning did not matter in the summer, and four contests dominated our days, the frog (including toads), lizard, turtle, and locust contests. The contests ran the whole summer, and we kept running totals of the creatures caught. I was record keeper, listing everything as I did later when I collected baseball cards. During a single summer the most contests ever won by a single person was three, Johnny and I both winning three. For the summer of 1950 or 1951, the record reads: "The most locusts Caught—J[Johnny]-46. Most Lizards Caught—S[Sammy]-4. The Most Turtles Caught—S-16. The Most Frogs Caught—H[Hank] & J-36." Among the other records, I caught the most locusts in one day, fifteen, these in the shell at Uncle Harold's. Hank caught the most frogs in one day, eight, while I caught nine turtles in a day. The most important contest was the locust or cicada contest, probably because there were so many of them and catching them on a limb was difficult. Through the summer, the cry "gotta live locust" echoed over Cabin Hill. Echoes incidentally disappeared at the end of childhood. Cabin Hill was quiet, and our voices enjoyed a momentary immortality, bouncing back at us across fields and through gullies. In a city the cacophony of living muffles and smothers words so that they quickly lose body and life and sink into nothingness, much like the person who spoke them. In any case sometimes a locust escaped before another of us could verify the catch, but that was all right, we always gave the boy credit for the catch, or at least I made that a rule after Hank disputed one of Johnny's catches. Johnny was fast, and he always won the locust contest, catching usually between forty and fifty locusts. Hank roamed streams and ponds, and he won the frog contest. I won the turtle and lizard contests. I had a knack for finding turtles, and the turtles I snatched off the road to Ashland counted. Fence lizards were quick, and Johnny should have won that contest. I had more patience, however, and after a lizard flicked out of sight I was more willing than Johnny to sit and wait for it to reappear. Because the locust contest was our derby, my records detailed several results, bent, it now appears toward my penchant for catching them before they hatched: the biggest locust caught in the shell and out, the "littlest" locust in the shell, the most live shells found in a day, and the biggest and smallest empty shells.

For country boys we were remarkably gentle and tried not to harm the creatures we caught, though most lizards cast their tails in trying to escape, something that intrigued us and made us envious. We speculated about what sort of arms would grow in the place of ones we tossed, if we were able to toss our arms. Catching the same creature twice was against the rules. Because turtles had distinctive markings and lizards clearly defined home ranges, enforcing the rule was easy in those two contests. As far as locusts were concerned, the rule didn't matter. Once a locust flew out of sight, it was free little game. Frogs and toads gave us more trouble because we also returned them to the place we caught them and they, especially the frogs, were hard to differentiate.

In 1954, Ga sold Cabin Hill. Childhood had passed. But, of course, childhood doesn't disappear. What vanish are memories and the keys to memory, items that spring the tumblers of association. Hanging on the wall in the downstairs bathroom of my house is a print of three cicadas, one view of the insect in the shell, the other two views showing the insect as seen from below and above. Published in London on July 12, 1792, by "F.P. Nodder of No. 15 Gower Street," the print is yellow and brown. Still, its lines are delicately drawn, and the insect seems almost lifted from rose medallion china. Three or four times a year, I remove the print from the wall and take it into the living room and examine it closely. My heart always jumps. What I see are not the filigree of line but rough-hewn memories of scratched and scabbed boys, dusty with dirt, playing in a place that today only exists in recollection.

My parents gave me a BB gun one Christmas. I took it to Cabin Hill, but I only shot one bird, a warbler. The warbler did not die immediately, and I felt terrible afterwards. I lined a shoebox with grass and lay the warbler inside on its side. By its head I put a soda bottle top filled with water. I caught beetles and dug earthworms and put them in the box. The warbler didn't eat them and the next morning it died. I freed the worms and beetles and buried the warbler in the box near my mimosa tree. Birds were safe around me until Ga sold Cabin Hill and married Bob Gwathmey. One day during my first visit to Bob's house, I shot four robins with a .22 rifle, probably because I was bored. I gave them to Peggy the cook, and she cleaned and cooked them for me after which I ate them. They were the last robins I shot. The next day a hawk perched on a fence bordering Bob's property. On my pointing out the hawk, Bob left the room to fetch his shotgun, even though he did not have chickens. While Bob was out of the room, I shooed the hawk away, not telling Bob of course. Later in life when I talked about going dove hunting with friends, Sam who worked for us said, "Mr. Sammy, don't you shot those doves. They are bible birds." I went hunting, but I was a terrible shot and missed every bird I aimed at. Mother taught several men in Nashville how to shoot, practicing on skeet. She had no luck with Father. He, like me, couldn't master the hand and eye coordination. Maybe he simply did not want to learn to shoot then be asked to go hunting and be almost compelled to shoot birds.

Odd matters cling to mind. One afternoon at Cabin Hill, Johnny discovered a snake curled in the shade under a cattle trough at the edge of a pasture. Johnny said the snake was a copperhead, a creature I didn't fear but which adults repeatedly warned us about.

Mealy would not go into the woodshed because she said copperheads lived there. One night Ga stepped on a snake in her bedroom when she went into the room to undress for bed. The terrified snake twisted around her ankle then wriggled off and coiled under a chair. Ga was standing on her bed when Mother rushed in. The snake was a black snake, brought upstairs, Mother decided, in basket of laundry that Mealy had folded then let sit outside while she did another chore. The basket was at the edge of a field; the day was bright and hot, and the snake crept between sheets seeking shade. The incident so frightened Ga that she had all snakes about the house killed, even those living in the basement that I liked to watch wind through the bricks like oily rope. The black snakes had kept copperheads away, and the next summer a copperhead appeared at the foot of the staircase in the front hall. No more black snakes were killed. Black snakes figured in the lore of Cabin Hill. Big Ga had an inside toilet built in the cottage because an earlier inhabitant refused to use the outhouse. She had just settled in comfortably, the words used by Mother being more explicit, when she glanced up. Slung across the rafters above her like a swollen hose was a huge black snake. The woman decamped rapidly, and Big Ga installed a flush toilet.

After Johnny assured Hank and me that the snake was a copperhead, we grabbed sticks and poked it. When the snake tried to wedge itself deeper under the trough, the poking became vicious. Eventually we killed the snake, discovering that it wasn't a copperhead but a hog-nosed snake. For years I have regretted the killing, and even now when I come across a snake in the woods that some thoughtless person has killed I wince, the truth in some strange way now being that the company of snakes appeals to me more than that of people. For me spring does not begin until snakes burst blossoming from their dens and sprawl nearby, mating, twisted together like blossoms around the stalks of ladies' tresses.

Our game No Bears was not our only source of excitement. One afternoon Johnny and I were sitting on a red bank overlooking the dirt road that curved downhill to the dairy barn. Johnny was holding my BB gun. Suddenly a small man came careening down the hill on a bicycle. On the handlebars of the bicycle was a long silver horn with a bulbous rubber ball at the end. When Johnny saw the horn, he yelled at the man, "Boot your horn." When the man heard Johnny, he spun his pedals backward, applying the brakes so quickly he slid into a big C. On stopping, he asked Johnny what he yelled. Johnny repeated the request, but instead of doing the normal thing and squeezing the end of the horn, the man stared at us and said, "You better not shoot my tires with your gun." "We are not going to shoot your tires," I said. "We just want to hear your horn." "You better not shoot my tires," the man said, adding, "I'm warning you. You better not shoot my tires." For a moment, the man was silent then he repeated himself, "Don't you shoot my tires. You'll be sorry if you do." Not only did the repetition irritate Johnny but it also tempted him, and he raised his gun and shot the man's front tire, the BB bouncing harmlessly off the rubber. Immediately the man dropped his bike and charged us. We ran as fast as we could, Johnny leaving me behind even though he was carrying the gun. Like a woodcock I circled and fell flat behind a log while the man chased Johnny. We both got away, and that, we thought, was the end. The next night the man broke into the dairy and used its phone to called our number at Cabin Hill. He said that some night he was going to come to Cabin Hill and cut my throat. Mother called the sheriff. The man had been released from the lunatic asylum a week earlier. Until the man was run to ground, Mother made me stay in the house at night. For two days the man eluded the sheriff and a posse of searchers. On the third day he was caught and bundled back into the asylum.

BB guns led to trouble, but trouble for growing boys is a natural part of idyllic days. On July 25, 1952, I wrote Father describing doings at Cabin Hill:

> Yesterday, we cut down a bamboo 33 1/2 feet high. The
> day before that we [Johnny, Hank, and I] built a hut in the

bamboo. We had our B.B. guns with us. Johnny saw a bike next to a tree. Hank shot up in the air and Mackie Norris and Alfred brother of the boy who chased us last summer came running out of the woods. Alfred chased us with rocks. He thought Hank shot at him. We came back and Johnny got into an argument with Mackie. Johnny got mad and shot a B.B. that hit the ground and bounced up and hit him in the leg [Mackie, I presume]. Well, he finally rode away, but Mackie said he was going to get his 15teen year old brother George and Mason Houston and bring shotguns. Johnny saw Mason and George from the hut. He also said something and Hank took out. Mason said, 'It's Johnny Johnson.' Johnny and I got behind the fort and they threw stones at us this big [here I drew a stone two inches in diameter]. One hit Johnny in the head and one hit me in the foot. The only thing that saved us was the fort. It held the stones back. They left when a truck came by. We hollered at them and they came back. We shot at them. I said Mason was coming behind us but nobody listened. Well here came Mason as I said we were trapped. James said, Look Mason and he went the other way. Mason chased him and we took out. One rock missed me by 1/10 of an inch. At dinner Hank said the boys were tearing the *hut down*! Well we built a better one. HERE IT IS.

Here I drew a hut that was round on the top like a mail box. Attached to the walls of the hut and protecting the front door was a barbwire fence.

Beyond Cabin Hill life was not idyllic. The new owners of the farm hired transient workers, mostly white. After they vacated the houses in which they lived, I explored the rooms, always finding three things: wire coat hangers, shoes, the heels of which had broken down and were splayed out like spoons, and on the wall calendars with Jesus stamped on them. For a while the house not far from the red barn was unoccupied. In the early years at Cabin Hill, I walked past the house on the way to Frogtown where many of Big Ga's colored workers and Ga's servants lived. After the Pearlys moved in, I stopped walking the road. Mr. Pearly had a large family and a large pack of beagles. He took better care of his dogs than his daughters. Perhaps the family was so poor that they could not afford both clothes and beagles. Anyway I often saw the Pearly girls walking about without shirts, their breasts more than buds. During the last summer in Hanover, Johnny told me the Pearlys wanted me to play with them inside the red barn. I walked to the end of the lane beside which our hut sat and looked across the road at the barn. One of the girls stood outside and waved. I waved in response then turned and walked away.

For a time Mr. Johnson was a hero to me. He had a rich imagination. One evening while we were resting after playing Steal the Pig, he pointed toward some bull bats, as he called swallows, darting about high above us. Then he told us he had spent a lot of time in the air, making over a thousand jumps out of airplanes as a paratrooper. Later I learned he'd played professional baseball. Drink aided Mr. Johnson's imagination, not something I ever realized while listening to his accounts of the high seas or low foreign lands. Like carpenter ants gnawing through a beam, drink destroys, as Grandmother Pickering might have put it, at first silently but eventually loudly as the public person collapses revealing private rot.

Initially the stories I heard Ga and Mother tell about the Johnsons were colorful and funny. The Johnsons planted big vegetable garden in a field just beyond the lane of cedars. Mrs. Johnson was a fine gardener, and during the summer the garden overflowed with watermelons, corn, squash, cucumbers, tomatoes, snaps, radishes, and onions. More than anything else Mrs. Johnson loved butterbeans, and down through the middle of the garden ran four rows in a long, thin hedge. Sadly Mrs. Johnson also drank, and late at night after drinking too much, she wandered into the garden in her nightgown and squatting amid the butterbean poles sang old gospel songs, tunes like "Bringing in the Sheaves," "Just as I Am," and "Pass Me Not Oh Gentle Savior." After his wife had been in the butterbeans for a while, Mr. Johnson appeared. He did not go into the garden. Instead he stopped at the edge, and picking up lumps of dirt, lobbed them high in the air above his wife and the beans. Occasionally a clump fell nearby, and Mrs. Johnson squealed and darted to a new spot. The singing and squatting ended not long before Ga left Cabin Hill. Beyond the garden the field sloped downhill into a gully. Across the gully grew two willow trees. Sometime earlier, drink inspired Mr. Johnson to cut the trees down. Limbs on the trees had dried, and this time instead of stopping at the edge of the garden and tossing clumps, Mr. Johnson carried a can of gasoline into the gully and sloshed it over the trees. He then ignited the gas, and fire skipped through the willows kicking up thousands of sparks, which because the wind was right, blew up the hill and fell in an orange rain on the garden. For a moment Mrs. Johnson was silent then she screamed and ran out of the beans toward the house, never to return again.

In a story-shaping family, truths are suspect, especially details resuscitated from memory. What is true is that the willows were chopped down and burned and the singing stopped. For me the tunes Cabin Hill played for and upon me were also ending. I suspect it was for my sake that Ga did not ask the Johnsons to leave once they began to drink heavily. I thrived at Cabin Hill. When my parents asked me if I wanted to attend summer camp like many of my Nashville friends, I refused. I explained that I did not want to attend camp because my friends had attended for years and could already swim well and knew how to paddle canoes and shoot bows and arrows. Because I was a poor athlete, I said I could never catch up. As a result I would not fit in and would be assigned to activities with younger boys. I told a truth but not all the truth. Cabin Hill had me by muscle and heart. Of course the Johnson boys and I would have gradually drifted apart as the children of the comparatively poor and comparatively well-off do in middle school in communities today. Through elementary school children play together, but in middle school the aspirations of parents diverge. The well-off know what they want for their children and, knowing how to get it, push their children. Other parents want good things for their children, but they are not sure how to get those things and are not sure they can afford them even if they know what the things are. Some children attend soccer or math camps; others do not. Suddenly everyone on the soccer team and in classes for the gifted is the child of a professional.

One night after drinking, Mr. Johnson beat his wife. After his father smashed his wife's head through the wallboard, Johnny took a stick from the woodpile and knocked his father unconscious, after which he and his mother and the other children fled to us and asked to stay the night. When Mr. Johnson woke up, he telephoned his friend Woody Jefferson. He came over and, after drinking some more, they loaded shotguns and starting hunting Johnny. For most of the night they stumbled through pastures and crashed through the boxwood in front of the house, shooting and yelling things like, "There goes the little son of a bitch!" Mother dissuaded Ga from calling the police because she said if the police came someone would probably be shot. Early in the morning the two men collapsed on the lawn then Mother telephoned the police. The police took away the shotguns and locked Mr. Johnson and his friend up for two or so days.

Later the events of the evening became part of family myth losing their sharp edges in the process. What suppurates in recollection is a Christmas, the events of which may have contributed to Ga's succumbing to Bob Gwathmey's importuning her to sell Cabin Hill and move into his house. After dinner I walked to the Johnsons' carrying a box of presents for the children. Johnny let me in. Stretched out on the couch in the living room was Mr. Johnson, an empty bottle of bourbon on the floor beside him, his pants down to his knees and his privates hanging to the side. Mrs. Johnson was standing on the bed in the room to the right. She was naked and shouting, "I want to fuck." Only in memory does the evening sear. At the time I was too young, too comfortable and innocent, too sheltered to be disturbed. After spending summer after summer on the farm, I did not know the facts of life. When a classmate explained sexual matters to me in the sixth grade, I did not believe him. When Judy "borrowed" one of her father's medical books and after sneaking it into school showed classmates and me drawings depicting a woman's private parts, I couldn't decipher the drawings. Colored pictures would have been more informative, but closest thing to pornography I saw growing up was an issue of *Sunshine and Health*, the magazine of a nudist society, its pictures featuring views of the backsides of fat middle-aged people.

Among the presents I received at Christmas in the sixth grade was a book entitled *for BOYS only*. In the book a Dr. Richardson lectured schoolboys on proper behavior with girls. "There are lots of ways of having good times with girls. Let's not choose the wrong ones," the doctor urged, cryptically from my young point of view. In the sixth grade following the doctor's advice was easy because my knowledge and inclinations were just as vague. No, what really disturbed me was late Christmas morning when Johnny appeared at the kitchen door. In his arms he carried toys his parents had bought for him and Hank. They were Christmas presents for me, he said. I didn't want to take them, for I realized that they had been sent out of pride, to balance the trinkets I had given them the night before and maybe to atone for the sights I saw. Pride has never mattered to me, its insignificance a reflection of the comfortable life I have lived. I had so much—a wonderful family and a happy untroubled life—that Pride was something I could afford to do without.

In any case the deteriorating behavior of the Johnsons probably contributed to Ga's decision to sell Cabin Hill. Not long before she sold, she wrote me:

> Ga has certainly missed you. The Johnson gang have been very quiet until today when they started playing in the hut. Johnny went to the store about dark last night and was waylaid by the Kits boys who asked him for $5.00. He told him that he didn't have any money so they kept Johnny and his bicycle on

the side of the road for more than an hour. Mrs. Johnson went after him and when they saw her coming they departed. Johnny was one scared boy. Johnny and Hank feel so bad about their Father's having been in jail. Several thoughtless people have asked them about it. Mr. Johnson goes to court Friday and I will write you what happens.

In the last letter Johnny wrote me, he said he had been to see a Roy Rogers movie. Years earlier Mother took Johnny and Hank to Ashland for their first movie. They were so frightened at first they buried their heads in their hands. Once we saw *Mighty Joe Young* together, but I suspect that first movie was a Western, a Gene Autry or a Hopalong Cassidy film. "I sure had a surprise this A. M. when I carried the mail in and saw your mother," Johnny wrote. "Wish you could have come with her." Mother had probably gone to Cabin Hill to help Ga pack. Johnny concluded his letter writing, "I will send you our new address soon as we move." In September, Ga sent me a birthday card. She had moved. "There are several boys your age who live close to me so you can have company when you come next summer," she wrote. "I think you are going to like Ga's new home." Cabin Hill had vanished. Ga was gilding the summer. I made no new friends. In the future I visited Virginia to see relatives in Richmond, accompanying Mother more because of duty than desire. The next summer Ga rented a cottage at Wrightsville Beach, North Carolina, for two weeks. During my high school years we went to Wrightsville. Some summers Sherry came to Wrightsville, as did Aunt Lucille, and they remained part of my life. But country Virginia was gone. New things beckoned, and for a time I probably didn't miss Cabin Hill.

Reading, Pets, and Toys

At Cabin Hill I spent as much time reading as I did roaming. In the attic I found a trunk filled with Uncle Buster's books, all written by Edgar Rice Burroughs. With John Carter of Virginia and Mars, I won the hand of Dejah Thoris. I bored into Pellucidar with Davie Innes and Abner Perry and fought the Mahars and Sagoths. On stormy afternoons, Tarzan was my good and great companion. He introduced me to Kala, his "Mother," and with him I was Untamed and Terrible. I saw the Jewels of Opar and met the Ant Men. I visited the Earth's Core and the City of Gold.

Books furnished daydreams, adding zest to my meanderings and for years making me imagine roaming West Africa. The spring of my last year at Cambridge I applied to the British Council and got a post teaching in Sierra Leone. When I told Mother and Father, they practically collapsed. Mother called me twelve days in a row from Tennessee, not something easily done in 1965. She begged me not to go to Sierra Leone and said my going would kill Father. If I'd had a gaggle of brothers and sisters, I might have persisted and gone to Africa. But I was an only child, and my parents were fine people whose only fault, from my point of view, was loving me too much for my own peace of mind, making me feel guilty when I conjured up visions of reckless and careless independence. Consequently I quietly jettisoned my plan of going to Africa, returned to Nashville, lived at home, and taught at MBA, a country day school, for a year. Old reading dies hard, though, and during my first year teaching at Dartmouth I wrote a biography of Tarzan, treating him as a real man. I packed Jane his wife off to Sweetbriar College and appropriated her description from another of my literary loves, Anthony Trollope. Later Jane became active in the Junior League, this during Tarzan's treks to forbidden cities. I enjoyed teaching, but I hoped the book would free me to spend days wandering places far from the Connecticut River. On finishing the manuscript I sent it to a press in Boston. An editor telephoned a week later and said the press was going to publish the book. Two weeks later, we learned that a biography of Tarzan by Philip José Farmer, the science fiction writer, was going to be published within the next six weeks. I made no more trips to West Africa, imaginary or real. I stuffed the manuscript into two manila envelopes and stored it in the attic where it still gathers dust. Of course, I have no idea where exactly in the attic the manuscript is. Youthful imaginings die easily. Life moves on, and the Moving Finger writes other things.

Sometimes I think I was born reading. Certainly I was my father's son. The stint at Kentucky Military Academy straightened Father's posture, but it did not slow his reading. Books furnished his life. Every night he read. He carried books to work and kept a book in the top drawer of his desk. When work was slow, as it often was, he opened the drawer halfway and read, to people passing by his office appearing thoughtful and concentrating so hard that they hesitated to interrupt him. At home, books perched on tables and lurked under beds and chairs. Much as she had given up setters, horses, and the horsy, hunting set, Mother adapted to Father's ways and became a great reader herself.

On the other hand, being an only child contributed to my reading. Books populated empty hours and colored slow days. Reading is a form of action, and at times I preferred playing inside with a book than outside with friends. Moreover I was sickly. "When I was sick and lay a-bed, / I had two pillows at my head, / And all my toys beside me lay / To keep me happy all the day," Robert Louis Stevenson wrote in "The Land of Counterpane." Jessie Willcox Smith's illustration for the poem in *A Child's Garden of Verses* has stuck to mind since childhood. A curly-headed little boy sits propped atop pillows in bed, his knees pulled up to form a table under his chest, his hands resting listlessly on top. On his immediate right a picture book lies open. Next to the book a camel stands peering up at the boy. Below the camel are a red ball and a small village, several of its trees toppled by wrinkles in the sheet. Toy soldiers wearing blue jackets trickle away from the village in a stream, forming a troop shaped like a puddle on the smooth area of sheet beyond the boy's feet. On the boy's left another group of soldiers drizzles toward the bottom of the bed, these wearing red jackets.

If Smith had painted a picture of me in bed, she would have raised the sheets into a tent and put a vaporizer inside. On the table beside my bed would be an empty bowl, one that once contained chocolate ice cream. In my house chocolate ice cream was a spirit raiser, if not a cure-all. In my hands would be a novel describing the adventures of the Hardy Boys and their buddy Chet Morton: *The Tower Treasure, The House on the Cliff, The Secret of the Old Mill,* or *The Shore Road Mystery.* The books cost a dollar and maybe eventually a dollar and a quarter. During eighth grade I sold my collection for fifty cents a book. Beside the empty bowl on my bedside table sat a small blue radio. On sick mornings I listened to the Arthur Godfrey show. During other times in the week I followed the doings of Amos & Andy, the Green Hornet, Sky King, the Shadow, and Sergeant Preston of the Yukon and his dog King. Once I bought a Sky King Magni-Glo Writing Ring, paying twenty cents and the liner from the top of a jar of Peter Pan Peanut Butter. Many of my favorite playthings were knick-knacks like the ring. I was especially fond of a small blue magnetic coffin, probably two and a quarter inches long. Inside the coffin lay a corpse. When the head of the coffin was thumped on a table, the corpse stayed in the coffin. Thumping the coffin on the bottom reversed the magnetic field, and no matter how I pushed the corpse would not stay "buried" and kept popping up. Among my favorite radio programs was the *Buster Brown Show,* advertising Buster Brown Shoes. A dog barked after which followed the jingle, "That's my dog Tige, he lives in a shoe! / I'm Buster Brown, look for me in there, too!" No creature made me laugh more than Froggy the Gremlin who greeted children in a high tinny gangster voice, saying "Hiya, kids, hiya, hiya." Froggy's magic twanger sounded like a veery suffering from the croup. Froggy's appearance always upset guest lecturers, these usually stuffy experts of one sort or another, and introduced glorious chaos into the dull order of school days. Froggy is no longer on the radio, but he does make guest appearances, usually appearing in the courses I teach about halfway through class, elevating high-falutin' subtle analysis into low common sense.

My parents did not purchase a television until I was eleven, too old to be seduced from books. Over the years I have been faithful in my fashion and have watched little television. Although I have never owned a stereo, I had a record player when I was a boy, a blue box that played 78 RPM records. My favorite album consisted of cowboy songs sung by Tex Ritter, among others, "Billy, the Kid," "The Phantom White Stallion of Skull Valley," the name of this last appealing more than the song, "Down in the Valley," "Whoopie Ti Yi Yo," and "Red River Valley," which I used to sing to myself, maybe because my "bright eyes" dreamed of wandering.

When I was small and we still lived in the Sulgrave, Father read to me at night. My favorite stories, at least those that cling to memory better than others, described the adventures of Uncle Wiggily, the rabbit gentleman, and then later Uncle Remus's tales. Uncle Wiggily always ended on the right note, optimistic and leading into a tomorrow rich with another story. "And now if it doesn't rain snips and snails and puppy dogs' tails in the clothes basket, so the little mousie has no place to sleep," Howard Garis concluded "Uncle Wiggily and the Pancakes," "I'll tell you next about Uncle Wiggily in a snowstorm." At night I slept with Nurse Jane Fuzzy Wuzzy, Uncle Wiggily's muskrat housekeeper. Before Father sold our house on Iroquois Avenue and moved into a condominium, Mother hired two men and a truck. She sat in a chair at the top of the attic stairs and supervised cleaning the attic, sending the detritus of generations to the dump, letters, linen, bricks used as ballast in the eighteenth century, trunks of old clothes, and most of the books and toys of my childhood. "You will thank me someday," she said. And I have thanked her, except I wish she had not tossed away Nurse Jane. The last time I saw her, Nurse Jane really looked like a muskrat, shapeless and losing clumps of hair. Of course if I'd kept her, my children would someday toss her into the trash, probably puzzling for a moment over the waste can wondering what child hugged her at night.

After nights with Uncle Wiggily came nights with Uncle Remus. To me Uncle Remus seemed real—kindly and loving like the colored people I knew in the country. Joel Chandler Harris's stories made me smile and appreciate life. Brer Rabbit was a trickster, an appropriate hero for the weak, slaves and children, a trickster who used his brain to triumph over those in power. Only the narrow-minded demand stories that instruct. Good stories are too various to be boiled down to palatable moral lessons. Still, in part I enjoyed Uncle Remus's stories because they taught the necessity of lying in order to escape the platitudes of society and live a life almost one's own. Only after children learn to lie, or "create," can they have lives of their own. Towering over the child, the ogreish adult says, "I can forgive anything but a lie"—a statement that is itself a lie, and a whopper at that.

Several of the first books I read have remained favorites, or at least, they have not sifted out of memory. How pleasant would it be to sit under the cork tree with *Ferdinand the Bull* and sniff flowers while down in the hot lowlands, only the ambitious trot about the ring, snorting, kicking up dust, and enduring the slings and lances of outrageous picadors. How sappy yet marvelous the depiction of a dreamer's hatching or accomplishing the impossible by being "faithful one hundred per cent" in *Horton Hatches the Egg*. Each semester I begin my course in the short story by reading *The Little Engine That Could* to students. I tell them that they might be able to understand the story. Of course they don't realize that outside the nursery the little blue engine never made it over the mountain. Disease, bad luck, misbehavior, a broken wife, husband, or child caused the Little Engine's boiler to rupture and spill the dolls and toys off the mountain, no matter the power of positive chugging. Nevertheless, I read the story. Truths are various and contradictory. Both the young man's optimism and the old man's pessimism are true, and thinking "I can" is certainly better than withdrawing into the dark of "I cannot." Sometimes I read *Scuffy the Tugboat* to the class. Bored by life in a bathtub, Scuffy escapes his owners, a man wearing "a blue polka-dotted tie" and his son. Floating along creeks and small rivers beside farms and woodlands and past deer and cattle, Scuffy was happy at first. But then as the river grew larger and Scuffy saw cities and approached the wide sea, he became frightened and wished he were back home. In children's books, one can sometimes return home, and just as Scuffy was being swept out to sea, the man in the blue polka-dotted necktie reached out from a pier, plucked Scuffy out of the water, and took him back to a happy life in the bathtub. Perhaps writing a memoir is a sort of returning home, particularly a memoir sliced off at the end of the eighth grade before life threatens to be tempestuous.

Father often recited Kipling, especially "Mandalay," quoting from the refrain, "On the road to Mandalay, / Where the flyin'-fishes play, / An' the dawn comes up like thunder / Outer China 'crost the Bay!" The only book of poetry which I reread as a child was Stevenson's *A Child's Garden of Verses*. The poems that appealed to me were Romantic and like "Mandalay" celebrated the imaginary and the faraway. "I should like to rise and go / Where the golden apples grow," "Travel" began. "Where below another sky / Parrot islands anchored lie, / And, watched by cockatoos and goats, / Lonely Crusoes building boats;— / Where in sunshine reaching out / Eastern cities, miles about, / Are with mosque and minaret / Among sandy gardens set."

For a dreamer I was remarkably content. In *The Wind in the Willows*, Water Rat contemplated wandering beyond "the great ring of Downs," "his simple horizon hitherto." He imagined what lay beyond home and the hills. "What seas lay beyond, green, leaping and crested! What sun-bathed coasts, along which the white villas glittered against the olive woods! What quiet harbours, thronged with gallant shipping bound for purple islands of wine and spice, islands set low in languorous waters." He met the Sea Rat who urged him, "Take the adventure, heed the call, now ere the irrevocable moment passes! 'Tis but a banging of the door behind you, a blithesome step forward, and you are out of the old life and into the new! Then some day, some day long hence, jog home here if you will, when the cup has been drained and the play has been played, and sit down by your quiet river with a store of goodly memories for company." Mole then appeared and sitting beside Ratty talked about the marvels of daily life at home after which he gave Ratty a pencil and a few half sheets of paper and said, "It's quite a long time since you did any poetry." At universities dreamers take courses in creative writing. They scribble for two or three years, graduate, and then like Father take corporate jobs and become "responsible" husbands and wives and parents.

Reading about exotic lands creates both discontent and its antidote contentment. Imagining not simply what lay beyond the horizon but journeying to such places kept me busy and happy. I spent hours thumbing the maps in *Hammond's Complete World Atlas*. Before falling asleep at night or stretched out on a rug in the day, I traveled far and had wondrous adventures. Another of my favorite books was Richard Halliburton's *The Complete Book of Marvels*. In a letter to readers, Halliburton said his favorite subject in school was geography. In class he pretended he had a magic carpet and without worrying about the minutiae of tickets and money he flew to China or the Grand Canyon. He imagined having a child and carting him off to "wonderful places." "Well," he concluded, "I'm grown now. But as yet I haven't any son or any daughter to go traveling with me. And so, in their places, may I take you?" Unlike Water Rat, I heeded the call and away I went, again and again, to Timbuctoo and Victoria Falls then to my favorite part of the world the Mid-East, to Petra and Palmyra, from thence to Persia and Isfahan and Shiraz, saying the names of the places aloud, the sounds almost hypnotizing. I walked into the lily pool at the Taj Mahal. At Madura I startled a colony of parrots, and at Angkor a king cobra. I climbed the Great Pyramid and explored old Rhodes, tame stuff, though, for one who had fed on honey-dew in Baalbek and amid the ruins of Babylon had sipped "the milk of Paradise."

Romance furnished only a shelf or two of my childhood reading. I read walls of inspirational biographies about young Americans. Bound in orange, many were published by Bobbs-Merrill and pointed the way to success and perhaps immortality, teaching that nothing lay beyond the grasp of the plucky and the industrious. Through impenetrable forest and desolate plain I accompanied *Daniel Boone, Boy Hunter* and *Meriwether Lewis, Boy Explorer*. With *The Mill Boy of the Slashes*, Henry Clay, I went to Washington. I was beside *Sam Houston, Boy Chieftain* when he caught Santa Anna napping and brought Texas into the land of the free and the deserving. With Wilbur and Orville Wright, *Boys with Wings*, I escaped gravity and soared above the earth. I read countless genre books: westerns, sports novels, and science fiction. After reading *Treasure Island*, I roamed landlocked woods hoping to find gold, not pieces of eight in a dead man's chest, but an abandoned car, money hidden in a suitcase under the front seat, or if not money, a body, preferably a skeleton, locked in the trunk. Forty years later when I found a Volvo in woods near our house in Nova Scotia, moss flaring up over the sides and planters of ferns on the roof and atop the trunk, I scattered forty "loonies," brassy dollar coins, throughout the car. The next day I led the children on a salamander expedition during which we just happened to discover the car and its golden treasure. A man does not become the books he read, but books can certainly contribute to the fun of being a parent.

I read Booth Tarkington, Jack London, Mark Twain, Louisa May Alcott, and a barn of Walter Farley's Black Stallion novels. I read Albert Payson Terhune's dog stories. My favorite dog story was Alfred Olivant's *Bob, Son of Battle*, the last of the Gray Dogs of

Kenmuir. Three years ago at a library sale I bought a copy of *Bob*. Although I shelved the book beside books I have written and I see it every day, I have yet to reread it. I know the book will make me sad, not for Bob's aging, his muzzle white and his gait stiff and slow, but for, as James Whitcomb Riley put it in "The Days Gone By," "When the bloom was on the clover, and the blue was in the sky." I also read comics, or as I called them, funny books, blending dollops of Superman with servings of Bugs Bunny and Porky Pig. I collected horror comics, but I refused to keep them in my room at night, and before going to bed stacked them in the hall outside my door. Eventually I banished the monsters to the trash and admitted I preferred the company of Uncle Scrooge and Donald Duck.

My parents did not to try to shape me by controlling my reading. They let me slip the educational bit after school and read randomly and for pleasure. They knew my hankerings, however, and often they gave me books I was certain to like. For Valentine's Day 1951, they gave me Raymond L. Ditmars's *Snakes of the World*. I read and reread the book and spent countless hours studying its pictures. Consequently I recognized milk and pine snakes as soon as I saw them. The photographs that really intrigued me though were of poisonous snakes: a litter of fifty day-old fer-de-lances, each a foot long, a close-up of the head of a bushmaster, its fangs looking big as ribs, and a Costa Rican rattler, a beaded forearm of snake pulled off the ground, the head fixed at the end of a curve, a javelin ready to hurdle forward. At Christmas that year my library of reptile books increased as I received the *Field Book of Snakes* by Karl Schmidt and Dwight Davis.

I am a counter. I count steps to my office, the times a student says "like" in conversation and the pieces of pepperoni on a pizza. In elementary school I kept lists of the books I read, not to measure myself against others but simply for the pleasure of listing. At the end of the school year I always threw the lists away. In eighth grade I read sixty-three books outside class. All I remember is the number and that one of the books was *Moby Dick*. I was too young, and reading the book was an ordeal, one that influenced subsequent readings of Melville. In later years I read *Moby Dick* two more times. Alas, I wasn't able to outgrow the effect of that first reading, my behavior resembling that of someone who becomes ill shortly after drinking grape juice and who refuses to drink grape juice again, although he realizes the juice and the illness were unrelated. By the by I haven't sipped grape juice since I was eight years old and got sick right after drinking a glass.

Among the scraps I turned up was a book report I wrote in the sixth grade on Nicholas Monsarrat's *The Cruel Sea*. The first paragraph was a trifle purple or tempest tossed:

> An ocean, treacherous and stormy, the Atlantic which is three thousand miles across and a thousand fathoms deep, bounded by Europe, Africa, and America; a war, World War II; a war to preserve civilization and a war for democracy; two ships, messengers of death; and lastly the men, a hundred and fifty men, strong men, weak men, honest men, crooked men go together to make *The Cruel Sea* which is the story of convoy duty during World War II.

The doings of children push parents back a generation transforming them into their own parents. I read so much that Father became Grandma Pickering and worried about my becoming a bookworm. He did not, however, send me away to boarding school. Toward the end of his life, he told me, "It is time you got the children a dog like the ones I got you." Almost immediately I became him and bought a dog, following his advice right down to the breed, a dachshund, several of which I had as boy. While I lived in the Sulgrave, I had a series of pets, all of which died: Winkie the cat, a chameleon who escaped from the nest I made in a shoebox and who slipped behind a radiator and was cooked, Quackie a duck that Mother forced me to give to my friend Jane when Quackie got too noisy for the apartment and which Jane's mother promptly backed over and crushed, Hammy a male hamster who turned out to be female and who ate her offspring after giving birth, and three turtles who did not survive long after having their shells painted at the circus.

I liked dogs. Once when Mother and I were in the elevator of the Jefferson Hotel, the singer Lily Pons entered. She wore a long fur coat, and on seeing it a beatific expression broke across my face. Reaching out, I stroked the coat, saying, "Dog, oh, dog." Shortly after moving from the Sulgrave to a house on Iroquois Avenue, Father bought me a cocker mix puppy. Because the dog was a mongrel, I named him Heinzie. On hearing about the puppy, Ga wrote mentioning my friends at Cabin Hill. "Johnny and Hank have a puppy named Tipsy. They brought him up to see me this afternoon so I told them all about Heinzie and they can't wait for summer to come. Sherry wanted to know all about Heinzie and you, what kind of dog he was." By the time summer arrived not only Heinzie but Heinzie number two was dead. Corea killed both dogs. The second dog was a black female dachshund sent to Father from friends in St. Louis. Shortly after Heinzie number two died, Father's friends sent Heinzie number three, a red female whose registered name was Fifi von Lister. Heinzie three lived with us for eight years. She was a wonderful tracker, and when neighborhood dogs started a rabbit, she led the pack. Her bloodlines were good, and we bred her three times to dogs owned by Herbert Sanborne, a philosophy professor at Vanderbilt. The puppies were born in a box in our garage, Heinzie producing eight, nine, and ten. Eventually a milk truck ran over Heinzie and killed her. Heinzie usually stood in the street and met the truck, running alongside it as it drove up our driveway. On this day the driver hurried down Iroquois and not stopping at our driveway ran over Heinzie. I was at home sick, but when Heinzie was run over, I got out of bed, shoveled her off the road, and buried her beside the toolshed in the backyard.

From Heinzie's second litter, we kept Oscar, or Pup Pup, as I called him. He was a huge amiable dachshund. He died at two. A man around the corner raised chickens, and when a fox began to prey on the chickens, he poisoned two or three chickens and tossed them into the woods behind his house. Pup Pup ate one. Father carried Pup Pup to the vet who pumped his stomach and told Father Pup Pup would recover. That night I dreamed about the dogs. When I called them, Heinzie came running. Pup Pup didn't respond, and although I searched for him, I could not find him. The next morning when I awoke, Father said, "Sammy, I have something to tell you." "I know," I said. "Pup Pup is dead." Such prescient moments have been rare in my life. I see and hear what is, nothing more. Only once have I seen fairies. When I was feverish, suffering from red measles, I woke up early one morning. The sky was sooty yellow, and a troop of fairies was dancing on my window ledge.

The last dachshund Fritzie came from Heinzie's third litter. Fritzie was born in the garage and lived eighteen years, from my elementary school days through high school and college and into graduate school. He was my companion. At night he ate oranges with me. When I read in bed, he burrowed under the covers and slept until he got hot. I tired to teach him to scratch my back, as I did my other dogs, but I failed. In my sophomore year in high school when Father picked me up after football practice, Fritzie stood atop the front seat. He recognized me as soon as I walked out of the gym. To say a dog is closer to one than any friend seems to imply that one's life is limited; yet, Fritzie was my close companion. He sat beside me when I read and did homework. I talked to him, telling him about school and my life. We wrestled in the living room. Once when we were wrestling, Fritzie got excited, and when he tried to bound over my head, his penis jabbed into my ear then bent backwards and double. Fritzie's jump collapsed in mid-air. Yelping, he rolled to the floor, howled then gathered himself and scurried out of the living room into the pantry where he buried himself beneath a pile of blankets in his box.

Dogs are good companions for children and middle-aged men. Children knead gloom away by rubbing a dog's back. Unlike wives dogs don't find the affections and company of middle-aged men inconvenient. Dogs don't judge. They don't nag and are satisfied with small things, a fallen grape, bits of cereal on the floor, and a quick scratch. Rarely do they ask for more than a rumpus or a walk. When I came home from school, Fritzie scampered gleefully around the house. No person has ever been so visibly happy to see me. On Iroquois, I also kept tropical fish in my room in three tanks, one holding ten gallons of water, another five, and the last three. Fish bloomed like flowers: black and red mollies, guppies, swordfish, loaches in their black and orange Princeton sleeves, cat fish, neon tetras red and blue, and angel fish, among schools of others. Watching fish slide between seaweed first relaxed me then made me marvel at the richness of life.

I liked animals, but some pets I never wanted, birds, for example. The sight of birds imprisoned in cages makes me melancholy. I have visited zoos around the world. I always leave elated and depressed, nothing depressing me more than the sight of silent caged birds, notwithstanding keepers' explaining that the birds were either born in captivity and not fit for independent lives or were brought to the zoo after being injured. For eighteen months I enjoyed my fish, but "the Great Blizzard" of 1951 dropped eight inches of snow and ice on Nashville. A forest of trees shattered; the electricity went off for a week, and we moved back into the Sulgrave boarding with friends. The aquariums froze, and when we returned were blocks of ice. I dumped the contents in the backyard and put the tanks in the attic. I am not sure why I did not restock the aquariums. After visiting me in Nashville, Grandma Pickering noted, "Your fish family is growing very rapidly and I never saw a wee tiny snail before. As you told me when I was down there before, 'a snail is very interesting.'" Earlier in the year I had bought seaweed, really milfoil, which was host to leeches. Ridding the aquariums of the leeches was work, requiring me to empty and scrub the tanks and water filters and throw weeds, sand, and snails away. Almost no smell or creature repulses me. I have crammed my hand through a hole in the side of a dead whale and pulled out a fistful of maggots without wincing. When I was ten, however, leeches turned my stomach. No longer do they do so; maybe when

I was ten I associated them with the "monsters" that thrashed through the horror comics outside my bedroom door.

Motivations, even those driving the present, are usually mysterious. Forging a satisfactory explanation for behavior, however, is easy and useful, invigorating a person and enabling him to move on to something else. An accurate explanation for behavior would probably lose itself in knotted complexity and confuse, perhaps paralyze, rather than explain. In one sense, tropical fish, the creatures I caught at Cabin Hill, the letters I found at Aunt Lula's, books, and the pets who ambled—mostly barking—through my early years were my playthings. Around ten or maybe even eight, I stopped wanting and requesting toys. For almost as long as I can remember I have not wanted anything material for either Christmas or my birthday, reflecting contentment or perhaps an affluence that so satisfied that it kept me at peace. I never suffered through an "identity crisis" and did not measure myself by or need material goods to define me. Around ten I became slightly willful, not unpleasantly so but in minor ways. I decided that straining not to break wind in the house was silly and so I, as the expression puts it, let fly rousers whenever I felt pressed at home, at the dinner table, in the kitchen—a practice which I have continued for fifty-five years. Aside from laughing, Mother didn't know what to do, so she consulted Ga. Ga's response was sensible: "For heaven's sakes, Katherine, that's just Sammy. Don't fret about such little things." Grandma Pickering's response would have elevated the matter to manners and a sense of the rightness of things. I should add that outside of the house in social situations and in the classroom, I have behaved conventionally.

Of course I received toys and enjoyed them, the train set being one, an English tricycle sent to me by Big Ga in 1945 being another. Father gave the trike away shortly after I mastered riding a bicycle. Indeed drink made Father wax generous, and over the years to Civil War buffs he tried to give away the pistol William Pickering carried during the war and all the papers I found at Aunt Lula's. The first time he asked for the pistol I objected strongly, in fact for effect I had a conniption fit. Afterward Mother hid the memorabilia and professed not to know where they were when ridden again by tipsy generosity Father asked for them. Of course I had toys, but toys were not me. In a picture taken when I was four, I am wearing a cowboy outfit, a handkerchief around my neck, a two-gallon hat perched on the back of my head, and a vest and chaps, both spangled with ribbons looking like those awarded at horse shows. I have a cap pistol in my hand. I liked cap pistols and one Christmas directed Father to buy Mother one as a present from me, the pistol, of course, being one I coveted. I had two sorts of pistols, the conventional type loaded with caps that came on a roll then my favorite with a revolving barrel one loaded with round wafers, the caps bumpy on and circling the surface of the wafer. The names of the pistols were stamped on their butts: Presto, Champion, Long Tom, and Texan, Jr. I had a Brownie Hawkeye camera, but taking photographs did not appeal to me, and I rarely, if ever, used it. My record player came with a device that slipped atop the turntable and enabled it to play 45s. I owned a few 45s, "Dim, Dim, the Lights," "Hearts Made of Stone," "Shake, Rattle, and Roll," and "Let Me Go Lover," but unlike schoolmates I did not build a collection of records. Electronic toys didn't appeal to me, and to this day I have never held a cell phone. One December I asked for a punching bag, the sort that stood chest high and was attached to pliable metal rod. Worried that I might not live until dawn, I crept into the dining room early Christmas morning to see if Santa Claus had brought me the bag. He had, and for a day and a half until the laces on the bag gave way, I was the lightest heavyweight boxing champion in history.

Attached to the garage on Iroquois was what once had been a maid's quarters consisting of a bathroom, the water of which had been turned off, and a small bed-sitter heated by a cast iron stove. For a time the room became my office. In it I glued together plastic models of old cars and battle ships. Eventually I tired of the models, and one day I lined them up along a wall in the backyard and bringing out my BB gun sank the ships and sent the automobiles to the car graveyard. One year my parents gave me a chemistry set. I tried to make stink bombs but failed, and thereafter I abandoned the set. In doing so I behaved like Father. From Father, Mr. McGinness recalled, he borrowed books by Ernest Thompson Seton, among others, *Rolf in the Woods* and *Wild Animals at Home*. When Mr. McGinness was twelve, Grandmother gave him Father's chemistry set, "an elaborate set containing many chemicals in wood pill boxes and glass vials, all packed together with sundry apparatuses in a beautiful wooded box—very little of the chemicals used." A child's microscope was part of my set. I used it very little. Although I wanted to study the wings and innards of insects, I couldn't force myself to capture and kill them. For years I have written about butterflies and dragonflies; I don't kill them. Instead I identify them on the wing, skipping after them along lanes and through brush, an activity that is probably good for my health. The inner workings of creatures have long intrigued me, and three weeks after I buried Heinzie Number Three, I dug her up to see what had happened to her body. At Cabin Hill I examined the bodies of dead creatures I found in the woods poking at them and turning them over to study maggots and burying beetles.

Not being able to make stink bombs did not disappoint me because living under the maid's room was a mother skunk and her kits. Occasionally they let fly, much to my delight. In fact I adored the fragrance of skunk on the night air and now associate it with good country matters. From a foot or two away the perfume overwhelms, but from almost any distance at all it rises into association, evoking memories of skunks pausing and raising their tails into curves before returning to the business of foraging for beetles and digging up buried hornets' nests.

I collected a small parking lot of metal cars, an ice truck with a canvas roof, a red and yellow convertible, the top of which rolled backward into the trunk, and then three cars from Germany given to me by Big Ga, none of the cars longer than my hand but with gear shafts that actually shifted gears. The cars intrigued me, so I dismantled them to study the workings. At the time I knew I was making a mistake. In any case I could not reassemble them. Most metal toys broke. No slinky lasted longer than a day. Generally after ten minutes of flowing down steps the coils were either twisted like dishrags or sprung open into question marks. Tinkertoys with their wooden parts endured better, and I never tried my hand at their metal equivalents.

Once we moved to Iroquois, I had a modicum of athletic equipment, for baseball a glove, a Louisville Slugger bat, then a football, but no soccer ball because soccer did not exist in Tennessee in the early 1950s. The family from whom Father bought the house had buried a home plate in the backyard, and until we were strong enough to hit the ball over the fence into Mr. Knox's yard next door, neighborhood boys and I played softball. The backyard canted downhill, but this did not stop Father from planting a basketball goal at the end of the yard. Games were fun because the slant almost leveled abilities, transforming baskets into matters of luck rather than skill at least for the first two or so times a person played on the hill. Off my "court" I was a terrible basketball player and never made a school team. Occasionally I played badminton and croquet. Generally I won croquet games because I planned ways to jam wickets while amassing extra strokes for myself. Many years later after Cambridge, I imported English croquet. Played with two balls instead of one, the game rewarded forethought more than force, the latter simply strength enough to whack an opponent's ball off the "court" and into woods.

In the 1950s schoolboys owned pocket knives with which we used to play Split, a game in which one threw his knife in the ground within a blade's length of the outside of his opponent's foot. If the knife stuck up, the opponent had to move his foot next to the blade. If the knife stuck in the ground more than a blade length away, an opponent did not have to shift his foot. The object of the game was to spread an opponent's legs gradually so that ultimately he could not stand. Sometimes the game took too long, and for the fun of it, one threw his knife at an opponent's foot.

A Comfortable Boy

Once or twice the tip of the blade jabbed through a sneaker and nicked a toe but nothing more.

I began tennis lessons once we moved to Iroquois, and I had an ersatz racket, not a Jack Kramer, the kind good players owned. When I was in sixth grade, Father bought me a football helmet when I played on the Parmer school team. The lower part of the helmet was leather and puffed around my cheeks while the top sunk into the leather then rose into reddish clay dome, making me look bald. Sports may not strictly be toys, but in effect I toyed with athletics, even when I was serious. What came easily to other boys came slowly, if ever, to me, and to be passable in any sport I had to work harder than almost anyone I knew. The effect of this was probably good, especially when translated beyond lines and playing fields into formless, often ruleless, life. Eventually I became a good swimmer, but I never learned to dive despite Mother's signing me up for diving lessons. In any case no one in his right mind enters water headfirst. The sane go in tentatively toe then heel then ankle. Only morons dive into pools, ponds, lakes, oceans, or bathtubs.

Someone once gave me a stamp book and an enveloped stuffed with stamps from foreign countries in hopes of making me collector. The attempt failed. Someone else gave me a coin book, filled with pictures of American coins. Although I liked looking at pictures of coins, particularly of old silver dollars, several of which Mother kept in a jewelry box, collecting coins did not interest me. Instead I collected baseball cards, this despite caring little about the game itself. I collected the cards because I liked making lists and tracking numbers. Cards from teams that vanished appealed greatly to me: the Boston Braves and St. Louis Browns among others. I did not care whether a player was good or mediocre; I just wanted his card. I listed every player I had on two or more teams, 236. I jotted down the percentages of each type of card in my possession. Thus on June 12, 1956, 12 percent of my collection were Old Topps while "TV" cards made up 7 percent. I packed the cards in cigar boxes—Garcia Delight, Tampa Nugger, and El Trelles, on the outsides of which appeared orange suns, long white beaches, palm trees, and sloe-eyed smoky maidens.

His daughters not being interested, Father's friend Bill Dearborn gave me his collection of lead soldiers, amassed during and just after World War I. He had made the soldiers from molds. Some marched; others charged while still others knelt behind machine guns, many of these French poilu wearing ridged helmets. Horses pranced; a pack camel stood motionless; a doughboy fired a rifle; and a Frenchman held a mortar shell. Accompanying the soldiers was a convoy of brown toy "Army" trucks and field pieces. Camouflaged, their barrels gray and their carriages splotched with color, some of the cannons resembled French 75s. An anti-aircraft gun turned high on a swivel. Other cannons manufactured by Marklin in Germany were siege guns with heavy treads on their wheels and long, thick barrels. From Britain came whippet tanks. Summer blue and top-heavy, they looked gawky and silly, as stable as newly hatched puffins. I added a few soldiers to the collection, primarily for color, Bengal Lancers astride black horses, yellow pendants streaming from their lances; swordsmen in red and black astride ponderous white horses; bagpipers, indeed Highlanders in sundry kilts, the most prevalent color being green and yellow; and Beefeaters, on their heads black hats shaped like hornets' nests. Among the soldiers I received was a troop of French Legionnaires worn from play and scruffy in faded blue; some of these I painted, dressing them in silver and red. I also owned a few Arabs, all on horseback, their robes flowing behind them in a breeze, and a squad of Confederate sharpshooters. Unlike the soldiers in Jessie Willcox Smith's "The Land of Counterpane," my troops didn't spill through ravines of sheets spoiling for a fight. Mostly I lined them up by type, foot soldiers in front, horsemen behind, then trucks and guns, as if I were quartermaster general. I liked looking at the soldiers and at *The First World War, A Photographic History* edited by Lawrence Stallings and published in 1933. I must have lifted the book from the attic at Cabin Hill because inside the front binding is a minute green and white sticker reading "Miller & Rhoads Book Department Richmond, Va."

Age may not bring wisdom but it assuredly brings change. Certainly becoming a parent alters the way a person thinks. Even without war life is fragile, at least the lives of one's children seem unbearably fragile. Today I would not even open *The First World War*. Of course, for a child born in 1941 the matters of war were inescapable. In first grade I drew pictures of American fighter planes shooting down Japanese zeros, the flaming sun of Japan bright on the fuselage, along with daffodils of fire marking places hit by bullets. One night during the Korean War and the accompanying scares of a nuclear holocaust, engendered by the rage to build bomb shelters and exercises in school in which children hid under their desks, I thought the rumbles of a distant thunderstorm the sound of atomic bombs exploding. And among my toys was a game with which I played in 1945 or '46. Manufactured by A. C. Gilbert Company in New Haven. The game consisted of a small four by three inch box, one inch deep, with a sealed, clear glass top. Under the glass at the bottom of the box were a drawing of Japan and two capsules, each with a BB inside. While Japan itself was black, spiky yellow flames exploded from nearby islands and burned across the drawing. Tumbling down through the drawing was an object labeled "Atomic Bomb." The names of three cities appeared in the drawing, Tokyo, Hiroshima, and Nagasaki. At the location of these last two cities were two round indentations, the object of the game being to shake the box so that the two bombs tumbled into the holes and stuck up straight, right on target.

The Sulgrave, Mrs. Little's, and Ransom

In spring 1950, Father paid $15,000 for a small clapboard cottage in the Belle Meade section of West Nashville. Until then I had lived in the Sulgrave Apartments on West End Avenue. A high-rise apartment building with almost no land attached has replaced the Sulgrave. In memory the Sulgrave seems a marvelous human place. Consisting of three or four brick buildings, the Sulgrave was three stories. Instead of facing West End, the buildings stood at a right angle to the road behind a stone wall and tangles of forsythia. The land on which the apartments stood was higher than the road, and to reach the sidewalk on West End one walked down stone steps cut through the wall. I used to sit atop the wall and look at people and cars, always hoping that the fire trucks in the station down and across the street would be called out to answer an alarm. On Saturdays Father took me to the station, and I clambered onto the front seats of tankers and pumpers and sat behind the steering wheels, growling like an engine.

The Sulgrave itself faced a driveway that circled in front of the buildings in a big oval. In the middle of the oval was a grassy area rough with trees, hackberries, and maybe cedars and magnolias. Across the far side of the oval a field sloped down to West End and in the other direction ran upward into a small wood. Through scrub on the far side of the field from the Sulgrave were the Royal Oaks Apartments. For a small child, even one who roamed miles during a summer's day, this was space enough. Behind the Sulgrave an alley ran parallel to Fairfax Avenue. Children are born recyclers and until they are educated into hygiene, and fear, are fascinated by alleys and dumps. Above the Sulgrave and behind the wood at the top of the "field" was Love Circle, a road that spiraled around a small knob. Osage or mock orange trees grew along the road, and accompanied by Jody, another boy who lived in the apartments, I pulled my red wagon to Love Circle and filled it with mock oranges. Sometimes we brought our booty home. Other times we spread the mock oranges across the road in a line then hid beside the road in bushes waiting for cars to drive over them, squashing them with a thump sounding like a blow to the chest of a big man. Some drivers slowed down, but no one ever stopped after running over a mock orange. Still, we titillated ourselves by imagining being chased through the woods by madmen and, of course, wild women. Along West End two or three blocks away were the Richland Market and Dr. Schwartz's Drugstore. Across the street a little farther down was Candyland. For a treat, Mother and Father took me to Candyland, and I ordered a double chocolate soda. We sat in booths festooned with the initials of spooning couples. What a treat it must have been, I thought, for a girl to have her initials carved into one of the booths. Mr. Pappas, a Greek, owned Candyland. He packed his ice cream so tightly by hand that it did not melt if we bought a quart and walked home with it. We always bought chocolate, although Mother sometimes ate a butter pecan or a peach cone.

Mr. Pappas's ice cream was the closest I came to ethnic food, Southern dishes of fried chicken, country ham, turnip greens, fried grits, sweet potatoes, rolls almost as big as softballs, corn on the cob, butterbeans, and pecan pie simply being food. We also ate food in season, strawberries, for example, when they ripened during the summer, not the whole year round. Food and seasons were bound together. Now that one can eat melons and tomatoes, asparagus, practically everything, year round seasons as well as foods have lost their spice. Raspberries lasted only two weeks. They used to burst on the palate exciting and delightful. Now that I can eat them throughout the year, they have lost their appeal. I ate my first pizza in Maine when I was eighteen years old and working at a summer camp. There were no Chinese, Indian, Thai, Ethiopian,

Mexican, or Japanese restaurants in Nashville when I was a boy. Fast food did not exist, and we ate meals at home. Once or twice a year Mother and Father took me to the Surf Restaurant two or so miles west of the apartments, and I ate red snapper. Later when we moved to Belle Meade and Mother and Father joined the Belle Meade Country Club we ate on Sunday lunch there after church. The food at the club wasn't very different from that at home; I remember liking chicken salad sandwiches on toast and Faucon salad, a Nashville specialty; Mother usually ate a caramel fudge ball, a dessert I refused to try because of the caramel sauce. Children are remarkably conservative and only age into liberalism. Circumstance arrests the development of some children, and they, alas, remain hidebound and conservative throughout their lives. Coconut cake made me a Democrat. For my birthdays Mother baked chocolate cakes. One year Dora baked a coconut cake. When I saw the cake, I had a tantrum and refused to eat it, pushing it away from me. Mother took the sweet and the sour in hand and sitting me on a stool in the kitchen demanded that I taste the cake. I took a nibble then a bite then a piece then another piece, and now on my birthday, to emend a line from one of Father's favorite poems— Tennyson's "Locksley Hall"—my thoughts lightly turn to thoughts of coconut.

Sometimes we walked to Centennial Park and fed ducks in the pond. Usually I played on the trolley that had gone off the rails except in the imaginations of children. The replica of the Parthenon attracted me less than the tall red calla lilies blooming in the middle of the boulevard leading into the park. Sometimes I visited the home of Ben West, a block away on West End. Ben's grandfather Mr. Meadows walked Ben to Ransom, and they often joined Father and me on our treks to school. Ben's father became mayor and in the early 1950s spoke out against segregation, a stand that encouraged Nashville businesses to open their facilities to all races. As a boy, that meant nothing to me. I visited Ben because he had an incredible electric train layout, one that in memory seems as big as a switching yard. Cub Scouts also met at Ben's house. I belonged for a year, but I'm not a joiner, particularly organizations through whose structure uplift and achievement course thick as clabber. For my yearly project Father, not I, made a kite. Afterward I stopped paying my weekly dues of ten cents and dropped out.

On Sundays I attended Sunday school at Christ Church in town at Ninth and Broad. After we moved, I attended St. George's at the entrance to Belle Meade Boulevard. I enjoyed stories from the Old Testament, the sorts of tales anthologized in *The Children's Bible*, published by the Golden Press, and a book I gave my children so they would know, for example, the fine old stories of Goliath and David the Giant Killer, of Joseph and the Coat of Many Colors, and of Shadrach, Meshach, and Abednego, the asbestos boys. I liked carrying but not filling mite boxes, in great part because I disliked asking people to donate, even pennies and nickels. I enjoyed Sunday school and made friends. When I became sick in 1946 and was in Vanderbilt Hospital, the class wrote me. "Dear Sammy," Garth Fort who has been my friend before I knew what a friend was, wrote, "we missed you at sunday school hope you get well soon and come on bak—from Garth." Except for misspellings the notes were the same, the children having copied them from a blackboard. With the notes, the teacher included lesson 14 from the *Primary Bible Folder*, entitled "At Home in Nazareth." On the front of the lesson Jesus appeared as a little boy wearing a golden headband and feeding a pigeon. Mary sat in a doorway to Jesus's left spinning while Joseph worked in his carpenter's shop behind, a stack of doors leaning against the side of the shack, the top door green. The lesson consisted of four pages. On one appeared the hymn "The Child Jesus," which read "The dear little Jesus once lay on the hay; / He slept and he smiled and he grew day by day / Until he could run and could play and could be / A help to his mother, like you and like me." On the back of the lesson appeared a sketch of a Kate Greenaway girl, her hair tousled into curls. In her left hand she held a small doll above the head of a baby boy lying beneath a comforter, a pillow under his head. Above the sketch was the poem "For a Very Small Baby," the

last two lines of which urged, "Teach us to live the way we should /
To help him grow up strong and good." Most of the *Folder*
consisted of "A Letter to the Parents," which preached the
importance raising children to be charitable and helpful. "Please be
thinking of little 'jobs' for which your child can be responsible, so
that when the class talks about ways of helping in the family, and
different tasks for which parents are depending on them, he can
contribute from his own experience." The lesson emphasized in the
Folder was admirable, albeit the prose slightly garbled. Great
portions of other folders consisted of drawings, all of which could
be colored. On one page appeared four drawings, two at the top
and two at the bottom. Dividing the two rows of sketches was the
sentence, "The children in Donald's class thought of all the people
who cared for them at home." In the upper left frame a man sat in
an easy chair reading a newspaper. Under him was the line "Donald
thought of his_____." I did not write *father* in the blank space but
I colored the man's suit brown and the chair and newspaper purple.
Above "Betty thought of her_____" stood a woman wearing an
apron and sweeping the floor. Again I did not write *mother* in the
blank, but I colored the picture, turning the mother's hair and
apron yellow and her blouse and dress blue. I did not spend much
time on coloring but only pushed my crayons back and forth like a
man sanding a small piece of wood.

I had fun in Sunday school, and I've often wondered with
momentary regret, only momentary, about my wandering from the
fold and the good shepherd. I admire the Sermon on the Mount
and think it the best guide I know to living a decent life. But I
loathe the doctrinal and am allergic to the highly organized. Only
the unthinking and adolescent are consistent. When I write essays,
strangely enough, I listen to gospel songs, old timers like "Sweet
Hour of Prayer," "How Great Thou Art," "Precious Memories,"
and "Shall We Gather at the River."

The problem in childhood, however, was that even though I
retired from belief in elementary school I did not have the words to
explain my retirement. Because I did not want to upset Mother, I

continued to attend church and Sunday school. When I was young, I was popular, and to my chagrin, people elected me to posts even when I did not want to be elected, some of the posts in church groups. Being unpopular is a burden in school, but being popular is also a weight, though perhaps not anywhere near so arduous. Perhaps, though, popularity drove me from the larger world into teaching and writing, into places where I could spend days with books, pencils, and paper for company, alone except for family, responsible not to a society but for that lesser thing classes. "For a handful of pages I left them," I sometimes think when I try to puzzle out why I didn't settle in Nashville amid friends and the familiar.

I may be wrong. Perhaps I really enjoyed being popular. Certainly the little things that drifted my way, most of which years had washed out of mind, only to be resuscitated in researching this memoir, pleased Grandma Pickering. Once after classmates elected me to something, Grandma Pickering wrote,

> I really was too proud and elated to quiet down for a good night's sleep. I really feel very humble, however, very proud, to-day as I contemplate the many happy moments, even days, which you continue to bring into our lives.... I am aware that these honors don't just happen, my Sammy, there are contributing reasons for each of them and to know that you have all the qualifications that one must have to win them is the best gift to us that could come our way.

Poor Grandma—she needed other grandchildren. Of course in a sense she had them. When I look at the pictures Mother took of me through my early years, I wonder what happened to all those little boys. On the wall of my dining room hangs a portrait of me painted in 1943. I sit in a frame decorated by gold leaf and measuring nineteen by twenty-three inches. I am wearing a double-breasted pink playsuit. The playsuit has short sleeves and at the end of each sleeve just above the elbow is a white ruffle. A ruffle also circles my neck. In my hands I hold an apple and am smiling. I have blond hair; my eyes are brown; my skin is soft, and my lips are full and redder than any apple. Only on Easter and Christmas or when a child brings a good friend home do we eat in the dining room. I have aged into gristle mentally and physically. Before dinner I swill a glass of wine in hopes of softening my words. Occasionally a guest asks about the portrait, wondering whom the canvas depicts. If I've had a second glass of wine, I answer, "A boy I used to know." If I haven't had a second glass, I say "me" then pour myself another glass.

That boy is only one of many who has disappeared from my life: a baby four months and thirteen days old wearing a white gown and propped up on a bed, pillows behind him, his hands together, fat faced, alert with laughter roiling his cheeks; a delighted slightly older boy holding a can brimming with chicken feed; a pirate in saddle shoes wearing a black hat with a cardboard skull pasted to the crown; another boy hunkering down watching a duckling bundle across a path; a tree climber perched high in branches forming a crow's nest; and then a five-year-old sitting astride an English trike, Christmas tree behind him, on the ground in front of him crayons standing on end like bullets. On top of the tree and not visible is Santa Claus. The same Santa Claus still decorates my trees. Color has leached out of his coat becoming more orange than red; his beard is dirty gray, and his right leg is shattered. Although we add shiny new ornaments to the tree each year, I refuse to put any other decoration at the top of a tree. In the picture the boy is smiling and is wearing a sweater over a white shirt, blue shorts, leather shoes, and striped socks, the stripes circling the socks in thin lines. The boy's hair is short, but the remnant of a widow's peak is visible. Behind the peak is a bare spot, the result of trying to trim his hair one afternoon. When his mother returned, he pretended to trip while holding the scissors, cutting his hair by accident.

Our apartment in the Sulgrave was on the second floor. The door opened into an entrance hall; to the left was Mother and

Father's bedroom, to the right a living room that stretched away from the door into a dining room. Across the entrance hall a door opened into a narrow hall. Straight ahead was the bathroom; to the left my bedroom; to the right a small pantry. Behind the pantry were the kitchen and a screened porch with stairs leading to the maid's quarters in the basement. Off the living room was a porch that faced the yard. The apartment was snug and warm, just right for an only child. Across the landing lived Mrs. McTigue or Tigue, Ewell, and Kaka. I am not sure if Jack Spore and Dave Aaron lived there but all were my great and good friends. In the morning after breakfast I hurried across the hall, and Tigie served me a cup of coffee, sugary and light. At Christmastime, Tigue rolled cotton down the top of a piano and set up a New England village, a steepled white church at one end of the town. Dave was in the navy during the war and sent me a naval officer's cap. He also enrolled me in the Imperial Domain of the Golden Dragon, my having crossed the 180th Meridian on January 17, 1945, on board the Dream Boat "By Proxy." Jack was in the army, and he wrote me from El Paso after the war, addressing his letter to 3rd Lt. Sam Pickering, Jr. He began by apologizing for not having written earlier, explaining that army life was "so tough on us 2nd Lt's, that I haven't had a spare minute till now." "I hope you have been a good soldier and have been obeying your Mother & Daddy and eating the proper foods—All good soldiers do that." "Tell Tigue & Kaka," he concluded, "I may be home sooner than they expect— and to have plenty of coffee on hand so you & I can drink our coffee together."

After we left the Sulgrave, I saw my friends infrequently. I'd like to say that I missed them. I didn't. The truth is that I miss them more now than then. Life was so exciting that I did not have time for regret or melancholy. Actually only the old have leisure enough for melancholy. If I died tomorrow, some members of my English department, not all, would say once or twice, "Gee, I miss old Sam. The place is awfully quiet without him." Within a week, however, I would be as far out of conversation as last spring's peas, as is fitting. I did run across Jack during a high school football game my junior year in high school. The game was important, and since I was a rarely used substitute, I did not expect to play. At the end of the third quarter, we led by two points, but the other team made a first down on our eight yard line and appeared certain to score. The evening was cool, and despite the excitement I was dreaming blissfully and anonymously in the middle of the bench when I heard, "Pickering, get in there at left tackle." The coach had made a mistake, and when the other team broke from its huddle, I prayed they would run toward the other side of our defensive line. Just before the ball was snapped, though, the referee blew his whistle and approached me. The referee was Jack Spore. "Sammy," Jack said loudly, "if you hurt any of these boys, I am going to tell your Mommy and Daddy." Then he blew his whistle again and shouted, "Play ball." I don't think the other team scored, but that's beside the point. Who wins and who loses doesn't matter a hoot in hell. What matters is warmth, niceness, humanity, fun—all of which Jack embodied.

Before Easter Big Ga sent a packet of cards to Mother who handed them to Kaka and Tigue. Throughout the day the Easter bunny knocked on the door, left a card, and hopped away before I could see him. When I was small, relatives sent me hundreds of cards, most of them sweet—birthday cards decorated with kittens in red, white, and blue sailor suits; a small dog wearing a green and white bow tie and riding a tricycle, printed inside "This little dog's riding as fast as can be to bring birthday wishes to someone who's THREE!"; a skunk smelling a flower, above him in red "Hi Stinky!"; or two squirrels holding onto the number six and gazing down at a birthday cake adorned with red roses and blue candles. On the front of one card a little black girl with curling hair stood barefoot on a broken brass headboard. The girl wore a pink and white smock. A halo circled her head and white wings sprouted from her shoulders. "Jessie," Ga wrote, "wants to see your new bed. A skunk came right to our window last night. I think he was looking for you." Ga put notes on her cards, on a Christmas card depicting two fat Santas on a bicycle built for two, she said she was going to put a red bow and a bell on Woozy the cat, adding, "he's so fat he can scarcely run." On Valentine's Day Hummel Cupids with pudgy thighs and cheeks swollen like marshmallows stuck arrows into pincushions shaped like hearts, and sailor boys waved blue and yellow semaphores with red hearts stitched in the middle. A kitten strummed a banjo shaped like a heart, and a puppy poked his head out from under a sombrero, the print reading, "My Valentine— Just can't keep it under MY HAT." A cocker spaniel with a blue bow around his neck held a heart in his mouth, "Just for you on Valentine's Day" printed on the heart. The hind legs of the spaniel bent backward so the card could stand on a table. "HOWDY PARTNER! I'd like to Lasso You for My Valentine," said a bear sitting atop a fence. The bear had blue eyes and ears thick as muffins; he wore a Stetson, a yellow handkerchief around his neck, a red-and-white-checkered shirt, blue jeans, and white cowboy boots decorated with hearts. A lasso dangled from his left hand. A fat cactus grew near his left foot; by his right a bluebird hopped along. The cactus lacked thorns, and much too gentle to eat bugs, the bluebird looked up, begging for a treat. On Easter a blond boy in a red and white striped shirt and blue shorts scrubbed the ears of the Easter bunny. Behind the bunny rose a necklace of soap bubbles, printed in the largest bubble "To a Fine Boy at Easter Time." Because I was often sick, I received scores of "Get Well" cards. On the front of card from Aunt Allie, the Worry Bird perched on a limb. He wore a straw hat and smoked a corncob pipe. When the card was opened, the bird's green tail feathers flew up. "He'll do all your worrying and you can just get WELL!" the card declared. The cards were sweet and affectionate, uncomplicated by wit, reflecting a simpler time, this even after granting that people rarely send edgy cards to small children.

Ga's sister Aunt Lucille wrote me after my fourth birthday, saying she would "just love to hear you tell about your birthday party." "Can't you write me a letter when you learn to write at the nursery school?" she asked. Initially Mother enrolled me in the nursery school attached to Overbrook School, run by Dominican sisters. I didn't stay long. Mother and Father were sensible. When I disliked doing something, they did not force me to continue. I lasted one morning at a day camp. At Overbrook, the sisters were mean, forcing all of us to put our heads down on our desks whenever a child misbehaved. Moreover older boys used the same lavatories kindergarteners did, and I felt intimidated. I then went to Mrs. Little's kindergarten on Crestwood Road. I kissed my first girl, learned to play the tambourine, and was happy. Kindergarten ran from nine in the morning until noon. I rode in a hookup, that is, with other children. Seat belts did not exist, and one day while I tickled Joy Yearwood on the back of her mother's car the door flew open and Joy tumbled out bouncing on the road. A car behind us swerved and missed her, and Joy only suffered a broken arm. In 1963 when I bought my first new car, a Plymouth Valiant, I stipulated that the car had to have seat belts, something Father thought unnecessary.

I have been in school for sixty-four years. I have learned and forgotten libraries of lessons. I have taught libraries of lessons that should and have been forgotten. I remember almost nothing about Mrs. Little's except the most important thing: it was fun. For Christmas that year I gave Mother a snapshot taken of me at Mrs. Little's. I stood beside an old, thick oak, furrows of bark running in trenches up the trunk. I wore a dark jacket, shorts, leather shoes and white socks fallen down around my ankles. On my head was a leather cap, flaps pulled down over my ears and tied under my neck. My mouth was open, probably because my sinuses were bothering me. My hands were balled into fists, and I looked tense, though I am sure I wasn't. Behind and to the right was the corner of a clapboard house, a window looking into the room where we played and sang. In a pamphlet Mrs. Little said that one of the things we would learn is "How to carry small chairs without the hazard of tripping or bumping into others and with a minimum of strain," no reading or writing, just moving chairs.

A Comfortable Boy

In 1946 I started first grade at Ransom. I was always a good student and a good boy, not causing trouble, making *A*'s with an occasional *B* tossed on a report card to vary appearance, and later getting my assignments done on time. In fact I was a girl, disciplined and quiet, the sort of little girl other little girls liked and who avoided risky behavior and who would grow into the kind of man parents wanted daughters to marry. Never did my parents put pressure on me about grades, in part because I did well without encouragement and in part because they didn't think grades important, not as important as parents think them today. Manners mattered more and until they died my parents lectured me on manners. When I was forty, Mother approached me near the end of a cocktail party and asked, "Sammy, have you thanked Snookie for inviting you? If not, please do so." Long after my schooldays ended, I decided that Mother and Father like many Southerners viewed ideas as play money. Ideas were cheap and easy to come by, the toys for conversation or the page. In contrast, becoming well mannered and socially responsive was difficult, the result of almost never-ending drills and lessons. For a time I thought Southerners had things backward. Instead of thinking about ideas and abstractions, they deflected analysis into stories, the result being that they lacked the inclination to ponder, a state of mind that led them to ignore important issues, say, exploitation of the environment. Now I believe I was wrong. I value order, manners, and structure more than in the past, not necessarily for myself because like all flawed humans I arrogantly exempt myself from ways of life I believe beneficial for others, but for my children and society. To probe deeply is to ignore the surface of things, a mistake because I suspect surface is the only reality. In contrast depth may be a delusion, an ornate fabrication that distances one from messy people, that is, pitiful, struggling humanity.

In first grade I did not consider such matters. I was too happy playing Red Rover and kick ball. At recess, Miss Courtney Hollins, my teacher in first and second grade, split the class in half and arranged us in two lines ten yards apart and facing one another.

Once we joined hands, Miss Courtney asked someone to begin the game. "Red Rover, Red Rover," I shouted, if I started the game, "let Linda come over." With that Linda who was in the line opposite released the hands she held and running at our line tried to break through. If she failed, she joined our side. If she succeeded, she chose one of us to return to her side and join her line. If a girl called a boy to come over, that was usually a sign of infatuation. If the boy returned her interest, he would run at her as hard as he could, in those days knocking someone down indicating true love. Linda, by the way, sat next to me at a table in class. I could not tie my shoes, and when my laces worked loose, she bent over and tied them for me. Kick ball was also a fine game, one I now think far superior to, safer than, and more fun than games children play later in school, football, baseball, and basketball, for instance. Dorothy was the best kick ball player in my class. She was also the strongest child in class and bullied the boys, all except me whom she liked. The behavior of boys, and men, is always scabby. Instead of urinals along walls, a long trough ran down the middle of the boy's lavatory, providing the opportunity for war games, shooting across the trough at one another while making "ack-ack" or "da, da, da, da" sounds. Peeing contests are a part of boyhood. At Cabin Hill the Johnsons and I competed in three contests: for height, distance, and endurance, perhaps endurance vile, but still endurance. Writing one's name in sand or dirt was a skill, but not a competitive event, smacking, perhaps, of something like synchronized swimming.

When I started to read, I read from right to left across the page, not from left to right, something that today might be reason enough to bundle a child off to special education. Concerned, Mother spoke to Miss Courtney. "Katherine," Miss Courtney said, "that's a small matter. Don't worry. I'll soon have him reading the normal way." And she did, though I should add that for years I have read most magazines from back to front, probably a quirk inherited from the Ratcliffes. I remember very little about my first years in school. At a Christmas pageant, one of the three wise men, fittingly played by Sarah, a Jewish girl, froze on stage, melting only after I crept between the curtains and tugged her sheet. Mother's scrapbooks are responsible for most of my Ransom memories; she kept enough papers from my school days to awaken sleeping recollection. When I wasn't drawing a wing of airplanes, their fuselages red, black, yellow, purple, and orange, and raining bombs on a Japanese fleet, the word *boom* scribbled six times across the sheet in thick black letters, I drew hills and plains bright with flowers. Six-colored rainbows curved above trees, the tops of which pinched together like those of evergreens. I liked gardens, and flowers blossomed in rows, sometimes with an American flag amid them. Often I drew Indians standing by teepees. Beside a purple teepee with a yellow interior stood three stands selling lollipops. Trees of lollipops at a small purple stand cost 98¢ while single lollipops at a big yellow stand cost only 6¢. Although six lollipops hovered over a green stand like balloons filled with helium, no price appeared on the stand. In another picture two eggs cost 20¢, all the eggs brightly colored, probably for Easter. Nearby, a girl with rags of yellow hair and bulging, laughing eyes sold toys for 10¢. A boy with brown hair and a mouth shaped like a staple walked an orange dog on a leash while a mother in a red dress swung a black purse and her daughter held a fabulous lumpy animal that looked a blend of turtle and parrot.

At the top of an assignment sheet, I colored in the outlines of a rail fence, a cow, pig, hen, and dog then Jack a boy and Jane a girl. I drew lines from the illustrations of the animals to the words that named them, from my brown cow to the word *cow*. On the lower section of the page I inserted the appropriate word into sentences, not getting them all right, for example, sticking *hog* into the sentence, "Jane's_____ gives her an egg." On another sheet, I colored a turkey yellow also giving him a few feathers colored like rainbow. At the bottom of the page I wrote, "turkey come turkey. Bill come my see Bill. He my my." On a page labeled "Beginner' Arithmetic Three," I colored ten apples red, writing the numbers one to ten underneath them. Next I colored eight fish brown under which I wrote the number eight, then nine hearts with charm bracelet attachments at the top, ten blue balls, five brown rabbits, seven yellow horns, four chairs with red seats, and lastly six yellow ducks. The directions for an exercise in Phonics 1A instructed teachers to use "Baa, Baa, Black Sheep" for ear training and speech. Later children were told to draw circles around pictures whose names began like "baa and black." Sixteen items appeared on the page, some clearly not beginning with the *ba* sound, cat, dog, horse, chicken, rat, and monkey. Only a few items began with the *ba* sound: baby, ball, box, boy, and boat. I didn't do well and circled every item that began with *b*, among other bus, bell, and book.

Mother kept several notebooks that I had filled with addition and subtraction. I rarely made mistakes. More interesting was the back inside cover of one notebook in which I traced my left hand. At the end of each finger I drew a face. Because the boys had short hair, their ears stuck out. The girls' long hair hung over their ears and draped down into my palm. Starting with my little finger and ending with my thumb, the fingers represented Pats, Sammy, Linda, Tomi, and Donna Lee. On the back of the cover, I drew three boats and forty-three trucks, most of the last tractor trailers, following different roads, however, driving across the cover then up and down, some turning sideways into right angles. I wrote S. P. on the sides of nine trucks and P. S. on one. Several trucks were numbered 17, 33, 44, 51, 77. Both trucks numbered 51 carried "Beer." Another truck carried "FOOD," and another "ROI-TAN" cigars.

The issue of *My Weekly Reader* for the week of January 17–21, 1949, announced the birth of "The Baby Prince," Prince Charles. The article informed second graders that "Princess Elizabeth is the mother of the baby prince. She is proud of her baby. The Prince is like other babies. He eats baby food. He laughs and cries. He sleeps much of the time. He is healthy and happy. Nurses give the Prince good care. They take him for a ride each day. He rides in an old baby carriage. His mother rode in the carriage when she was a baby." The other three pages of the issue were devoted to a silent reading test. The test consisted of fourteen sections, seven with illustrations. Making up each section was a paragraph followed by two sentences for which the second grader chose the final word, choosing from among three. Until the last section all my selections were correct. "Mr. Toad sits in the cool shade of some garden plants," the section read. "He puts out his long, sticky tongue. He catches grasshoppers and crickets. He eats insects by the hundreds." "Mr. Toad eats hundreds of plants insects potatoes," the first sentence stated. Alas, I circled *plants*.

Mother saved several of my first-grade exercise notebooks. One was an "Old Hickory" Pencil Tablet, with three-fourths of an inch between lines and manufactured by Southern Woodware Company in Nashville. The cover was green, and the face of Andrew Jackson appears on the front, underneath him the entrance to his home The Hermitage. Most of the exercise booklets were the Blue Horse tablets. Near the top of the cover in a frame three and three-quarters inches square, the blue horse stood in a corral, ears erect, nostrils flared, bit between the teeth, and eyes calmly intelligent, ready for whatever first grade brought, ready to trot the rocky trails of arithmetic and writing, computations like four plus five and seven take away three, and sentences such as "I love my Father" and "I love my Mother." Blue Horse tables were popular, partly because the manufacturer, Montag Brothers in Atlanta, offered prizes to children who amassed quantities of covers. For the contest ending on June 15, 1945, Montag supposedly offered 350 bicycles, 125 "R. V. A. Licensed Radios," 500 footballs, 500 Note Book Covers, "1000 Victory Prizes and 13,525 Other Valuable Prizes." To become a contestant a child had to send the company "a minimum of 25 covers." "For many years Montag's has given prizes like these to children all over the South," the company stated at the bottom of the cover of a tablet I used in spring 1948. "We know they're the kind of prizes you like and so we hope that all of them can be secured when this year's contest ends. As you know, the war has made it hard to get many things. If some of these prizes shouldn't be available, you will receive a prize of equal value or money equal to the cost." Classmates collected covers, but no one ever gathered enough to win a prize. In one of the notebooks, I found a get-well card from Miss Courtney. "We miss you very much," she wrote. "Almost everyone in our class has measles. With love for you, Miss Courtney."

Twenty-five years ago I bought a house in Storrs. In my second collection of essays, I mentioned attending Ransom. A neighbor read the piece and immediately sent me a copy of the Ransom school song, noting that we were fellow alumni. The song is innocent and optimistic, just right for my time there. "There is no school like John B. Ransom School," the song began, bouncing along to the tune of the "Washington and Lee Swing."

We do our lessons 'cording to the rules,
We can read and write and cipher, too.
And we do just what our teachers tell us to.
We have a Mothers' Club that's hard to beat.
They gave us sidewalks so we keep dry feet.
They gave us flower beds and shade trees, too.
Shade trees, too——Ransom Sch——ool.

Schooldays at Parmer

In the summer before fourth grade, we moved to Iroquois Avenue. The house was a modest white clapboard, consisting of two bedrooms, mine facing Iroquois, Mother and Father's set back in a wing; a narrow room that could function as a guestroom but which was really a swollen hall linking the bedrooms to the kitchen, two bathrooms, a long forearm of a living room, the elbow of which connected to the kitchen and served as a dining room, a kitchen itself and a small pantry then a screened-in back stoop, from which stairs climbed into the attic. Our dogs slept in a cardboard box under a table in the pantry.

Across the front of the house ran four windows blinkered by dark green shutters. Two dormers opened in the roof like eyes. Mother planted boxwood along the foundation both in the front and along the driveway that ran along the right end of the house. The front yard wrinkled down to the road in a series of gentle terraces. Behind and set higher than the house was a two-car garage. Father walked to Belle Meade Boulevard at the end of Iroquois and rode the bus to town every morning unless a friend picked him up, a common occurrence, and we didn't get a second car until Mother and Father bought me a used Plymouth in 1957 so I could drive to high school. Attached to the garage were the maid's quarters, which became a storeroom, boxy with attic overflow, and a battered chicken house that Father used as a tool shed. A white trellis ran beside the shed. In front of it Mother planted red hollyhocks, one of my favorite flowers. Behind the house and blocked on three sides by the screened stoop, the back of the house itself, and Mother and Father's bedroom was small brick terrace. In front of it was a flowerbed in which Mother planted pansies in the spring.

About an acre of land came with the house, and the backyard ran uphill into a wood brambly with saplings. Oddly, as I look back, I seemed to have chopped years into blocks of activity. I rambled all over Cabin Hill, but I never really explored the woods behind our house on Iroquois. Neither did I wander the lot next door, which was vacant when we first moved to Iroquois. Later the Silvers built on the lot, and during the blasting for their house I brought home slabs of conglomerate filigreed with fossils, mostly sea shells. The blasting cracked the foundation of our house. Afterward snakes appeared, pouring themselves glistening between stones, a sight that thrilled me but upset Mother.

Of course I explored occasionally. One spring I crawled through culverts, several so filled with gravel that I was forced to roll onto my back and push myself forward with my feet. Children—and adults—are remarkably stupid. Our house sat under a lid of land. Above the house Westview Avenue ran perpendicular to Iroquois. In winter I sleighed down Iroquois from Westview. On one occasion I stood on the sled. Halfway down I became frightened and stepped off, with the result that I bounced bottom over head to the foot of the hill. To an extent cuts and bruises were the showy boyhood equivalent of "salad," the bars and ribbons with which career soldiers decorate their dress. Once in a while a scab was so ornate that a boy charged friends a nickel for removing his bandage and showing it to them. Bicycle crashes caused harmless but sensational wounds, sanding patches of skin away. I rode a J. C. Higgins bicycle, on the handlebars of which I attached squirrel tails. For the tails I traded a Barlow pocketknife, getting the short blade of the bargain Father thought.

I attended Parmer, a neighborhood school on Leake Avenue less than a mile from our house. I wanted to ride my bike to school. Sensibly, or so I think now from a parent's point of view, Mother refused to let me ride, protective helmets not being available. In eighth grade when a gaggle of friends got motorbikes, she refused to let me have one. In fact I knew asking for a bike was futile, but I asked nonetheless. Only once in my life have I ridden a motorcycle. I rode behind a friend and was so terrified that I clamped myself tightly to him and the bike, the exhaust pipe searing the skin off my right calf, something I did not notice until I dismounted. I have told my children that if one of them ever rides a motorcycle I will disinherit him, not that he would lose much if I did so.

I entered Parmer seamlessly. I made friends swiftly and never felt out of place. School was easy, and good grades came effortlessly, as they had done at Ransom. What had changed, however, were friendships, not probably the result of changing schools but the result of growing from the fourth through the eighth grade. Suddenly people my age populated, perhaps crowded, my world, people whose names I have not forgotten even though I haven't seen many of them since 1955. My closest friends remain classmates from Parmer. Time and distance have beaten the ties between us to airy thinness, but the tensile strength of emotion still links us. Two years ago I drove to Monteagle, Tennessee, to celebrate Bill Weaver's sixty-fifth birthday, a Parmer boy and my oldest and dearest friend. At the party were Garth Fort and Jeffrey Buntin, classmates, and then Margie Dortch and Em Keeble (maiden names both), two or so years behind us in school but Parmer and neighborhood friends nevertheless. When I saw those men and women, no, boys and girls, my emotions skipped. On the other hand, the affection I feel for old friends and the number of people I knew and liked at Parmer may be Southern or may just reflect my nature. Vicki, my wife, grew up in Princeton, New Jersey. Neither does she have friends from her school days in Princeton, nor can she can remember the names of classmates. I could hardly get through the scrapbook in which Mother pasted pictures and notes from my Parmer years. Each page awakened memories and regret for not having seen my classmates for so long. Would that I could list all my classmates and beside their names write, "You were swell. I hope life has treated you well."

The down side of growing into friendships is that a person grows into society simultaneously and becomes a conformist, not necessarily bad but not good if one finds himself unconsciously mouthing and living platitudes that don't suit him. Rarely are responsible parents nonconformists. Duty wraps parents and good husbands and wives, heck, good neighbors, like a spider wrapping a moth in its web. Rejecting obligation and affection can, if a person is not careful or sentimental, turn one bestial. No matter, I was popular at Parmer and instead of running from popularity as I did later in life in order to have my version of my life I embraced popularity. I enjoyed school and friends. I attended scores of square dances, skating and tea parties, get-togethers for visitors from out of town, hops, and formals. The Thirteen Club sent engraved invitations; the club being, I think, for thirteen-year-olds in their last year of elementary school. My picture appeared repeatedly on the social pages of the Nashville papers, often dancing in a sport coat and tie. In Storrs my children never went to a skating party or hayride. They never had the chance to square dance, and for the most part, did not attend junior and senior proms. Only once in four or five years do Vicki and I eat dinner at an acquaintance's house. For three months in the summer we disappear into Nova Scotia into a part so boggy that it would cause electronic mail to short-circuit if I had a computer, which I don't. We have a telephone number, but I share it with few people, the children in case an emergency arises and the English department in case someone calls and needs to contact me. During the past decade, only a handful of people have contacted me.

Late in elementary school, athletics almost kick children into conformity, imposing not simply the discipline of training but determining inclination and directing desire. Occasionally Father took me to watch the Nashville Vols at Sulfur Dell in 1952 with Al Worthington pitching, Ralph Novotney catching, Buster Boguski at second, Rance Pless at third, and Dusty Rhodes in the outfield. I liked going to the games but because I was a terrible batter and fielder I never entertained thoughts of playing at any time other than recess in school. The enjoyment did, however, impress itself upon me, and in later years I occasionally attended a game. About halfway through games I inevitably became bored and antics took over. During one game in which the Vols went blind and couldn't hit, I began yelling "Put Pickering in." Pickering, I told spectators around me, had just been brought over from Fayetteville in the Carolina League. He was hitting .370, and because he knocked so many balls into the brickyard beyond the park, his nickname was "Brickyard." Once people sitting near me began yelling for Pickering, I moved to another section of stands and shouted for Pickering. After a couple of innings, the cry for Pickering was tumultuous. "If the team has a good hitter, why not play him," a man said to me, his tone exaggerated and his voice raspy from yelling for Brickyard.

On sunny spring days, Father sometimes took me to Vanderbilt track meets, probably a holdover from his watching Coleman run. I enjoyed dozing in the sunlight, and each year I go to one or two meets at the University of Connecticut and aimlessly while away an afternoon, lounging in the stands, watching my students hurry toward finish lines. For two years during the late 1920s Father operated the scoreboard at Vanderbilt football games, and when I was in elementary school, Father bought me a season ticket in the end zone and I accompanied Mother and him to games. Vanderbilt usually lost, and I remember skipping back to our car, Father walking slowly and muttering. Tickets did not cost much, and going to Vanderbilt games was fun, no matter who won or lost. Many years later Father's great friend and our neighbor across the street David Keeble died at a Vandy game. "What better way could there be to go," Father said later, "than at halftime sitting in a box on the fifty yard line and Vanderbilt ahead of Tennessee?" For the record Tennessee won the game.

Athletics did not harry the rambler out of my system. I knew that no matter how I trained I would never be good at any sport. Consequently I recognized that devoting myself to a game was futile. Sitting on benches allowed me to ponder, for example, the

197

mathematical impossibility, and insanity, of directing 110% of one's effort to any enterprise. Starting at Parmer, sports taught me the valuable lesson of being satisfied with small things, getting into a game for three plays. The person who finds the little, ordinary things of life enough is probably going to enjoy daily living more than the person who hankers for big accomplishments. Moreover, the person down to trifles is rarely up to no good. The miracle of the loaves and the fishes is not about miraculously feeding a multitude but about being satisfied by the partial and the small, a fist of bread or a hunk of fish. I also learned that I'd probably have more fun in life if I wandered alone outside boundaries and social hash marks rather than if I joined teams. Lack of talent then became a saving gift, or maybe even itself a talent, that for failure but ultimately for common sense. At Parmer I played football for three years. In the sixth grade I was a fullback. I never ran the ball in a game, and I am not sure if I ever got into a game. In eighth grade I got upset the day before the first game when the coach decided to start a seventh grader, not me, at left tackle. I did not let sports upset me again. After the end of practice, I went home and ate a slice of cake. Then, I went into the front yard and, assuming a three-point stance, began blocking a tree, batting my head against the trunk until blood ran down my face. Mother could not persuade me to stop, so in desperation she telephoned the coach then coming to the door and calling me said the coach wanted to speak to me. I went to the phone dripping blood but bleeding embarrassment. The coach asked if I were ready for the game. I said I was. The next afternoon the coach put me in at left tackle in the second quarter. On the first play from scrimmage the boy opposite me bowled me onto my backside and jumping over me into the backfield, intercepted a lateral, and ran for a touchdown. Parmer lost by a touchdown.

Lessons were easy. The age of national tests and unending measurements had not darkened the school day. To be sure we read, wrote, and learned the multiplication tables, but more importantly, we aged, for the most part easily and contentedly.

Years, not books, bring wisdom—and foolishness. Classes usually had between forty and forty-three children in them. The two classes that composed Parmer's graduates my year added up to eighty-two. Classes for the gifted and special education did not exist. Some children, always it seemed country boys, failed year after year, grinding to an academic halt in sixth grade where they hung until they could drop out of school. In retrospect it seems clear they suffered from dyslexia, not something diagnosed at the time, at least not in Tennessee. The mixing of children of all academic inclinations doesn't seem to have stymied any budding Milton or Einstein. I never thought the pace of learning too slow or felt frustrated. I didn't think about such things; I just did the assignments. The same teacher taught us all subjects, and we did not have special art or music classes. The lessons did not pound good study or work habits into the fibers of our beings. Children who were organized by nature and had always worked hard, perhaps more than necessary, continued to do so, provided they had the leisure. Children not constitutionally disposed to studying found different, maybe better, or worse, things to do. Our teachers liked us, and we liked them and despite celebrating promotions almost always regretted leaving Mrs. Bonney, Mrs. Rich, Mrs. Taylor, Mr. Bass, or Mrs. Harris.

One night after I was elected to the school board in Storrs in the 1990s, I overheard myself talking and realized that I had gone around the bend. I had forgotten my days at Parmer and found myself discussing studies as if they really mattered to middle schoolers, instead of to parents who had caught the onward-and-upward-for-my-child influenza. How nice it was to amble through school at a time when neither parents nor children overly concerned about lessons. The lost and found column in the seventh grade, "Spotlight," seems an emblem of another age, perhaps even a poem.

1. LOST—Green Pencil—Alice Orr
2. LOST—A Red Ruler—Judy Hansberger
3. LOST—Yellow Pencil—Carolyn Shaver
4. LOST—A lunch ticket with name on it.—Margaret (Sissy) Brown
5. LOST—Red Plastic six-inch ruler—Patricia Nunnelly
6. LOST—a coca cola ruler—Edith Head
7. LOST—History Book—Mary Lee Rogers

Of course we had concerns. Those boys among us who were less hirsute than others waited anxiously for the appearance of pubic hair. Bare parts made undressing before classmates an ordeal. To help things along Jeffrey rubbed a blend of Vigoro and Peat Moss across his lower regions. Jeffrey had a knack for the laughable. One summer he earned money by mowing the grass of neighbors when they went away for vacations. In lawns he wrote "bad" words using gasoline for ink, not knowing that gas killed grass. On returning from vacation and mowing the grass themselves, a couple of Jeffrey's neighbors were disturbed when the word "shit" appeared in their lawns, the letters big as those on billboards. To Jeffrey's friends and our mothers and fathers, if not especially to Jeffrey's parents, what Jeffrey did was wildly funny.

The jokes we told each other were innocent and sweet. On the first day of school a new teacher asked the class to say their names. When the teacher reached the end of the first row of students, a boy said, "Honeychild Jones." On the teacher's asking him to stop playing around and tell the truth, he repeated "Honeychild Jones" whereupon the teacher sent him from the room. The boy got up from his desk and walked toward the door stopping only to speak to a boy sitting at the end of the fourth row. "Come on Chickenshit," he said. "If she won't believe me, she'll never believe you."

On the weekend at Rock Island during which Hayes taught us that skill so conducive to calm of mind, we bought jockey straps. We planned to swing out from a cliff over the river on a rope then let go and drop into the water. Worried that the water would smash into our privates like a driver whacking a golf ball perched on a tee, we went to a sporting goods store. On our telling the clerk what we wanted, he looked at us and said "small?" We didn't realize that small referred to the waist size of the strap or belt not the cup. We looked at each other then as a group said "large." "Are you sure?" the clerk asked. "We are sure," we answered. The straps were so large that they could have been used as slingshots in siege warfare.

Many of us had crushes on girls but these were crushes that did not lead to fleshly indentations. At some parties we played Spin the Bottle, an antiseptic, and the way we played a sanitary game. I was Big Ga's grandson, and I didn't care for the game, something I wrote Sherry. "I agree with you on those kissing games. I'm getting tired of them also," she wrote back, adding, "I've avoided the last couple of parties." My distaste did not, however, prevent me and Mary Trabue, and if my partner was not Mary it should have been, from setting a record one weekend at Beersheba Springs. We kept our lips glued together for over two minutes, not continuing longer because breathing was inconvenient. The record did not last beyond the next spin of the bottle. For the record I did not progress past Spin the Bottle until college graduation, and at times I wish I'd never learned the new games, at least the ones that transformed the level tenor of life into fleshly dizzying chaos. At Parmer, though, puppy love never howled. For two years Alice was my girlfriend, the "Believe It or Not" endeavor at Beersheba not constituting a dalliance but being for the record book alone. For several months many of my classmates and I attended Fortnightly, a dancing school on West End Avenue, not far from the Sulgrave. At Fortnightly we learned to waltz and foxtrot. We had a new dance card for each session. The card contained space for ten dances and before the evening began we scheduled partners by signing cards. Matters were well and kindly organized so that everyone's card was always full, and nobody had to sit out a dance, no matter how tall or short he or she was. One evening more boys than girls must have appeared because my partner for the first dance was Garth Fort. The fifth and tenth dances were special, and almost always I danced those with Alice. Alice and I were such good friends that one Easter after apologizing for not being able to think of a present other than money to send me, Ga wrote, "take this little bit and buy Alice a soda."

Matters amorous peppered the gossip column of the class newspaper, intriguing bits such as "Wonder why Roger is always laughing with Doris Templeton," "At the '13' dance Raymond and Catherine really had a twirl," and "There are three girls who sit together in Mr. Bass's room that like three boys that sit together in Miss Brownlee's room." Doris incidentally precipitated the only time I was sent into the hall. We rode together to school everyday in the same hookup. Familiarity leads to delight or the inappropriate. In sixth or seventh grade Doris sat in front of me in class. One morning she scooted about the seat of her desk so much that I became irritated or intrigued, I am not sure which, and I jabbed her in the bottom with the sharp end of my pencil. She screeched, and I went into the hall. No adult ever spoke to me about poking Doris, not even the teacher. If Mother or Father heard about the reason I was in the hall, they never mentioned it to me, and I suspect if they had heard they would have laughed and thought about giving me a supply of new, sharp pencils.

My classmates got along smoothly together. Bullying, for example, almost did not exist. Once I stopped a classmate from teasing a weaker boy. The classmate was stronger and bigger than I, but he backed down meekly, probably because I was well liked, popularity being potentially more threatening than muscles. In fact I had almost no muscles and weighed 118 pounds when I graduated from eighth grade.

In school, I don't think dress mattered much, but then I may remember little about clothes because I've never paid attention to fashion. Basketball shoes, especially Keds, were popular, the company's insignia forming a moon disk over ankle bones. Also boys liked Janzen shirts, the ones with alligators sewn over the left

A Comfortable Boy

breast. In later years a menagerie wandered onto shirts, among others, dogs, skunks, horses ranging free and others with polo players astride them. In an essay I once proposed driving the zoo into sartorial wilderness and sewing nipples on shirts, the size and color variable in order to accommodate diverse tastes. "Every male in college in the nation would purchase a shirt, probably a wardrobe as clothiers would create shirts for sundry occasions, formal and informal, for picnics and dinner on Easter Sunday, to wear to stock car races and to weddings."

Next to No Bears and Steal the Pig, the eraser game is the best game I have ever played. We never watched films in school. In seventh grade when recess was rained out and we had to stay in our classroom, we played the eraser game. Two children played at a time, the pursuer and the pursued. Both had blackboard erasers on their heads. Through the aisles separating rows of desks they ran, one chasing the other until one of the participant's eraser fell off or until the pursued caught his prey by touching him. The winner played another round while the loser retired to his desk. Occasionally we had arithmetic tournaments in which two children went to the board. The teacher then shouted out a problem, and the first person to write the correct answer down advanced to the next round. "We have had several tournaments in arithmetic," Jo Ellen Scott wrote in the "Spotlight." "The winners were Hayes Noel, Roger Grimsley, Ralph Spencer, Sammy Pickering, and Charlotte Adams." On the next page of the "Spotlight" appeared "Girls Only" commenting on the tournaments. "Do you realize girls that out of five winners only one has been a girl? That girl was Charlotte Adams. Let's take after Charlotte by getting to work and show those boys that we are really *Brains*!!!"

Once a week, on Friday morning I think, the school met in the cafeteria for an assembly. Teachers made announcements, and I suppose students must have performed, turning the assembly into a little talent show. The real talent show took place at the Belle Meade Theater on Saturday afternoon. Tickets to movies cost 13¢, the show usually a Western, perhaps Gene Autry on Champion,

203

Hopalong Cassidy with his sidekick Gabby Hayes, maybe the Lone Ranger and Tonto or Roy Rogers with Trigger and Dale Evans. Before the movie the Happiness Club met, and aspiring young singers and dancers performed. Afterward movie-goers sang, "Happy Days are here again. / The skies above are clear again." In school assembly we sang about America, songs like "America, the Beautiful" and "Columbia, the Gem of the Ocean." We also sang rollicking military songs, among others, "Anchors Aweigh" and "The Halls of Montezuma." My favorite was "Caissons Go Rolling Along." Even today on a long trek, I sometimes break into song, shouting, "Over hill, over dale / As we hit the dusty trail / And the Caissons go rolling along." At Parmer, noise lapped under the roof when we reached "It's hi! hi! hee! / In the field artillery." One night in the fifth grade, I won car seat covers in a drawing sponsored by the PTA. Since then the value of prizes I have won has sunk. Twenty years ago at a drawing held after a ten-kilometer road race, I picked up a case of Coca Cola in cans, and last month my one-dollar ticket won two dollars in the Connecticut Lottery.

Occasionally the auditorium was host to a school musical or more official talent show. Because I had no talent except getting along with people I did not participate. Still, assemblies must have been various. Unfortunately I recall little about them or the Parmer School song, except for the final phrase of this last, "For we are Parmer bred." Nevertheless while rummaging about before writing this memoir I came across one of my many lists. On it appeared fourteen things I did at Parmer, one of which was appearing onstage in assembly seven times. What I did onstage remains a mystery. Among other items on the list, I discovered that in seventh grade I nominated Raymond Pirtle for president of the student council. "He won." I also noted that I ran second to John Clay for "Athletic Representative to Mr. Jackson" [the director of athletics], perhaps giving the lie to my recollection of disdaining sports. In any case John was a fine athlete, and I suspect that I stood against him only to tack a line onto my list, something that nags at me, making me fear that I have written my books and articles only to add lines to my vita, the adult's version of the list.

Class Day was Tuesday, May 31, 1955. We marched in, and the day began with a devotional, the Lord's Prayer sung by girls and followed by boys giving a choral reading of the twenty-fourth psalm. At the end of the program, Alice presented a gift to the school. I gave my farewell address. The class sang the alma mater, and we walked out. In between were piano solos, songs, and recitations. Some of the material appeared three days later on the final day of school in the *WOP*, the eighth-grade newspaper, among other matters the class history and a section entitled "I'll Never Forget the Day," in which students described memorable incidents, most of them in which they got into trouble but wildly harmless from the prospective of now. "Last fall five or six boys including myself were coming in from recess and we got a drink of water," Jackie Hooper wrote,

> but the bad thing about it, we weren't swallowing the water—instead we spit on each other just as Mrs. Harris came in. Just as soon as we could say Jack Robinson we were in Miss Talley's office. Mrs. Harris gave a graphic description of the incident and then Miss Talley [the principal] spoke up and asked me how I would feel if I walked into my father's office and all his employees were spitting water on each other. In the midst of their anger, we almost got tickled, but together they made us feel like we had committed a major crime. Boy, from that day on we nearly strangled trying to swallow that water.

"Advice to the Seventh Graders" included "Don't make the notes you pass mushy unless your natural color is red" and "If you want a longer recess, just look out the window and you'll be put out." Among class "Resolutions" were that students should receive "no less than $500 per annum for their services"; "*All* students shall have freedom in speech, which heretofore has been abridged somewhat"; and "There shall be a well regulated militia and freedom to keep and bear arms in the event of violence on the part of teachers." In the "Last Will and Testament," I left my flocks of girls and wolfish ways to a seventh grader. The will was tongue and molar in cheek; I clearly had no girl, the romance with Alice having ended, and I couldn't have been a wolf even if I took howling and gnawing lessons.

Shortly before graduation, Grandma Pickering wrote me:

> Here it is Monday and in many ways it might be just another one like the others, however to us—those that love you—it is much more important for today is your beginning of the last week at Parmer and the passing of another stepping stone in your life, so this is just to say that Grandma is looking back over your elementary school days which we have followed with so much affection feels very grateful for the great satisfaction which your conduct along all lines has given to us. Always remember that wherever you may be, I glory in all that you do well. Just keep it up, Sammy!

Grandma Pickering sent a check along with the letter. I suspect that I pocketed it and perhaps didn't read the letter, at least not carefully. If I did read it, I hope I winced. Certainly reading it now makes me both wince and feel a little sad, sad not for myself but for Grandma who, on paper, made too much out of me and who wanted me to make more out of myself.

At the start of the summer before the eighth grade, Johnny wrote me, saying, "The locusts are coming out now. I wish you was up here so we could have our annual competition." The next two words he wrote were "ha! ha!" I didn't laugh; I missed the country. In the fall, classmates elected me president of the eighth grade. I was pleased, but the contest I really wanted to win was the locust contest or so I think now having meandered far and paradoxically maybe not so far from Cabin Hill and Carthage and Nashville. Who knows? Anyway, I have now reached the age at which people talk more about colons than culture. Three weeks before I started this book I had a colonoscopy. As I was lying on the table, the nurse noticed my name then asked, "Pickering? Do you teach at UConn?" On my saying that indeed I did teach at the university, she said, "You taught my daughter Stacy. She loved your classes. I will write her and tell her that I saw you." "Yipes," I thought, "and how will she describe the meeting, looking down on me with my rump bulbous in the air, six times as big around as my head, maybe seven or even eight." Health was too much with me. I was ready for anesthesia and slicing my way out of the present and into the past with a pencil.

On a hot August morning, the kind when the heat lies hazy and blue, a countryman sat on his front porch and gazed across his yard toward the road. A neighbor came walking along the road, and, so the story goes, seeing his friend, stopped and said, "What are you doing?" "Thinking," the man on the porch answered slowly. "What about?" asked the neighbor. "Don't know, just started," the man replied. The story stops here and to me is wonderfully satisfying. This remembrance ends similarly, with my strolling out of Parmer, not thinking but ambling, just getting started, life's morning hour, as Nannie put it, not yet beginning to heat up. "Our mothers were wonderful blessings," Jeffrey wrote me some time ago. "They guided us with light hands and never asked us to grow up before we wanted to." Ahead lay growing and heavier hands, schooling and teaching, marriage and children, traveling, and a few, but not many, things, as the General Confession puts it, that I ought not to have done. For two years at Parmer I was on the School Patrol. I held a pole with a yellow flag on the end and standing by a crosswalk, stopped traffic, and helped younger students cross the road. Now that really was something!